THE ARAB PSYCHE AND AMERICAN FRUSTRATIONS

MONTE PALMER

ISBN: 1468150057
ISBN 13: 9781468150056

Library of Congress Control Number: 2012900166
CreateSpace, North Charleston, SC

Dedication

To Princess
Wife
Best Friend
Editor-in-Chief
Co-Author
Arabist
Novelist
Gourmet Cook

Preface

Every time that the U.S. gets involved in the Middle East, or so it seems, things turn sour. Perhaps this is because the U.S. has either ignored or misread the psychological realities of the Arab world.

With this thought in mind, the objective of this book is to help Americans and Europeans better understand how the Arabs view the world and why they behave the way that they do, their psyche if you like. Along the way, the book provides those who are about to embark upon an adventure in the Arab world with a sketch of pleasures and pitfalls that awaits them. There are plenty of both.

Observations presented in this book are based upon my participation in some twenty research projects with Arab colleagues focusing on various dimensions of the Arab psyche. They also draw upon my association with a variety of Arab institutions including the American University of Beirut and the Al-Ahram Center for Political and Strategic Studies in Cairo. Even more insightful were the thousand or so hours spent drinking coffee with Arab colleagues who shared freely of their knowledge and their concerns. I thank them all, but will resist the temptation to list names. Errors are mine alone.

In addition to personal experiences gained in more than forty years of studying the Middle East, I had hoped to provide a complete bibliography of the works of other students of the Middle East that have done so much to deepen my knowledge of the region. Sadly, this list reached more than 100 pages of fine print and had to be abandoned. Reluctantly, the only references provided are those required by quotations and related passages that demanded documentation.

This is a continuing project, and I encourage readers to share their insights with me at *www.arabpsyche.wordpress.com* and at *arabpsyche@gmail.com*. This is not a blog, but I will list readers' comments on the website to the best of my ability.

Special thanks is due to Princess Palmer, companion, critic, editor in chief, and co-author of *At the Heart of Terror* and *Islamic Extremism*. Special thanks is also due to Diane Palmer whose commentary on the manuscript broadened my horizons. She also did a diligent job of proofreading.

Table of Contents

CHAPTER 1

SEARCHING FOR THE ARAB PSYCHE

Every time that the U.S. gets involved in the Arab world, or so it seems, things turn sour. Islamic extremism and anti-Americanism are soaring. The U.S. has retreated from Iraq, the cornerstone of its dream of building a new Middle East free of terror and religious extremism. Far from becoming a beacon of peace and tolerance, Iraq has become a swamp that breeds terror, as have Yemen, Algeria, Lebanon, Somalia, and the Sudan. Other countries may not be far behind. America's pet tyrants in the region have fallen to popular revolutions and its favored kings and princes get shakier by the day. This includes Saudi Arabia, the source of one-fourth of the world's oil reserves. If present trends continue, America's frustrations in the region will only grow deeper.

With this thought in mind, the objective of this book is to help Americans better understand how the Arabs view the world and why they behave the way they do—their psyche if you like. Along the way, the book will provide those of you about to embark upon an adventure in the Arab world with a sketch of pleasures and pitfalls that await you. There will be plenty of both. You may also gain insight into how the Arab psyche has defeated conquerors in the past and how it will continue to frustrate American efforts to control the region.

The task is not new. The British and French studied the Arabs in order to conquer them. The Americans and Israelis have now taken up the quest, albeit with no better results. The U.S. is still smarting from its debacle in Iraq, and the Israeli occupation of Palestinian territories has

1

brought the Jewish state little but grief. Read *Haaretz* (English edition) and the *Jerusalem Post* for a few days, and you will get the picture. Both discuss the woes of occupation with a brutal frankness that one seldom finds in the American media.

The Arabs, themselves, are obsessed with the study of their own psyche. They, too, are brutally frank in describing a psyche that is in disarray. Prince el Hassan bin Talal, uncle of the king of Jordan, bluntly acknowledged that "the state of the Arab nation leaves much to be desired," and that "confusion and disappointment reign" (Talal, 2007).

Some Arab commentators even fear that the Arab psyche might not survive. The deceased poet Nazar Qabani posed the question, "When will they announce the death of the Arabs?" The 2008 meeting of the Arab Organization of Cultural Development wasn't willing to pronounce the Arabs dead, but it worried that the future of Arabism, despite its rich history, "raises a thousand and one questions" (Al Jazeera, 2008).

Few Arab scholars deny that their psyche is in disarray. Rather, their concern focuses on two critical questions. First, what explains why a culture once renowned for its power and creativity now finds itself mired in social and political decay? Second, what can the Arabs do to revive glories past and claim their rightful place in the world community?

Were the Arabs really that enlightened? Absolutely. Jim Al-Khalili, a British physicist and producer of a four-part BBC series on medieval Islamic scientists, notes that the golden age of Arabic science occurred between the ninth and thirteenth centuries. It was during this era that the Arabs and the broader Muslim community led the world in the areas of mathematics, physics, astronomy, chemistry, medicine, and philosophy. The author's favorite among the Arab scientists was Ibn al-Haytham, now regarded as the father of the scientific method, with its emphasis on controlled experiments and replication of results (Al-Khalili, 2009).

RED-FLAG ISSUES

The popular revolutions that shook the Arab world in 2011 may unleash the Arab genius of the past and again cause Arab enlightenment to play a leading role in the world community. It is also possible that these revolutions will lead to even greater confusion and disappointment.

Then again, they could lead to extremist rule that looks to the past rather than the future. All options remain open.

Much will depend upon the ability of the Arab psyche to solve the riddles of extremism, violence, fragmentation, tyranny, inequality, and economic stagnation that have plagued it since the collapse of the era of enlightenment some six hundred years ago.

How the Arab psyche deals with these critical issues will also have much to say about American frustrations in the Arab world and broader Middle East. What the U.S. is doing now is not working, and it can only benefit from an Arab world in which extremism gives way to moderation, violence to reconciliation, fragmentation to internal cooperation, tyranny to democracy, inequality to equity, and economic stagnation to economic growth.

The ebb and flow of these key issues over the course of Arab history is part of our story and should provide a helpful guide for dealing with the present and the future. Those who refuse to benefit from the lessons of the past are fated to keep making the same mistakes over and over again. Thus it was that U.S. Defense Secretary Robert Gates quoted General Douglas MacArthur in warning, "Any future defense secretary who advises the president to again send a big American land army to Asia or into the Middle East or Africa should have his head examined" (Shanker, 2011).

ONE ARAB PSYCHE OR MANY?

The search for the Arab psyche follows its evolution through eras of tribalism, Islam, colonialism, flawed independence, resurgent Islam, and terror and reprisals, into the unfolding era of popular revolution. It is important to view each stage separately, for each has left an indelible mark on the Arab psyche that persists today. Many sins that the West attributes to Islam, for example, are actually the legacy of tribalism. It will simply be easier to deal with the Arab psyche if we know what is causing what.

As the following chapters will illustrate, the Arab psyche becomes increasingly complex as it attempts to cope with an ever more complex world. Assuming that the Arab psyche today is the same as it was in the era of tribalism or Islam has led to tragic mistakes in dealing with the Middle East.

Many of the Arabs that you encounter may not conform to our evolving portrait of the Arab psyche. There is simply too much diversity in the region for one size to fit all. The rural psyche often differs from the psyche of the region's massive cities, and the gap between fundamentalist and secular psyches can be huge. As the discussion unfolds, you will encounter the tribal psyche, the Arabo-Muslim psyche, the Arab nationalist psyche, and the psych of the fox, among others.

This said, several themes in the Arab psyche are sufficiently prevalent to cause both the Arabs and the Americans a great deal of frustration. It is they that are the main focus of this book.

Because of the prevalence of these themes, the Arabs are seldom surprised by the way they behave and find themselves to be quite predictable. They don't always like it, but at least they know what is coming. The Americans are usually surprised by the way Arabs behave. If American frustrations in the region are any indicator, they have no idea of what is coming. Neither did the British or French, for that matter. And the Israelis? You be the judge.

While I can't promise a uniform Arab psyche, there are some things that I can promise. Those who enter the Arab world with an open mind will find it the most fascinating of places. Challenging to be sure, but not as hostile to the United States as one might believe.

I can also promise that those of you who are venturing into the Arab world to dominate it will clash with the Arab psyche. If history is any guide, you will lose. Maybe not immediately, but time is on its side.

Materials presented in this book are based upon forty years of working with the Arabs and my participation in some twenty research projects with Arab colleagues, focusing on various dimensions of the Arab psyche. The book also draws upon personal observations made while working with a variety of Arab institutions, including the American University of Beirut, the Al-Ahram Center for Political and Strategic Studies in Cairo, the American University of Cairo, Bir Zeit University in Palestine, and the Arab Development Institute in Libya. Particularly insightful was my close association with graduate students from all areas of the Middle East. More illuminating were the thousand or so hours spent drinking coffee with Arab colleagues, who shared freely of their knowledge and concerns.

Even with all of the sources drawn upon in preparing this book, a knotty question remains. Is it really possible for a person raised in Wisconsin to understand the Arab psyche? I hope so, but admittedly, Wisconsin is a long way from Cairo.

Arab colleagues have helped to bridge the gap, but it is possible that their vision of the Arab psyche is also flawed. The Arab scholar Wafiq Raouf poses the question, "How can anyone brought up in the Arab culture be objective?" (Raouf, 2005, 7).

WHY DO ARABS BEHAVE THE WAY THEY DO?

The answer to this question begins with the observation that most people, Arabs included, spend a great deal of time seeking pleasure and avoiding pain (Howard, 2006). The pain-and-pleasure principle is as old as the hills and boils down to two key elements: the environment and the psyche. The external environment stimulates people to behave while the psyche thinks about how to respond to environmental stimuli in a manner that provides the best balance of pain and pleasure.

Sometimes, the environment outweighs the influence of the psyche, and people's behavior is quite predictable. Other times, the psyche reigns supreme, and people respond in the most unpredictable of ways. If you sit on a tack, finding the link between stimulus and response doesn't need a great deal of thinking. Figuring out the best way to serve God, by contrast, may take a great deal of thinking.

The environmental component of the equation requires little elaboration. The environment is simply all of the external forces that push people to act one way or another. It could be mountains or rivers, the teachings of your faith, the laws of the land, the price of bread, or the people that you deal with on a daily basis. People can be a source of joy. The French existentialist philosopher Jean Paul Sartre, by contrast, defined hell as other people. Whatever the form of the environment, it is hard to escape. Just for the record, the title of Sartre's play was *No Exit*.

This, in turn, brings us to the discussion of the psyche, that wonderful unseen thing that determines when, why, and how Arabs and everyone else respond to the environmental forces that are playing with their minds. Unfortunately, no one is quite sure what the psyche is. For some, it is the soul or emotional heart of an individual. For others, it is the brain, the mind, the unconscious, the ego, the self, the internalized values of society, cognition, or anything else that helps individuals decide, consciously or unconsciously, how they are going to respond to the millions of stimuli that the environment throws at them during every waking hour and beyond.

To make things even more complex, psychologists have invented so many ways to study the human psyche that it is hard to keep them straight. It would be helpful if the diverse branches of psychology used a common vocabulary or shared a basic set of principles that guided their quest to understand why people behave how they do. Sadly, they don't (Romero and Kemp, 2007, xxv.) They can't even agree on a list of basic human needs and motives (Pervin, 2003, 137–141).

ANALYZING THE ARAB PSYCHE

Our search for the Arab psyche focuses on the Arab identity, motivations, social conscience, emotions, traits, and cognitive thinking process. As such, it incorporates insights from various branches of psychology, including brain-mind analysis, social learning, behaviorism, cognition, and social psychology. Feel free to quibble with this approach, but it does capture the essence of modern psychological theory (Pervin, 2003; Howard, 2006; Gross, Sheppes and Urry, 2011).

The analysis of the Arab psyche begins with identity, because it is hard for Arabs, or anyone else, to plot strategies for maximizing pleasure and minimizing pain until they figure out who they are and how they fit into the world around them.

Most Arab scholars agree that the pillars of the Arab identity are the Arabic language, a common culture that finds its roots in the tribal customs of the Arabian Peninsula, a sense of Arabism forged by a common history, and an Islamic faith that is embraced by about 90 percent of the Arab population. Christian Arabs downplay the role of Islam in shaping the Arab psyche, but they agree that the Arab psyche is religious to the core.

Many Muslim Arab scholars find language, tribalism, historic traditions, and Islam to be indivisible. It is language, it their view, that distinguishes Arabs from other peoples of the region. Arabism provides the foundation for nationalistic sensitivities that play such a crucial role in our story. Islam provides the foundation for the religious revival sweeping the region, and tribalism provides the foundation for the intense family ties that continue to permeate all dimensions of Arab society.

Loyalty patterns also tend to follow identity patterns, a fact that underscores much of the tribal and sectarian conflict so prevalent in the Arab world today. Arabs may share a common sense of Arabism, but Arabism often plays second fiddle to sectarian and tribal identities.

Most Arabs, like the rest of us, are motivated to pursue their diverse needs and wants. I like the word "wants" because it includes basic human needs such as security, sex, food, shelter, and belonging as well as the appetites that they spawn, including greed, lust, envy, and power. All are part of the human condition, and you can't understand the Arab world without them.

Many people consider faith to be an innate need. Innate or not, faith is a profound motivator that is propelling the fundamentalist revival sweeping the world. Military strategists of all religions now use religion as a "faith force multiplier" (Baigent, 2009). On average, people of intense faith are willing to fight with greater ferocity than people of little faith. This principle is not new, but returns to the Old Testament.

The Arab psyche learned other wants from parents, peers, preachers, and poets, not the least of which were honor, dignity, and freedom. It is they that are fueling the populist revolutions reshaping the Arab world.

Emotions

The motives discussed above are all about what people want. They strive to achieve their wants, and when they get what they want, they feel good. When they don't, they may feel frustrated, angry, or depressed. Pain and pleasure are often referred to as the building blocks of emotions. The more intense the pain or pleasure, the more intense the ensuing emotions (Howard, 2006).

Emotions are critical to the search for the Arab psyche because emotions trigger behavior. If wants motivate behavior, it is emotions that serve as the sparkplug. The difficulty is that you can't always predict the type of behavior that any particular emotion will trigger. An exchange of insults, for example, may lead to an explosion of anger, apologies, or turning the other cheek. It might also result in latent vows of revenge. The point is, something is going to happen.

Of the thousands of emotions that psychologists observed, several are considered universal (Pervin, 2003, 346). Others may be limited to specific cultures or individuals. I believe that all of the sixteen emotions listed in Table 1.1 fall into the universal category, but I can say with confidence that they are all part of the Arab psyche. Each of the sixteen emotional categories listed in the table is arranged from lowest intensity of arousal to the highest level of arousal. Aggravation, for example, is likely to trigger a mild rebuke, while anger could lead to a brawl, and rage to war or revolution. The intensity of these and related emotions have ebbed and flowed throughout the course of Arab history, but they have never been more intense than in the ongoing era of revolution and rage.

Table 1.1   The Emotional Component of the Arab Psyche
Mild Arousal → Medium Arousal → High Arousal

awareness → interest → excitement
happiness → joy → ecstasy → rapture
surprise → startle → astound
distress → anguish → despair
disgust → revulsion → contempt
closeness → affection → love
aggravation → anger → rage
shame → humiliation → mortification
concern → worry → anxiety
wariness → fear → terror
lonely → secluded → abandoned
disappointment → frustration
sadness → anguish → grief
dislike → aversion → hate
acceptance → moderate expectations → rising expectations
guilt → self-reproach → repentance

Guilt and Shame

Do Arabs have a conscience and suffer from guilt like most of us? It couldn't be otherwise, for Islam, like Judaism and Christianity, are Abrahamic religions that preach guilt, repentance, and redemption. You can't understand the wave of fundamentalism sweeping the Arab world without it. This issue is discussed more fully in Chapter 6, "Islam Resurgence and the Arab Psyche."

Morality is also part of the Arab psyche, but the Arab vision of morality focuses more on family and faith than on political institutions which are generally viewed as immoral. Be warned, the Arab vision of morality does not extend to occupiers. To the contrary, the Arab psyche considers the defeat of occupiers to be a moral obligation.

While guilt is part of the Arab psyche, most Arabs rely more on shame than guilt to keep people in line. Shame has deep tribal origins and remains the preeminent mechanism of social control in the Arab world. God is forgiving. The peering eyes of neighbors are not. Some Arabs suggest that shame dominates Arab relations with each other, while morality heavily influences issues such as personal salvation and opposing foreign invaders. If this is the case, shame pits the Arabs against each other while morality unifies them against foreigners and members of rival sects. The issue is too complex for present purposes, but it will be discussed at length in later chapters.

Traits

Emotions tend to decrease as people's needs have been met or the source of their euphoria has dissipated. This is less the case for traits or psychological predispositions that have evolved over time as guides for maximizing pleasure and avoiding pain.

The traits frequently cited by Arab commentators as being an integral part of the Arab psyche include authoritarianism, mysticism, hero worship, and the search for a Mahdi or savior (Mahmoud, 1984). Arab scholars often mention other traits such as freedom from authority, collectiveness, and suspicion of anyone outside of their immediate family. These traits evolved during the tribal era and are very much in evidence today.

Such a litany of traits would appear to be a bundle of contradictions, but as you will see when the story unfolds, the Arab psyche has a logic all its own. It is this logic that the U.S. and other conquerors find so frustrating. Traits do change, but it may take a long time, far longer than those hoping for radical changes in the Arab world may wish.

How the Arab Psyche Thinks and Reasons

The psyche's efforts to maximize pleasure and avoid pain requires a great deal of thinking (cognition), a process that includes perceiving everything taking place around it, evaluating what it perceives in terms of pain or pleasure, and organizing its evaluated information into manageable categories such as friend or foe. Once the information assaulting the psyche is processed, it is used to reason the best strategies for getting what it wants with the least amount of pain. And so it is with the Arabs.

Let's start with the process of perception. Is it really possible for the Arab, or any other person, to keep track of the millions of bits of information spinning around his head at any particular moment? Now, add the processes of evaluation and categorization, and then filter it through all of the emotions and other components of the psyche discussed above.

Freudian psychoanalysis simplifies things by suggesting that all individuals possess an ego that navigates them along the treacherous path between pain and pleasure. You can't see the ego, but the vision that comes to mind is that of a miniature elf sitting behind the control panel of the brain, doing its best to maximize pleasure while it protects the individual from pain. It's not very scientific, but psychologists have broadly adopted the term to describe the human pursuit of pain and pleasure.

Whether you call it reasoning or ego, the human effort to maximize pleasure and protect the individual from pain often leads to psychic defenses that help people avoid the harsh realities swirling around them. Defense mechanisms also have their origin in Freudian psychology, but have now been modified to serve mainline psychology. Among the defense mechanisms that play a prominent role in our search for the Arab psyche are projection (blaming others), cognitive dissonance (accentuating good news while discounting bad news), denial (blocking out painful information altogether), and rationalization (making dumb decisions seem logical). We will add others as circumstances dictate.

IS THE ARABIC LANGUAGE THE SOUL OF THE ARABS?

I ask the question because almost every commentary on the Arab psyche that I have encountered, in more than forty years of researching the topic, stresses the link between the Arabic language and the way Arabs behave.

"No people of the world," writes Philip K. Hitti, "have such enthusiastic admiration for literary expression and are so moved by the word, spoken or written, as the Arabs. Hardly any language seems capable of exercising over the minds of its users such irresistible influence as Arabic. Modern audiences in Baghdad, Damascus and Cairo can be stirred to the highest degree by the recital of poems only vaguely comprehended.... The rhythm, the rhyme, the music produce on them the effect of what they call lawful magic" (Hitti, 1943, 21).

This should not seem too strange to Westerners familiar with Gregorian chants, opera, and modern rock concerts. The words aren't clear, but their message is conveyed by the mood and emotion that the music generates.

Raphael Patai devotes an entire chapter in his *The Arab Mind* to the impact of language on the Arab psyche (Patai, 2002, 43–77). Much of Patai's commentary focuses on the above quote from Hitti and stresses the tendency of the Arabic language to encourage exaggeration, emotionalism, embellishment, overassertion, and repetition.

Patai, however, takes Hitti's observations one step farther by embracing the Sapir-Whorf hypothesis which suggests that the grammar and structure of a language guides an individual's mental activity (Patai, 2002, 43–77). Research on the topic is spotty, but having struggled with the Arabic language for the better part of a lifetime, I am reluctant to dismiss the Sapir-Whorf hypothesis out of hand. The influence of language on the thinking process becomes particularly evident in translating Arabic into English. Basic words like dog and cat are no problem, but abstract words seldom have a direct English equivalent. This is particularly the case of Western terms dealing with psychology, the social sciences, religion, and mysticism. Arabs and Americans may think that they are discussing the same topic, but there is little meeting of the minds, a legal term suggesting that people are talking past each other.

Mohammed Jabri, in turn, has made language the central focus of his analysis of the Arab psyche and the way that it grasps and evaluates knowledge (Jabri, 2007). In particular, he notes the dichotomy between pronunciation (sound patterns) and meaning, the former often being more important than the latter. Never mind what the words say. The message, or at least a large part of it, is conveyed by the emotions, music, and rhythm of the spoken word. What you see in print may not be what the Arab psyche hears. This is certainly the case with eloquent readings of the Koran, the spirit of which far transcends the written word. Arab Muslims understand this point better than anyone else because the Koran is written in the language of their soul.

My own interest in the topic stems from a lifetime of attempting to measure Arab attitudes and opinions, with varying degrees of success. Having soon learned that answers to sensitive questions were bound to be flawed, my colleagues and I used Arab proverbs that Arab graduate students generated and evaluated to measure attitudinal predispositions. The project was a tremendous success in the sense that our respondents in a Saudi Arabian pretest welcomed the questionnaire and answered it with enthusiasm. So much so, in fact, that they wanted to keep the questionnaire in order to share its proverbs with relatives. The trouble was, the responses didn't make a lot of sense. We had overcome suspicion of the questionnaire only to realize that the proverbs weren't measuring what we thought they would measure.

In line with Jabri's views outlined above, a specialist in Arab proverbs later explained that the words were less important than the rhythm, emphasis, and timing of the proverb. The point is that Americans take words literally, while Arabs are reading between the lines and keying on emotional signals. It is all very frustrating for U.S. intelligence services. Believe me, a crash course in Arabic isn't going to help.

THE PSYCHIC ROAD MAP AND ARAB POKER

These, then, are the basic components of the individual's psyche that will guide the analysis of the Arab psyche and its frustration of U.S. efforts to manage events in the Middle East. Collectively, it is these components of the psyche that motivate individuals and guide their efforts to find pleasure and avoid pain in an ever-changing environment.

"Guiding" is the tricky part. People can't be sent out to pursue pleasure and avoid pain in a helter-skelter manner. The environment would eat them alive. So the psyche provides individuals with a road-map (schema) for navigating their environments in a way that provides the most pleasure with the least pain. Each time the environment changes, the roadmap has to make the necessary adjustment or suffer the consequences.

Seeing that the Arab psyche loves to play games with Americans, it might be easier to think of the Arab psyche as a board game, such as Monopoly, in which each throw of the dice ushers in a new set of opportunities and dangers.

No, that's too random, and not enough thinking is required. Thinking, after all, is the psyche's job. Besides, life in the Arab world is too dangerous to leave things to a role of the dice. Planning and plotting are essential. Perhaps, a game of chess would be more appropriate. Wits are matched against wits, and decisions have to be made with an eye to future moves.

Sorry. That won't work either. There is no chance involved. The players are in almost total control of their environment which is hardly the case in the Arab world. Who can predict the next sandstorm or when raiders will appear from behind the dunes or in the skies?

How about a game of poker? It has everything: skill, the luck of the draw, bluffing, and the chance for huge gains and losses. Poker also has the virtue of simplicity. Anyone can play. All the psyche has to do is decide when to hold 'em and when to fold 'em.

This, of course, assumes an element of rationality. Is it possible for a psyche, Arab or otherwise, to be rational? The answer is probably yes if the psyche's goals are clear and well defined, its motivation strong, its information ample and accurate, and its reasoning process not subverted by curious emotional states (conscious and unconscious), or clouded by flawed perceptions, conspiracy theories, defense mechanisms, misplaced expectations, and untested assumptions about how the world works.

Because the requirements for pure rationality are so strained, it would be folly to assume too much rationality from any psyche, be it Arab, Muslim, American, or Israeli. Under the best of circumstances, the information available to the psyche is limited and distorted. The psyche's processing of that information is even more so. One way or another, the psyche must place its bets with a high degree of uncertainty. The same is true of those who would predict what the Arab psyche is likely to do.

A wonderful example of the dangers of prediction in the Middle East is to be found in the Arab joke about the frog and the scorpion. The scorpion approaches a frog sitting on the river bank and asks for a ride across the water.

"No," replied the frog "You would bite me in midstream, and I would drown."

"That's not logical," replied the scorpion. "If I bit you, we would both drown."

The frog was persuaded, and began swimming for the other shore when the scorpion bit him.

"Why did you do that?" asked the frog in bewilderment. "It's not logical, and now we will both drown."

"I know that it's not logical," replied the scorpion, resigned to his fate. "But what the hell. It's the Middle East."

FROM THE PSYCHE TO BEHAVIOR AND BACK AGAIN

Having introduced the environment and the psyche, the way has been prepared for analyzing the behavior patterns that you are likely to encounter in the Arab world on a frequent basis. Some are political, while others are social and economic. Be warned, it is virtually impossible to draw clear lines between political, social, and economic behavior in the Arab world because all blend together in a seamless web.

This section is titled, "From the Psyche to Behavior and Back Again" because the way Arabs behave becomes part of their environment, and their psyche has to adjust to it. It's all a continuous and unending circle. That is what makes the Arab world so interesting and so frustrating.

For the sake of simplicity, the key elements of Arab behavior to be examined in this book are outlined in Table 1.2

Table 1.2   Frequent Patterns of Arab Political, Social & Economic Behavior

Political Behavior
1. Expressing nationalism, ethnicity, tribalism, and other forms of collective identity.
2. Expressing spiritualism.
3. Searching for a strong basis of group support.
4. Expressing loyalty.
5. Displaying an obsession for control.
6. Expressing satisfaction and discontent.

Social Behavior
1. Conforming to the pressures of culture and tradition.
2. Dealing with others in a dominant-subordinate society.
3. Deviating from the pressures of culture and tradition.

Economic Behavior
1. Displaying behavior that reflects economic productivity.
2. Displaying patterns of distribution and sharing.

FROM THE INDIVIDUAL PSYCHE TO THE GROUP PSYCHE

How did we get from talking about individual psyches to talking about the psyches of groups, nations, cultures, and civilizations? Surely not all members of a nation or civilization possess an identical character and march in lockstep.

Perish the thought. Groups, small or large, are collections of individual psyches, each of which is unique. The more clusters of individual psyches have been shaped by common cultures, share common interests, and face common hurdles to the fulfillment of their needs and fears, the more likely they are to reflect similarities in the way they respond to the circumstances that confront them.

The Arabs, for example, constitute some 250 million individual psyches that manifest observable similarities resulting from a similar history, culture, language, and for the most part, religion. This does not mean that 250 million Arab psyches march in lockstep or even that they get along very well. They do, and they don't. The history of the Arabs is littered with war and violence, and yet, even the marauding tribes of pre-Islamic Arabia would set aside a few weeks each year for contests of sport and poetry reading. The situation is much the same today. Rare is a speech by an Arab leader that doesn't pay tribute to the dream of Arab unity. Alas, the dream remains elusive, and their squabbles make them easy prey for their foes.

ARAB PSYCHE OR MUSLIM PSYCHE?

If you want to add the psyches of neighboring Muslim areas such as Turkey, Iran, Pakistan, Afghanistan, and the Muslim countries of Central Asia to the number of psyches that the U.S. has to deal with in the Middle East, the figure more than quadruples. Add the entirety of the Muslim world to the equation, and the figure jumps to a staggering 1.5 billion, or about one-fourth of humanity.

Why include Muslims when the vast majority of Muslims are non-Arabs? The answer is simple. Islam, the religion of Muslims, was revealed in Arabia to an Arab, the Prophet Mohammed. It was the Arabs who spread their faith by conquest, and with it came their culture. All of the major historical figures in Islam are Arabs, and the Koran, the revealed word of God, is written in Arabic.

This is not to suggest that the Muslim psyche is the same as the Arab psyche, but merely to point out that one has influenced the other. It is certainly not to suggest that Arabs and their ethnic neighbors like each other. They don't. Thus, we see a curious dynamic at work in the Middle East as resurgent Islamic emotions are softening ethnic jealousies of the past.

What can be said is that the responses of neighboring Muslims psyches to American efforts to control the region are likely to be very similar to those of the Arab psyche. Nothing is written in stone, but it is something to think about. The Arab psyche is the focus of the book, but occasional examples are drawn from neighboring Islamic countries to illustrate similarities within the region.

LET THE JOURNEY BEGIN

As the discussion progresses, it may seem that you are being taken into a world that bears much in common with *Alice in Wonderland*, a world in which things seem familiar, but nothing is quite what it seems. Perhaps a more appropriate guide for those of you concerned about American frustrations in the region would be Mark Twain's *Innocents Abroad*. Even more interesting might be Twain's *A Connecticut Yankee in King Arthur's Court*. The hero of the story brings Yankee know-how to medieval England, replete with telegraph polls and Gatling guns. All goes well until so many people have been killed that the hero suffocates under the bodies.

CHAPTER 2

THE TRIBAL FOUNDATION OF THE ARAB PSYCHE

Probably the best place to start the search for the Arab psyche is with the struggles of beni Adam. The name may not sound familiar, but you know him well. *Beni* is the Arabic word for son, and beni Adam is the son of Adam. For the Arabs, beni Adam represents humanity and all of its failings. Beni Adam also symbolizes the common bond between the Arabs and the rest of humanity. His failings are those of all of God's children.

Adam, as the story is recounted in the Torah, Bible, and Koran, gave way to the temptations of Eve. He was cast from the Garden of Eden into a grim universe of pestilence, poverty, and predators. Beni Adam's struggle for survival in this most hostile of environments was guided by the same basic needs, appetites, and instincts that guided most advanced creatures. Unlike other animals, he was graced with the gift of reason, much of which was devoted to the task of maximizing pleasure and avoiding pain.

Beni Adam's first venture into social activity, like that of most of humanity, was buoyed by the instincts of nurturing and bonding and followed the lines of kinship. Small nuclear families gave way to broad extended families and they to clans and eventually tribes. The myth of a common ancestor united them all. There had to be some basis for trust and cooperation between people. Blood, while imperfect, was stronger than water.

Society helped beni Adam meet his basic needs, but the price was high. Unlike the days of yore, he was no longer a free spirit who could rape and pillage at will, not that the temptations didn't remain. There were rules to follow, and he had been stamped with a social identity that he could not escape. He was what his tribe was. If his tribe suffered, he suffered. It was all very confusing, and so beni Adam developed a mental roadmap, a psyche if you like, for gratifying his basic needs with minimal pain. In the process, beni Adam evolved into beni tribal. He was the son of the tribe, and the tribe was his family.

And how did beni tribal deal with his new world? Most of the time, his behavior simply reflected the social pressures that surrounded him. The dull grind of survival dominated life, and he kept his nose to the grindstone. It was terribly boring and very predictable.

Other times, however, beni tribal gave vent to the most devious of psyches. Wealth had to be sheltered from the eyes of envy, and potential adversaries had to be lulled into error. Revenge for past affronts required the most careful planning, as did schemes for seducing the girl in the tent next door. One could not survive in the cruel world of the tribe without being clever. The Arabic movies and soap operas exploit these themes to the hilt. Invaders should take note.

THE IMPORTANCE OF TRIBALISM TODAY

Tribalism, for better or for worse, remains a key element in understanding the Arab world and the broader environs of the Middle East today. To paraphrase a frustrated American officer in Afghanistan, "After nine years in Afghanistan, we still don't understand tribalism" (Shanker, 2011).

Saudi Arabia and the Gulf sheikhdoms are all tribal monarchies. The politics of Yemen are largely tribal, and tribes or large clans dominate the rural areas of virtually all Arab countries. When you take the long drive from the Amman airport to Jordan's capital, you pass through lands controlled by one of the most powerful of Jordan's tribes. It is one of a group of native Jordanian tribes that dominate the security services and assure the survival of a tribal monarchy that rules a population that is about 70 percent Palestinian in origin. Jordan's king is himself a member of the Hashemite clan of the Kuraysh tribe and a direct descendent of the Prophet Mohamed. How did a member of this most illustrious tribe from what is now Saudi Arabia become heir to the throne of Jordan? It is quite simple. The British put his great-great grandfather on the throne when they created Jordan in the aftermath of WWI. Why are there so many Palestinians in Jordan? They were refugees from a long succession of Arab-Israeli wars that began in 1948. The Palestinians do most of what gets done in Jordan, with the exception of the army and security services. They remain tribal. It is much the same in Kuwait, a tribal monarchy whose halting steps toward democracy are slowed by the predominance of tribalism in voting patterns.

U.S. forces in Iraq, for their part, attempted to use tribalism to their advantage by aligning themselves with the country's Sunni tribes in the hope of breaking the grip of al-Qaeda and other terrorist groups in this war-torn country. The tribes cooperated when it served their interests, and they deserted the U.S. when it didn't. Similar strategies were applied in Pakistan and Afghanistan, albeit without notable success. Tribes view themselves as independent nations, and alliances with the U.S. last only as long as they serve the purposes of the tribal sheikh.

Whatever its form, tribalism is of far more than historical interest. It is part and parcel of the Arab psyche and, from all appearances, is likely to remain so for a long time to come. Bitter conflicts between powerful families and clans beset even the most modern areas of the Arab world. The interminable chaos in Lebanon, for example, is as much a conflict between clans as it is a conflict between religions.

The Arabs, themselves, are ambivalent about their tribal past. For many, it symbolizes the virtues of pride, generosity, bravery, hospitality, rugged individualism, freedom, and innate intelligence so dear to the heart of the Arab psyche. To others, it smacks of savagery, superstition, and the fragmentation of the Arabs into thousands of groups perpetually in conflict with each other. For them, tribalism is the source of all of the woes of the Arab world today, but none more so than a legacy of conflict and mutual distrust that makes it seemingly impossible for the Arabs to forge a unified nation. The progressive Gulf website *Al-Shindagah* expressed this view in its lengthy series on the Arab psyche: "This means that our [modern] culture is just a whitewash which has no influence on our behaviour. Rather, our behaviour is governed by ancient precepts that go back to pre-Islamic times; namely, tribalism with all its biases" (*Al-Shindagah*, 1999).

Ghazi Al Gosaibi, the noted Saudi poet, philosopher, diplomat, and politician, offers a much kinder view of tribalism. He traces the rise and fall of the Arabs to the status of the poets and poetry in the Arab world. The pre-Islamic poet, according to Al Gosaibi, was the revered king of the intellectual world and the fount of all wisdom. With the rise of Islam, the role of the poet was reduced to that of a prince, and today, Al Gosaibi laments, to that of a hired publicity agent (Al Gosaibi, 2010).

Al Gosaibi bluntly states that Arabs have a great deal to learn from their tribal past, and he quotes the following lines from Amal Donqul that, in Al Gosaibi's view, "describe the story of a generation, and summarizes the history of the Arab nation in this century (Al Gosaibi, 2010, 14).

> *We are the generation of war*
> *Swimmers in blood*
> *Thrown by our aper ships*
> *Over icy mountains of death*
> *The generation of pain*
> *We saw Jerusalem in paintings*
> *We spoke the language of Arab conquerors*
> *And carried the flag of Arab refugees.*

Philip Hitti, the dean of modern Arab historians, shared Al Gosaibi's profound respect for the pre-Islamic poets. "In battle his tongue was effective as his people's bravery. In peace he might prove a menace to public order by his fiery harangues.... Besides being oracle, guide, orator and spokesman of his community, the poet was its historian and scientist, in so far as it had a scientist" (Hitti, 1956, 94-95). Hitti goes on to note that poets were endowed with knowledge of the unseen. Their voices conveyed not only words, but also mystical meanings. Words were often less important than the mystical meanings hidden in the rapture of the sound.

WHAT IS TRIBALISM?

The profound influence of tribalism on the politics of the Arab world today requires that we probe deeper into the foundations of tribalism and its influence on the Arab psyche. This is not an easy task, for tribalism is not a "thing" that you can reach out and touch. Rather, tribalism is a complex system of interdependent relationships, none of which can be understood without reference to the others.

Understanding tribalism begins with the physical, social, cultural, economic, and international environments in which it evolved. It couldn't be otherwise, for people had to adjust to their environments or perish.

Environmental conditions, in turn, gave shape to a tribal psyche intent on maximizing pleasure and minimizing pain in the most difficult of environmental circumstances. There wasn't much slack, but a history of blood feuds, honor killings, and power struggles suggests that there was a whole lot of thinking going on, much of it focusing of deviance from tribal norms. Even beni tribal might risk all for love. One of the most fascinating books on the topic that I have come across is Al Adnani's *Adultery and Homosexuality in the Arab History* (Al Adnani, 1999).

Finally, tribalism is the way in which the environment and psyche interacted to shape the way that tribal Arabs generally behaved. The goal is not merely to understand tribal life in early Arabia, but to understand the persistence of tribalism as a key political element in the politics of the Arab world today. Today's environment bears little resemblance to early Arabia, but the roots of tribalism are the same.

The Origins of the Arabs

The Arabs and the Hebrews are the lone remaining descendants of an array of Semitic-speaking peoples who settled in Yemen between 3000 and 1000 BCE. Their precise origins remain a matter of debate. Yemen was the destination of choice because of its fertile lands and abundant rain. Civilization flourished, and Arab historians often consider Yemeni civilization, with its prosperous cities and advanced agriculture, to be as significant as the ancient civilizations of Egypt and Phoenicia. Whether or not this was the case, Yemen stands as the earliest example of Arab development and was the work of a very sophisticated people. The prosperity of Yemen, with its frankincense and myrrh, were well known to the Romans, who referred to Yemen as Arabia Felix, or "Happy Arabia."

Alas, not everything was happy. Abundance led to an exploding population, and the weaker Arab tribes were pushed into the scorched lands of the desert, where they combed the harsh terrain in a desperate search for water and pasture. The Bedouin (nomadic) tribes ascended the mountains in the brutal days of summer which often topped 140°F. In the winter, they descended to the valleys searching for food, pasture, and water. There were no rivers to speak of, only wadies, empty river beds that channeled the sparse rains that did fall into the barren wastes, where they either evaporated or reemerged as an oasis spring or natural well. Both were rare.

In a curious irony of history, the weakest of the Arab farmers survived to become the strongest of the Arab warriors. It was the warriors' creed that shaped the Arab psyche that fueled the Islamic invasions of later years.

The Yemeni Arabs trace their ancestry to Qathan, the leader of the tribe that initiated the settlement of Yemen. In their view, they are the purest of Arabs, and they taunt their northern brethren with the phrase, "I am more (A'arab) than you."

The Northern Arabs consist of pre-Islamic tribes who had been Arabacized by their interaction with the pure Arab tribes of the south. That didn't lessen their feeling of Arabism, and all northerners trace their origins to Nizar bin Maad ben Adnan.

The difference between the northern and southern tribes is largely of historical interest, but the distinction exists. While the southern Arabs may have the pride of ancestry, it was the northern Arabs who gave birth to Islam and who now rule the thrones of the region.

Tribalism as an Organizational Framework

Arab tribalism originated as an organizational framework designed to coordinate beni Adam's struggle for survival in a harsh and rudimentary environment. Much like a pyramid, the base of a tribe consisted of small nuclear families that merged imperceptibly into vast extended families of innumerable aunts, uncles, and cousins, and they merged into clans (collections of related families) until they eventually came together as a tribe.

The preeminence of the family in the tribe is easy to understand. You didn't join a tribe; you were born into it. The individual worked with the family, was protected by the family, was cared for by the family in times of illness and infirmity, and was provided a spouse by the family, often a relative designated at birth. There was no one else to rely on, nor was there any place else to go. You were branded with a family identity at birth, and you were what your family was. Child rearing was collective, and orphans, the inevitable result of war and disease, were raised by the family.

The point to be stressed is that tribes were confederations of independent families that had coalesced into ever larger units until they reached the optimal unit for survival in the harsh environment of the desert. Each family retained its sense of independence and was responsible for controlling its members. The family came before the clan, and the clan came before the tribe.

Aside from being a pyramid in which stronger families dominated weaker families, the organizational structure of tribalism was essentially that of the extended family.

Positions within the family were largely a matter of age and sex. The eldest male of the family ruled as a patriarch as long as he was able and, baring abnormalities, ceded power to his eldest son. The head of the family, clan, and tribe was respectively the fount of all authority. He was king, commander, chief financial officer, judge, and jury. The rules were clear, and power struggles were reduced.

This was not a matter of minor concern, for rare was an empire built by an enterprising sheikh that was not threatened by conflict among his sons. Ibn Saud, the founder of the present state of Saudi Arabia, went so far as to force his sons of different mothers to swear on the Koran that they would accept the rule of the eldest, albeit least talented, of their brothers. The family has survived, but its future may be in doubt.

The hierarchy of families and clans within the tribe reflected their power which flowed naturally from their lineage, wealth, courage, and religious aura. All had a great deal to do with the size of the family and the number of sons it could field in battle. And sons there were, for polygamy was the norm.

The sheikh ruled the tribe, but he was required to consult with elders in critical matters such as warfare. Thus, while patriarchal, tribalism also involved the seeds of democracy based on consultation. At least some Arab scholars argue that the tribal principle of consultation is the best hope for democracy in the Arab world today.

Tribalism, then, contained the seeds of both cooperation and conflict. Survival required cooperation among families, while competition for scarce resources within the tribe created tensions between families. It was the same within clans and families. Hence, we have the famous Arab proverb, "Myself against my brother, my brother and I against the family, the family and I against the clan, and the clan and I against the tribe."

The picture remains much the same today in the tribal monarchies of the Arab world. The royal family of Saudi Arabia, for example, is reputed to have some thirty thousand members, depending on how you count. The very name "Saudi Arabia" smacks of tribalism, and the direct descendants of Ibn Saudi, the founder of the Saudi dynasty, tightly control its affairs. Even they, however, are a study in the tension between cooperation and conflict that permeates all tribal societies. They struggle for power within the ruling family, and they cooperate enough to keep themselves in power. Examples from Saudi Arabia will be provided throughout the book because the Saudis represent the most vivid example of modern tribalism and its weaknesses. They also control about one-fourth of the world's proven oil reserves and represent one of the two major centers of power in the Arab world. The other is Egypt.

While Saudi Arabia provides the most graphic example of tribalism in today's world, the family continues to be the core of Arab society throughout the region. It will remain so as long as the family is vital to the survival of the individual.

The Culture of Tribalism: What Society Taught

The kinship framework sketched above was much like an iron frame, designed to keep people in line while organizing them to survive in the harshest of environments. That was the easy part. The trick was getting people to accept their fates and play their assigned roles in an effective manner. This was not an easy task, for beni Adam was a free spirit and inclined toward rebellion and excess. He didn't like being forced to toe the line and was frustrated by a system that allocated everything on the basis of age, sex, and linage. This was fine for those in positions of power, but it did little for a majority of tribal Arabs relegated to a life of subservience by the accident of birth.

The answer for the Arabs, as for most people of the time, was the evolution of a culture that taught them that their world was the best of all possible worlds. Their culture also helped them to make sense of their world by explaining how it came into existence and how, by following its traditions, they could achieve true happiness and security.

The starting point of Arab culture, as for most cultures, was the belief that their social arrangements had been forged by their ancestors, the wisdom of whom was not to be questioned. This, of itself, made their society the best of all possible worlds, and the ancestors, as portrayed in poetry and myth, became role models to be emulated. The role of Qathan and Adnan as the founders of the southern and northern Arabs, respectively, has already been noted. The poets went one step farther by making Seth, the son of Noah, the founder of the southern Arabs, while the northern Arabs claimed the Prophet Ismail, a resident of the holy city of Mecca, as their founder.

The lessons that the ancestors taught were clear and unambiguous. Of these, the most important was that individuals could not survive without the support of their family, clan, and tribe. Loyalty and morality resided with the family, clan, and tribe, in that order. There was no loyalty beyond the tribe.

The next lesson dictated that the survival of the tribe demanded obedience to superiors, be they the father, elders of the clan, or the chief (sheikh) of the tribe. Obedience was ordained by the ancestors and was not a matter of debate.

The third key lesson was that the survival of the tribe depended on its honor. Honor was everything. For males, the test of honor was bravery in battle and sexual prowess. For women, it was giving birth to large numbers of male children.

Along the way, tribal Arabs were taught right from wrong (ethics), the essence of which shines in the proverbs of the era:

Men perish as a victim of their greed.

Words are deadlier than the sword.

27

Prudence starts with seeking advice.

A free man honors his promise.

Whims are the enemy of wisdom (Al-Shindagah, 1999, 1- 6).

Other values such as integrity, hospitality, and generosity abounded. All were matters of pride linked to the central theme of survival in an unforgiving desert. As a sign of their hospitality, pre-Islamic Bedouins (nomadic Arabs) would light bonfires on hills to guide the way for those without shelter. Again, in the words of a pre-Islamic poet:

I am a slave to my guest so long as he is my guest,

but I have no other trait that brings me closer to being a slave

(Al-Shindagah, 1999, 7).

Tribal culture supported its visions of history and morality with specific instructions on how members of the family and tribe were to play the roles that fate assigned them. Basically, boys imitated their fathers, and girls imitated their mothers. Arab culture also scripted the rituals of birth, marriage, and death. It regulated relations between the sexes, allocated economic and political responsibilities, resolved conflicts between individuals and families, and dealt with issues of crime and punishment.

Just to be on the safe side, Arabic culture also taught a heavy dose of fatalism and conformity. Both were praised as godly virtues. Questioning and curiosity were discouraged. Doubting the established order was condemned as blasphemy, and revolt was portrayed as futility. Acceptance and conformity were the order of the day.

Tribal culture was probably an easy sell because there was little reason for the pre-Islamic Bedouins to question their ancestral myths. Desert life was remote, and wandering Bedouins had little contact with the civilized cultures of the era. Tribal life was all they knew, and it had been ever thus. It was just the way things were.

Even the cities and agricultural settlements of the era were organized along tribal lines, and they offered little in the way of enlightenment, other than superstitions that justified the established order.

Intellectuals in settled trading and religious centers possessed a broader cultural perspective than the Bedouin, including a general idea of Judaism and Christianity, both of which were tribal peoples in the region. It was the culture of the Bedouin, however, that provided the core of the Arab psyche.

The International and Economic Environments of Tribalism

The international and economic environments of the Arab Bedouin were inseparable. The international environment consisted largely of other tribes, each pitted against the other in a desperate economic struggle for whatever water and pasture that the desert had to offer. There wasn't enough to share, so they raided neighboring tribes.

In the process, raiding became a passion play of bravery and manliness, the victors eulogized by the poets in streaming verses of hyperbole. In the words of the poet al-Qutami, "Our business is to make raids on the enemy, on our neighbor and on our own brother, in case we find none to raid but a brother" (Hitti, 1956, 25).

Passion plays have their rules, and so it was for the Bedouins. Killing was minimal, and hospitality was a sacred obligation. If raiding were an economic necessity, so too were hospitality and the protection of caravans and traders. The caravans paid for their passage, and the tribes were dependent on the manufactured goods of settled areas that they raided and with whom they traded. You might think of it as a curious ecosystem in which both violence and cooperation were essential for survival. Keep this duality in mind, for it is one of many contradictions that will be encountered in the search for the Arab psyche.

The passion for survival and raiding was rivaled only by the passion for an Arabic language believed to be the essence of the Arab soul. It was the poet who was the master of the Arab soul, for he was master of the language.

According to the rules of the passion play, "one month or so a year was set aside for competitions in warrior skills and poetry reading. On the final day of the assembly, the victorious poet would mount a hilltop and sing the great deeds of his tribe and the nobleness of its chief; now he would describe the joys of vengeance; sometimes tell of courage, always of honour. At other times he stopped to describe the wonders of nature, the solitude of the desert, the scents of the oasis and the freshness of cool springs. Hanging on his words, his hearers surrendered to all the emotions that the poet wished to inspire. On their attentive faces was reflected admiration for a hero, contempt for a coward" (Sedillot in Benoist-Mechin, 1854, 11).

The poetry era was erotic, for manliness required more than the power of the sword. Whatever their content, the annual poetry competitions intensified the passion of the Arabic language while assuring its unity and purity. More than anything else, it is language that identifies the Arab. As the noted anthropologist Carleton Coon writes, "The Arabs had no special development of music, no painting, no haute cuisine, little architecture, no sculpture, and no drama. Their artistic equipment had to be portable.... Hence to the Arabs language is much more than a means of communication. In its classical form, it is the vehicle of the greater part of their aesthetic expression" (Coon, 1958, 58-59).

THE DESERT ORIGINS OF THE ARAB PSYCHE

Tribal culture helped to shape the Bedouin psyche, but the mere existence of a tribal culture didn't mean that everyone was going to behave as scripted. The tribal psyche remained that of beni Adam, who did his best to maximize the simple pleasures of tribal life while minimizing the pain of social ostracism. Maybe that meant following the rules that life had always taught, and maybe it didn't. There wasn't much room for slack, but the psyche did its best to keep things interesting.

The components of the tribal psyche during the pre-Islamic era were the same as the components of the Arab psyche today. For that matter, they are the same for all human psyches. While the bottles were the same, the wine was still pretty raw. The discussion starts with identity and then continues through the motivations of the Arab Bedouin, their reasoning process, and their submission to the wiles of the Arabic language.

The Tribal Identity
The Bedouin Arabs knew who they were. They were Arabs of such and such tribe, and such and such clan and family within that tribe. There were no identity crises here. The stamp was permanent and indelible. They also knew their status within the hierarchy of tribes, as well as their assigned position and roles within the family, clan, and tribe. They

couldn't dodge their identity even if they wanted to, because there was no place to go. Neither other families nor other tribes welcomed strangers, and they viewed people who had forsaken their kin with the deepest of suspicion. Kinship was the foundation of trust which meant that people who had deserted their family couldn't be trusted. Such was the nature of the kinship system.

What Motivated the Pre-Islamic Bedouins?

The biologic needs and appetites of beni tribal were the same as all human beings and require little elaboration. This is not the case of the motives instilled in the Bedouin by their culture. Rarely were people so motivated by pride, honor, compulsive loyalty to the family, and courage as the Bedouin Arabs. All these traits were obsessions.

Reflecting the above motives, tribal culture taught everyone that they were their brother's keeper. It didn't matter who committed the sin, because responsibility was collective, and all members of the family could be killed for the misstep of a close relative. If worse came to worse, the family or even a clan could be locked in a blood feud that would last for generations. An eye for an eye and a brother for a brother. Such were the rules of the game. By their very nature, these cultural values invited conflict.

Now, add two additional elements to the formula. First, the desert environment forced tribes to raid one another for economic survival. Conflict was inevitable. Second, human appetites being what they are, temptation lurked beneath the surface. The tribes were a pretty tight ship, but for those willing to take the risk, poets and peers had some interesting ideas on the topic.

The image of women in early folklore ran the gamut from loving mother to a beguiling seductress possessed of mystical powers. Sometimes she was a witch or priestess, but she was never a passive plaything. Rather, she was an equal partner who captivated the heart of the hero and inspired his bravery and miraculous deeds, often fighting at his side (Khourshid, 1991, 27-28).

While deviance was prevalent, a larger problem was the tendency of the Bedouin to become slaves to their culture. Pride and honor became passions built on survival of the family. There was morality, but morality was linked to kinship, beginning with the family and ending with

31

the tribe. There was no morality beyond the tribe and clan, and not too much beyond the family.

This meant that conflict in the service of the family was moral and encouraged. Tribal morality also condemned greed, lust, and the rest in the name of survival and tribal cohesion, but to what avail? Beni Adam's appetites came with Adam's fall from grace and knew no time or place. Then, as now, they simply had to be dealt with.

But how? The West attempted to solve the problem of deviance in society by increasing guilt, promising damnation in hell, building jails, and becoming more permissive. The Bedouin didn't have jails, heaven and hell were remote concepts, and permissiveness couldn't be allowed without inviting feuds that could destroy the family and its larger extensions.

The answer was shame. Everyone watched everyone as if his or her life depended upon it. Even when violence wasn't involved, the concern for family honor was pervasive and compelling. It had to be. The status of a family was linked to its honor, and the slightest indiscretion of an errant daughter had to be cleansed by the family if its honor were to be restored. Woe to the tribe that didn't avenge the murder of a kinsman for "a bird named 'al Hama' would come out of the victim's skull and hover over his grave shrieking, 'Satisfy my thirst!'" (*Al-Shindagah*, 1999, 5). Remember, status and honor were tied to survival and were not simply misplaced emotions. To again cite our unknown pre-Islamic poet, "I shall wash disgrace with the edge of my sword, no matter what this may bring about" (*Al-Shindagah*, 1999, 5).

The Conscience of Beni Tribal

But what did beni tribal do with the rules of right and wrong that he had learned so diligently? Did he incorporate them into his personality in the form of a conscience or superego that lashed him with guilt whenever he strayed from the true path, or did he use his knowledge of the rules as a guide for not getting caught?

Doing good out of fear of getting caught is not a conscience. It is merely a fear of pain that disappears when no one is looking (Hussain, 2009). Did this mean that morality in pre-Islamic societies was driven solely by shame and that guilt and conscience played no role in keeping people on the straight and narrow? You can judge for yourself.

Emotions: Triggers of Action

Without repeating the discussion in Chapter 1, suffice it to say that emotions are intense psychological imbalances that demand action. For the moment, we will deal with those emotions that formed the core of the Arab psyche, as portrayed in the folklore and anthropological studies of the era. Incidentally, they continue to be among the dominant emotions in the Arab world today.

<u>Fear and Honor</u>

The discussion starts with the emotion of fear because beni tribal was surrounded by the constant threat of death. Predators and pestilence lurked, and war and raiding were part of desert life, as were blood feuds and honor killings. The fear of war offered the choice of fight, flight, or submission, but to what avail? Flight or submission brought hardship, a loss of honor, and cries for revenge. For a true warrior, death was preferable to shame. His bravery would be eulogized by the poet, while the coward would remain forever a blemish on the saga of the tribe.

The fears of women were no less brutal, but seldom eulogized by the poets. Sanitation was rudimentary, and death in childbirth was common. Even then, only the hardiest of infants survived to adulthood. Yet, women braved death rather than suffer the dishonor of remaining childless. It was all part of the pageant of tribalism, for the survival of the tribe required a continual replacement for those who died.

If the Arab Bedouins weren't responding to the fear of ever-present dangers, they were worrying about indiscretions committed by a relative. It was an eye for an eye and a tooth for a tooth, and death for a woman accused of adultery.

Adding to their fears were the peering eyes that followed their every move. Who knew what they saw or invented? But at least the peering eyes were human. Not so the jinn (or jinni) and other evil spirits who lurked in every rock, bush, and animal. Who knew where a date pit thrown carelessly into the garden of an oasis might fall? Perhaps it would kill a jinn and trigger the revenge of his sons? Such was the story of the "Merchant and the Jinn" in *The Arabian Nights* which came later, but I mention it now because the Bedouins were big believers in jinn and spirits of all sorts.

The greatest of beni tribal's fears was the shame of being ostracized from his tribe. Rugged individual that he was, the Bedouin still could not survive without the support of the group. As Hitti writes, "No worse calamity could befall a Bedouin than to lose his tribal affiliation. A trible-less man, in a land where stranger and enemy are synonymous…is practically helpless" (Hitti, 1956, 26, 27).

Love and Pride

If fear were linked to honor, perhaps the same was true of love, that most universal of human emotions. That, at least, was the most common of themes in pre-Islamic folklore. The story of Kalb and Jalilah is one of the most famous tales of Arab antiquity, and it blends conscience with the emotions of love and pride. The story begins with a bitter conflict between two clan leaders who, as stepbrothers, were locked in a bitter conflict for the leadership of the tribe. Tensions were to be eased by the marriage of their children, who were deeply in love and had vowed that they would marry no other. The father of Jalilah, fearing that the marriage would work to his disadvantage, canceled her marriage to Kalb, killed his father, and gave the hand of Jalilah to a powerful but less esteemed sheikh, whom he had turned to for protection against the forces of his stepbrother.

Kalb followed the wedding procession from afar, and in conspiracy with Jalilah, he entered the wedding tent in disguise, killed the would-be bridegroom, and claimed Jalilah as his queen. He then returned victorious as the sheikh of his tribe (Khourshid, 1991). Love was served, the murder of the father revenged, and the unity and honor of the tribe restored. Disgraced, the father of Jalilah vanishes into ignominy.

And where does conscience come in, if it does? Weren't the two lovers upholding the deepest values of their society and smiting evil? What else could conscience ask of them?

Frustration and Anger

Was beni tribal frustrated? The harshness of the tribal environment suggests that frustration was inevitable. There wasn't much to have, and what the Bedouin did have was in short supply. Arranged marriages, as the story of Kalb and Jalilah portrays, were an obvious source of frustration, as were the Bedouins' fierce sense of independence and abhorrence of being fenced in. The early Arabs may have longed for freedom, but the discipline required for survival in the desert didn't provide much scope for individual whim.

Yet, maybe the Bedouin were not as frustrated as one might expect. Frustrations are the product of stifled expectations, and Bedouins tended to accept their fate as the will of the ancestors. As such, there was little cause for frustration. It could also be argued that what frustrations the tribals did have were spent in the grueling struggle for survival and the relentless raiding of neighboring tribes. According to the advocates of the frustration-aggression hypothesis, frustrated warriors make fierce warriors.

Perhaps the most famous story in pre-Islamic folklore, "The Romance of Antar," is preeminently the story of love frustrated. As the story unfolds, Antar, the son of a black slave, falls hopelessly in love with his stepsister, the beautiful Iblah. Alas, Antar is refused recognition by his father, an Arab king. Marriage is out of the question, for Iblah is a princess, and Antar is the unrecognized son of a slave. He pleads for the love of Iblah and the recognition of his father, but he receives neither. Antar's only hope is to become the best horseman, warrior, and poet of his generation. And so he does. Love conquers all as the fame of Antar's sword strikes fear in the enemies of his tribe, and his poems are of such dazzling beauty that they are hung from the Kaba, the holiest of religious shrines in pre-Islamic Arabia. The father relents, and Iblah is swept away by love of the youth who she had once rejected. Samples of the poem can be read on *PoemHunter.com*.

Like all good Arab folklore, Antar is the story of love, honor, bravery, and cleverness, but frustration was the driving force in Antar's pursuit of his impossible dream. The story of Antar is more than that. It is also a story of hope, rebellion, and the ability of people to change their life if they put their minds to it. In a society that controlled its members by locking them in an iron frame and doping their mind with passivism, the popularity of Antar, the King Arthur of Arab folklore, stands as testament to the ability of individuals to change their world if they want to. The popular revolution of the present era suggests that the spirit of Antar still lives.

If the Bedouins were frustrated, the chances are that they were also testy much of the time. This doesn't mean that anger necessarily resulted in violence. To the contrary, displays of anger often served as an early warning system to assure that others would rush in and quell a dispute before it did erupt into violence. Don't forget, the family and tribe were all subject to reprisals and couldn't allow violence to get out of hand.

Thrill of Victory and Agony of Defeat

The thrill of victory and the agony of defeat ranked high on the hierarchy of Bedouin emotions, as did righteousness and envy that buoyed attacks on neighboring tribes. Add the vows of hate and vengeance that eased the agony of defeat, and you can begin to understand the passion for raiding in Bedouin society. Later chapters will find the same emotions at work in the Middle East today.

This doesn't mean that tribal life was without its joys. Weddings, feasts, and the birth of a male son were times of great joy. Most happy memories, however, were fleeting and soon dulled by the tedium of daily survival. Not so the thrill of victories past and the daring feats of Antar and other poetic superheroes. They were the stuff of dreams in a society that longed for superheroes.

The moral values expressed by the pre-Islamic poets provide vivid pictures of a lusty society in which superstition reigned and the heroes worshiped wine as well as idols. Such is the story of Amriolkais, a hero who pined in vain for the love of the beautiful Onaiza. Sir William Jones recounts the story:

> One day, when her tribe had struck their tents, and were changing their station, the women, as usual, came behind the rest, with the servants and baggage, in carriages fixed on the backs of camels. Amriolkais advanced slowly at a distance, and, when the men were out of sight, had the pleasure of seeing Onaiza retire with a party of damsels to a rivulet or pool…where they undressed themselves and were bathing when the lover appeared, dismounted from his camel, and sat upon their clothes, proclaiming aloud that whoever would redeem her dress must present herself naked before him (Jones, n.d., 2–3).

The story ends with the morning chill forcing the girls to submit, and when they complain of cold and hunger, the hero builds a fire, kills the young camel on which he had been riding, and the wine flows. Onaiza, after much begging by Amriolkais, takes the prince to safety on her camel. His mission completed, the hero moves on to other conquests, including the seduction of a maiden from an enemy tribe.

Poetry was stripped of its pagan ways with the advent of Islam, but the emotions of beni Adam, not to be denied, gave way to *The Arabian Nights*.

The Missing Emotions: Curiosity and Innovation

The Bedouins may have dreamed of superheroes, but curiosity ranked low among their emotions. They were resigned to their fate, and like other creatures of the region, they lived at one with the desert. They accepted what the fates provided and made little effort to change their environment. How could they? They were helpless against nature. It was hard enough just to get along at it was.

The exception to this rule were remarkable feats of animal breeding, but even these adaptive innovations did little to alter the delicate balance between the Bedouin and the desert. The priest and sages condemned change, and who was the Bedouin to question the wisdom of the past?

Cognition: Navigating Between Pain and Pleasure

The stories of Antar and the two lovers suggest that the Bedouins, for all of the rigidity of their routine, did a great deal of thinking in their pursuit of pleasure and avoidance of pain. Every move in the two stories was based on intricate knowledge of their societies and included an endless chain of if-then sequences. "If I do this, then they will do that."

Did the tribal psyche have an ego or self that cleverly guided its relentless search to increase pleasure and reduce pain? I raise the question because some early anthropologists suggested that the group so controlled tribal individuals that they lacked an individual ego capable of operating independently of the group.

This view is no longer in vogue, but I raise the question because many works on the Arab psyche assume that the Arab psyche of today is merely a carbon copy of the Arab psyche of the pre-Islamic era. This is a very dangerous assumption and could go a long way in explaining American frustrations in the region.

The Limitations of Tribal Logic

Did the presumed simplicity of the tribal reasoning process during the pre-Islamic era suggest that it was rational? It was certainly rational in its ability to adapt to the harshness of the desert environment, but there is enough evidence from the folklore of the era to suggest that at least some of the defense mechanisms and other mind games of today were well established during the tribal era.

Particularly important was projection, the tendency to blame others for everything. To accept blame was to bring the pain of shame on self and tribe, not to mention the risk of feuds and honor killings. How could you blame the elders? They were beyond reproach and most vindictive when their decisions were questioned. Hostile clans and tribes were the logical candidates to blame.

Paralleling projection was displacement, or the process of discharging painful feelings of frustration and anger on innocent individuals unable to fight back, be it a wife, slave, or conquered village. The pain of anger and frustration would be alleviated for the moment, but nothing was resolved. The pain returned, as did the abuse of innocent parties.

This process was facilitated by making the target individuals seem inferior and unworthy of concern. Key to this process was the need to create "emotional distance" between the assaulter and the victim in order to desensitize any guilt or pangs of conscience on the part of offender (Grossman, 2009, 156). In psychological terms, this is called compartmentalizing. Guilt is avoided because the victim has been desensitized. Grossman illustrates this point by titling a chapter in his book *On Killing*, "To Me, They Were Less Than Dogs" (Grossman, 2009, 156).

Things were more a matter of status or "social distance" during the tribal era, but took on moral tones with the advent of Islam. Conflicts in the Middle East today are all moral pageants, each side slaughtering the other in the name of moral righteousness.

Another defense mechanism of lasting interest was the tendency of the Bedouins to seek escape from the dismal hardships of the present by identifying with the superheroes of the poets. Imaginations soared, as did hope that a strong leader with superhuman powers would emerge to lead them to victory over their foes. This was a dominant theme in tribal culture and diverted attention from thoughts of changing a way of life that offered little more than a hand-to-mouth existence.

Finally, we come to denial, the process of avoiding pain by unconsciously denying that the source of pain exists. One reason that Bedouins adapted to their environment rather than attempting to change it was their reluctance to search for evidence suggesting that their tribal lifestyle wasn't the best of all possible worlds.

Arabic as a Tribal Language

Applying our earlier discussion of language to the pre-Islamic era, we see that the Arab scholar Wafiq Raouf begins his analysis of the Arab psyche with the observation that poetry was the literary foundation of Arabic culture and, as such, stamped the Arab reasoning process with the emotion, embellishment, and illusion for which pre-Islamic poetry was so famous (Raouf, 2005, 16–17). The same could be said for *The Arabian Nights* and Arabic folklore of later eras. The Arabs are not unique in this regard, for most poetry is full of illusion and ambiguity. I mention the point because the Arab psyche has yet to dispense with the emotion, embellishment, and illusion of tribal Arabic.

Tribal Poker

Such then was the tribal psyche that sketched a mental roadmap that the Bedouin used to identify friends and enemies, assess their relative power, weigh the penalties for deviation, and otherwise assess and evaluate the information that came his way from parents, peers, priests, elders, soothsayers, and star gazers.

It was a poker game at both the individual and group level. Pursuit of pleasure required risks, most of which required reliable information. The question was, "Who to believe?" Parents, siblings, and elders, fearing a blood feud, were bound to be conservative, especially when it came to affairs of the heart. But not the poets, who tempted youth to destruction by eulogizing the amorous conquests of their heroes. Stargazers and soothsayers also inclined in that direction, but they went one step farther by giving gamblers a timeframe and some odds based on the stars. It was all very dangerous, especially when adding time and space into the reasoning process.

The jokers in tribal poker were time and space. Time for the Arab psyche was dictated by the seasonal migrations and rituals of birth, maturity, marriage, and death. No one seemed to worry about it. Time just happened, and every deadly, boring day followed another. No wonder people thrived on stories of Antar and the other superheroes of Arab mythology.

That is, unless a raid was pending or temptation beckoned. Raiding required that the psyche plan with great precision. Surprise was of the essence, and even a lapse of a few moments could alert the enemy and result in disaster. The timing of lovers had to be even more precise. There was little time for words, and while the eyes of family and neighbors peered, the eyes of lovers flickered with secret messages (Hamady, 1960). Discovery spelled doom, but what could the psyche do?

Space was trickier. Survival depended upon adequate space for pasture, and struggles for space were a prime source of tribal warfare. Large spaces had to be covered, and the terrain was difficult. Nothing could be left to chance. It was even harder for lovers. They had to find empty space away from the peering eyes, and yet they managed, at least for one glorious moment.

HOW MOST BEDOUIN ARABS BEHAVED MOST OF THE TIME

Beni tribal behaved much as you would expect him to behave, given the environment in which he lived and the way his psyche attempted to cope with its universe. There weren't many options, and there wasn't much slack. The behavior patterns sketched below were the norm, and they serve as a baseline for examining how the Arab psyche and Arab behavior have evolved over the course of centuries. Be warned, however, that there were many exceptions to the patterns described. Indeed, virtually all folklore of the era stressed deviance from the norm.

The typical behavior of pre-Islamic Bedouins was shaped by the convergence of their Arab environment and their psyche. It is difficult to draw a clear distinction between political, social, and economic behavior in Bedouin society, for all were geared to perpetuating the tribal way of life and blended together in a seamless web, each drawing upon the other.

Political Behavior

Expressions of Nationalism, Ethnicity, and Tribalism

Aside from a vague sense of Arabism, expressions of identity focused on the family, clan, and tribe, in that order. Families and clans squabbled within the tribal framework, but stood as a cohesive unit in the face of danger. Pre-Islamic poetry left no doubt about the matter:

> *I am nothing but a member of my tribe*
>
> *If it goes astray, I will too,*
>
> *and if it follows the right path, so will I (Al Shindagah, 1999, 4).*

It wasn't quite that simple, but suffice it to say that no one wandered around in a state of mental anguish wondering who they were, what they were, or where their loyalties lay. Identity crises would come later. In the meantime, most of the waking hours of beni tribal were devoted to supporting the family and protecting its honor. Raiding, an economic necessity, was part of that picture. Those really interested in the topic might find Smith's (1903) *Kinship and Marriage in Early Arabia* to be of interest. The book also illustrates the marked similarities between the tribal traditions of the Arabs and the Hebrews of the era.

Spiritualism

Because life was harsh, the Arabs of the pre-Islamic era prayed to a variety of gods in the hope that one or another could ease their woes, smite their enemies, and protect them from the evil spirits that lurked behind every bush and tree.

The stuff of fantasy? Not for people of the era. Gods and spirits were real and had to be accommodated. Gods resided in heavens, and evil spirits lived in the earth. It was almost as if humans were a battleground. The gods entered through the head, and the evil spirits through the feet (Nathan, 1995). Blood sacrifices were common and are often portrayed in Islamic dramas to illustrate the barbarity of Arab life before the revelation of God's message to the Prophet Mohammed.

Each tribe had its favored gods, and often each clan or family did as well. This diversity of gods assured that faith, such as it was, would fragment the Arabs rather than serve as a basis for Arab solidarity. There was no shared religious identity. Yet, there seemed to be a pervasive awe of all gods. Mecca, the location of a unique black stone believed to have spiritual powers, had emerged as a center of spiritual pilgrimage long before the advent of Islam.

In the most curious of ways, spiritualism also promoted the sense of informal equality for which the Bedouins were famous. The patriarch ruled with an iron hand, but always with the certain knowledge that jinn lurked among the oppressed. The evil eye played no favorites.

Just to be on the safe side, pre-Islamic tribes sought the guidance of prophets, some forty thousand of whom were known prior to the Prophet Mohammed, the true prophet. If a prophet couldn't be found, witches or soothsayers would do. It wasn't wise to leave home without consulting one.

Establishing a Strong Support Base and Offering Expressions of Loyalty

As groups were essential for survival, the first step in the Bedouins' struggle to meet their basic needs was establishing a strong support base.

The only support groups available to beni tribal were kinship groups extending from the family. As a result, beni Adam became the ideal family man. What choice did the Bedouin have? He could conform or be ostracized from the family and die in humiliation. He couldn't run, and he couldn't hide.

It was only to be expected that Bedouin loyalty patterns followed the family, clan, and tribal sequence because it was these units that shaped the Bedouin's identity and were the key to the Bedouin's physical survival. The existence of family and tribal gods were all part of the formula for assuring kinship solidarity. Kinship loyalty was not only a practical necessity, it was a religious obligation.

Control and Submission: Keeping What You Have

Being a fatalist in dealing with the universe didn't mean that beni tribal wasn't preoccupied with security and controlling everything that could be controlled.

One might be tempted to say that beni tribal was paranoid. That probably is not accurate. Paranoia is irrational fear, and beni tribal's fears were quite rational. He put his family first and did his best to tear down outsiders. Why, then, was it irrational to assume that others would do the same? Besides, vengeance in tribal societies was collective. Who knew what indiscretions his brothers had committed in an effort to get closer to the girl next door?

Such fears made beni tribal very authoritarian. He ruled those under him with an iron hand, micromanaged their affairs, delegated authority grudgingly, and punished those who brought shame to the family. In the case of clan and tribal leaders, much was to be gained by playing one family against another. One could never be too careful. In a later time, some of the Turkish sultans took the precaution of assassinating their brothers upon assuming office.

For all of his authoritarian behavior, beni tribal could be the most compassionate of people. Compassion just had to be expressed in the right way. Generosity was not a sign of weakness, but a source of pride, wealth, and honor. So it was that wives were well fed and children pampered. Beni tribal, himself, was not too thin. Fat equaled wealth and success and was worn as a badge of honor. I recall reading ads for fat pills in the Kuwaiti press during my early ventures in the Middle East, and Saudis continue to mock themselves about being too fat to hold meetings in small rooms.

Authoritarianism could also be comforting. A strong father brought security and eased the burdens of responsibility. One merely followed orders, and conflict was avoided.

However authoritarian beni tribal may have been, an easygoing sense of equality existed within the tribe. They were family, after all, and first names or affectionate nicknames were the norm. Fancy titles would come later.

Finally, beni tribal clung to his lands as the ultimate form of security. This was invariably the case of sedentary cultures, but even the tribes of Arabia fought jealously over their migration routes. In both cases, survival depended upon the control of land.

Expressions of Satisfaction and Discontent

Because beni tribal was fatalistic, he didn't expect much. His sorrows were those of the family, and the family elders conveyed them to the head of the clan and tribe. Elections and opinion polls were unknown, but tribal leaders were anxious to have consensus in the tribe and were wary of dissent among the elders. As a result, issues that required tribal cohesion were settled by consultation.

Social Behavior

Conforming to the Pressures of Culture and Tradition

Getting along in tribal society meant conforming to the rules of tribalism, as stifling as they might be. So people usually did what people always did. They clustered within their extended families, bowed to age, accepted the authority of the eldest male, did what their gender was expected to do, worked their fingers to the bone, shared what they had with relatives, sought the approval of their peers, avoided the evil eye, and had lots of children.

Gender roles were as clear as everything else. Men searched for pasture, raided their neighbors, spent a lot of time socializing with their male friends, and sired as many children as nature would allow. I recall being introduced to an elderly Bedouin in Jordan who was holding a baby in his arms. My first instinct was to congratulate him on a new grandchild or great-grandchild, when my host whispered in my ear that the sheikh had sired the child and that he was about to fulfill a lifelong wish of dying with his child in his arms. Bearing and begetting children were vital to the survival of the family and matters of intense pride.

Women weren't veiled or secluded. They couldn't be. There was work to do. Women cooked, cleaned, cared for the children, worked beside men in the fields, and in the case of the Bedouins, did their part in preparing for the semiannual migrations. Often, they also fought beside their warrior husbands. This didn't mean that they weren't watched with care, because they were.

Women also worried a great deal about being able to bear a large number of sons. It was their honor, their security, and their identity. The inability to bear sons carried the stigma of failure and threatened divorce or additional wives. Could the man have been at fault? Not a prayer. It was a matter of honor.

Women lived through their sons, and they were her glory. Sons also brought daughters-in-law, whom she could control, and grandchildren to be pampered. Many women died in childbirth. Those who survived spent a great deal of time mourning the death of their infants, few of whom survived to adulthood. Raiding and turf wars also took a horrendous toll on the male population, as did pestilence and disease. In most cases, this meant accepting a new husband.

A special place in a woman's heart was reserved for her brothers, with whom she shared a bond of blood and collegiality. Her father, while not necessarily unkind, was remote and to be served. She had little choice in the selection of her husband, who treated her as private property and demanded obedience. Love sometimes flourished, but marriage was a social and economic contract. If she came from a different tribe, the bond was not one of blood that required special kindness or the need to deal with her brothers. Marriage of a cousin helped, but it was to her brothers that she often turned for advice and support. She could have more children and remarry, but brothers were finite.

Submission to age played a key role in conformity of both genders. In the words of the most timeworn of Arab proverbs, "One day older, one year wiser." I recall the story of a Libyan friend who had five sisters, all anxious to be married. Unfortunately, the elder sister had fallen in love with a man below her status (my friend was the son of a tribal sheikh), and all weddings had to be postponed until the matter had been resolved. Eventually, the father threw up his hands in despair and turned the matter over to the eldest son, who, checking the suitor out, rejected him.

Dealing with Others in a Dominant-Subordinate Environment

In one way or another, the pressures of culture, kinship conformity, and spiritualism combined to produce four indelible hallmarks of tribal behavior: honor, hospitality, conformity to tradition, and passivity. You can't understand the Arab world today without them.

Beni tribal was obsessed with honor and dignity because he had to be. Appearances were everything in a world of peering eyes. Beni tribal, accordingly, played his cards close to his vest, careful to hide weakness and often disguising his true intentions. He was macho to the extreme and given to embellishments in boasting of his sexual prowess and praising the feats of his lineage. The more he boasted of his lineage, the more he had to protect it by avoiding marriages beneath his status, killing sisters and daughters who brought shame on the family, and glorifying herding while rejecting the menial tasks of the cultivator.

The importance of honor and dignity also meant that affronts came easily, especially in the presence of others. A challenge was a challenge, and beni tribal couldn't back down. How could he? To back down was to lose face and shame his family. More often than not, bravado gave way to anger, if not aggression. Hopefully, others would rush in before the confrontation resulted in disaster.

Beni tribal was equally the most vengeful of individuals. Affronts, if not rectified, were carried forward, smoldering until they became feuds, the origins of which were often lost in history.

Because affronts to pride and dignity were so dangerous, beni tribal could be the most polite and solicitous of individuals. One was effusive in the praise of others, and rare was a conversation that didn't begin with concern for their well being, all the while avoiding interest in another's wife or daughters that might lead to misunderstandings and conflict.

In much the same manner, beni tribal was the most generous and hospitable of people. Misers were abhorred, and honor and the rigors of tribal life demanded no less. Even potential adversaries had to get along to survive in the harsh environment of the desert.

Deviating from the Pressures of Culture and Tradition

Beni tribal's main strategy for increasing pleasure and reducing pain was getting along by going along. There wasn't much choice, and as we have seen, the children of beni Adam were locked in an iron frame and programmed to accept their fate as the will of the gods and ancestors.

This didn't mean that beni tribal didn't push things on the margins when no one was looking, especially if the girl in the next tent was exceptionally beautiful. Who could blame him? The beauty of human women had tempted even the angels of God.

Was beni tribal sex crazed? No more than the rest of us. He certainly didn't have access to the 2.5 million porn sites on today's internet (Ogas and Gaddam, 2011). This said, the impression that beni tribal was sex crazed is easy to understand. It was the stuff of folklore, *The Arabian Nights*, *The Perfumed Garden*, and most Western movies about the region. Polygamy added to the impression of sexual excess, as did the need to be macho. How disillusioning it is for those of us raised on *The Arabian Nights* to learn that male-enhancement drugs have become top sellers in the Arabian Peninsula.

While beni tribal's scope for maneuver was limited, a clever fox could always manage to get a bit more than his allotted share of the cake, however meager it might be. I introduce the fox at this point, as the fox becomes one of the key actors in the Arab drama as it unfolds over the centuries.

The fox instinctively knew that the best pickings were near the seats of power. But how was he to get close to his prey when the positions of power were allocated on the basis of lineage, age, and sex?

Based upon the folklore of the era, there were four ways for the fox to hover near the seats of power. The first was honor and glory. War heroes captured the public imagination and had to be accommodated. If this proved difficult, one could excel by becoming a priest or mystic, or better yet, a poet who claimed inspiration from a mystical friend from the netherworld (Al Gosaibi, 2010). For foxes that could neither fight nor rhyme, the door was always open for a spy. Rare was a sheikh or tribal king who didn't worry about his back.

The lowest of the foxes were the sycophants, bowing and scraping before the wielders of power while screaming their praise to the heavens. Were the sheiks fooled? No, but they loved adulation and enjoyed humiliating bootlickers just to see how far they could make them stoop.

Whatever the case, the closer the foxes were to the center of power, the easier it was for them to sample the pleasures of power, promote the interests of their families, and tear down the reputation of their adversaries. Slandering rival families and clans was vital because resources were scarce, and there was only so much room at the top. Besides, they were playing the same game, and what choice did the fox have but to follow suit? Offense, for those locked in this dangerous game, was the best defense. The more the fox invented salacious rumors, the less time his enemies, including relatives, had to worry about him.

For those subject to vile gossip, the path was clear. Deny, stonewall, scapegoat, and fly into a rage, inviting confrontation. People already thought the worse, and giving credence to their suspicions could be fatal.

It all sounds rather venal, but what other options were there for getting ahead in the tribal environment?

A curious equilibrium was thus established between the need for a strong support base, founded on solidarity against external threats, and the need to serve oneself by playing the fox. It was a complex game that would get even more complex with the evolution of Arab society.

It could also be a deadly game with no exit except rebellion. In the tribal world, rebellion meant the splintering of the tribe and family, a dangerous option in an environment that equated power with size of the family and tribe. More often than not, splintering occurred when the death of a patriarch precipitated conflict between sons of different mothers. This was the story of the two lovers. It is also a story being played out today in Saudi Arabia and other remaining tribal kingdoms.

Economic Behavior

Bedouins worked from sunrise to sunset just to keep starvation from the door. They worked as a family unit, most of it devoted to the task of herding, hunting, and raiding. Sedentary labor was beyond their dignity.

Yet, for all of their hard work, they seldom survived at more than a subsistence level. Drought and disaster washed away the prosperity of abundant times. There wasn't much to save, and acquisitions of wealth were soon dissipated on feasts of birth and marriage. Whatever was left went to the priests and soothsayers. It was all part of the tribal plan for keeping poor families from acquiring more wealth than the tribal sheikh. Wealth was part of his powerbase, and it had to be preserved. Anthropologists refer to squandering of wealth on feasts and religious ceremonies as leveling devices (Nash, 1966).

RED-FLAG ISSUES: WAS TRIBALISM ALL BAD?

Was tribalism all bad? Perhaps the answer to this question is to be found in the relationship of the red-flag issues of extremism, violence, fragmentation, tyranny, inequality, and economic stagnation. It is these issues that today's Arabs find so detrimental to their dream of an Arab revival and that Americans find so frustrating to their dream of controlling the Middle East.

Extremism Versus Moderation

Let's start with extremism, seeing that it heads the list of America's frustrations in the region. Extremism, theirs and ours, begins with authoritarianism and the tendency of people to see their world in stark terms of black and white with few shades of gray in between. Because the Bedouins tended to perceive their world in terms of absolutes and opposites, it is there that we look for the seed of extremism that is so prevalent in the region today.

Of these absolutes and opposites, none was greater than the Bedouin's tendency to judge other people as being either good or evil or friend or foe. Either way, there was little room for compromise. Fear and frustration added to extremism, as did the emotion of self-righteousness that placed the glory of the group above all. Temporary alliances could be made, but most were a matter of expediency and fragile at best. All were inflamed by a culture of superheroes and mystical gods who urged excess rather than moderation. Underlying all of the above was the economic austerity of the desert that pitted family against family and tribe against tribe in the struggle for survival. It was a world in which you either won or lost, and there was no turning back.

Despite the Bedouin's extremist tendencies, the logic of mutual aid managed to prevail, and hospitality became one of the crowning Arab virtues. The seeds of moderation were clearly evident in contests of poetry and horsemanship that prevailed over the course of history. Religious extremism was also muted by the mutual respect for multiple and competing gods, none of which was almighty or particularly effective. If serving one god proved ineffective in fighting the jinn or the evil eye, others could be consulted. Choice, by its very nature, leads to moderation.

Violence Versus Reconciliation

Religion didn't necessarily lead to violence in pre-Islamic Arabia, although human sacrifices were common, and faith played its role in the pageant of raiding and tribal conflict. More likely to trigger violence were the emotions of fear and honor so prevalent in Bedouin society. The peering eyes were either attempting to destroy your honor, or they were locking you in a social vice to protect theirs. The former called for revenge, and the latter produced frustration. Neither guaranteed violence, but the prospect of both loomed large in a society that glorified raiding. Now add hate to the formula and the assumption, not unrealistic, that everyone was out to get you and your family. This led naturally to suspicion and often to violence, especially when offense was the best defense and no one was willing to back down for fear of losing face. Political economists are content to attribute tribal violence to a struggle for scarce resources. Economic conflict, however, doesn't explain the persistence of blood feuds over generations or Arab generosity in times of severe adversity.

For all of the emphasis on raiding and violence in pre-Islamic Arabia, it is important to keep in mind that raiding stressed posturing and war cries rather than killing and maiming. The desert pitted all against all, but it also taught the need for tolerance. Thus it was that tribalism contained complex rituals for settling conflicts without violence. Unrestrained violence was as threatening to the survival of the tribal system as it is to the future of the region today. Maybe that is what Al Gosaibi meant when he said that the Arabs had a lot to learn from tribalism. Perhaps he was also referring to the tribal values of integrity and freedom.

Fragmentation Versus Solidarity

Tribalism, by its very nature, fragmented the Arabs and created a psyche that, for all of its sense of Arabness, couldn't extend feelings of loyalty beyond the limits of the tribe. It is the Bedouin fixation on the family and clan that leads the Arab nationalists of today to condemn tribalism so bitterly. How, they ask, can you build an integrated nation when people put family and clan above the interests of the state and use their positions of power to channel resources to their kin while undermining the influence of competing families and tribes? Their answer is simple. You can't. What passes for an Arab state is little more than a collection of kinship power centers (Sharabi, 1988).

Perhaps tribalism also contains the seeds of American frustration in the Arab world. It is far easier to control a unified country than it is to deal with an endless number of hostile groups always at each other's throats. If America pleases one, it alienates untold numbers of its rivals.

Tyranny Versus Democracy

Tribal society was collective, and thoughts of "one man, one vote" weren't part of the process of deciding who gets what, when, and how. It was also a most rigid authoritarian society that prized conformity and submission, and it placed the rights of the group above the rights of individuals.

This said, each family and clan controlled its own affairs, and consultative councils, consisting of clan elders, discussed the issues of importance. The sheikh was dominant, but he couldn't go against the will of the tribe and retain his power. The elders didn't vote, but it wasn't hard to read their moods.

In pursuing this point, the Arab scholar Mohammed Shahrour argues that the tribal tradition of consensus continues to be the Arab's best hope for democracy (Sharour, 1994). Consensual democracy differs from Western liberal democracy which is based upon individual choice, but at least all major groups in society, stakeholders in modern parlance, are represented. That will not change, Shahrour argues, until individuals feel secure enough to think independently of their core support groups, a situation that has yet to be achieved.

Human rights are a little trickier. The Bedouin's "for me or against me" mentality was not compatible with human rights. People were either friends or enemies, and in the Bedouin's view, enemies deserved no rights. The rigid social structure of the era relegated women to inferior positions and made mobility among classes almost impossible. You were what your family was, and status categories persisted over generations.

As always, there were exceptions, including the superb treatment of strangers, discussed in the early part of this chapter, and the casual relationships that prevailed within the tribe. Family heads were authoritarian, but it was a pastoral authoritarianism in which members of the family had rights and were generally free to express their views.

Inequality Versus Equity

Members of a tribe were family and, as such, were entitled to a reasonable share of the tribe's wealth. The tribe worked and raided as a unit. The more the tribe prospered, the more its members prospered. Powerful families did better than weaker families, but the differences weren't great. It was all part of building tribal solidarity, and it remains so today as individuals are honor bound to put kin before others. Slaves were property and seldom entitled to more than subsistence.

Economic Stagnation Versus Economic Growth

The Bedouin subsisted, but little more. The means of production didn't change because they, like all other dimensions of tribal society, were calculated to resist change. This included myths that proclaimed the tribal world to be the will of the ancestors and promoted the idea of fate as well as feelings of fearfulness, suspicion, resignation, fatalism, and low self-volition. The physical isolation of the desert insulated them from external pressures that might have precipitated change, and constant raiding created an atmosphere of social isolation that precluded the free flow of information from tribe to tribe. Physical and social isolation, in turn, created a sense of psychological isolation that made it difficult for tribals to visualize themselves in any environment other than their own. Things were ever thus, and no one thought about changing a system that, in their limited view, provided admirably for their basic needs. The few who did speak of change were ostracized as deviants or written off as mystics better suited to putting curses on their enemies than leading a social movement.

While the pre-Islamic Bedouins showed little interest in changing the tribal system, they showed great ingenuity in adapting to the demands of the desert. They used basic astronomy to predict the weather and time their migrations. The demands of survival were also reflected in skilled animal husbandry and exceptional skills of warfare. These adaptations enabled the Bedouins to survive their desert environment without changing it. However, this didn't mean that Bedouins were averse to settling in a lush oasis when the opportunity presented itself.

THE DESERT VERSUS THE SOWN

Most of the discussion in this chapter has focused on the nomadic Bedouins of the Arabian Peninsula, for it was their culture and their psyche that stamped the Arab psyche of the time. It is one of the curious ironies of history, as suggested earlier, that the weakest of farmers became the bravest of warriors and would totally dominate those who had forced them into a desert existence.

A second curious irony of history is that the impetus for change came from the settled populations and not storied warriors of the desert. Settled populations soon inclined toward commerce and had greater exposure to the outside world.

It is also probable that the daring actions of Antar and other folk heroes made the creation of settled populations possible. As Freud points out in *Moses and Monotheism,* the plot was the same for all super-heroes of ancient times, beginning with Sargon of Agade and including Moses, Cyrus, Romulus, Heracles, and others (Freud, 1955).

Recall that all forty thousand prophets spawned prior to Mohammed emerged from settled agricultural and trading communities. So it was with the power and prosperity of the Kuraysh, the tribe of the Prophet Mohammed, who had become international traders as well as the guardians of the holy sites of Mecca (Said, 2006). Unlike the Bedouin, they had acquired an enhanced sense of self-volition and had developed a sense of empathy that enabled them to see and appreciate the possibilities of change. The settled populations were tribal and shared most of the attributes of the Bedouin, but the urban environment allowed the entry of ideas that were closed by the physical, social, and psychological isolation of the Bedouin.

The economy of the urban environment also inclined villagers to be more concerned with protecting their crops than raiding their neighbors. This didn't mean that they enjoyed greater peace of mind than the Bedouin. Fear was more intense precisely because they couldn't flee. They fought bitterly when threatened, but they found it easier to pay tribute to marauding tribes than risk destruction of their crops and livestock (Coon, 1958, 193).

Tribalism, then, provided the foundation for authoritarianism, fatalism, distrust, violence, and many of the other negative characteristics associated with the Arab world today. Tribalism, however, also contained the seeds of many laudable Arab qualities such as honesty, hard work, cooperation, moderation, adaptability, bravery, prudence, hospitality, and generosity.

CHAPTER 3

THE ARAB PSYCHE FROM TRIBALISM TO ISLAM

If tribalism laid the foundation of the Arab psyche, it was Islam that took a fragmented and conflicted people and molded them into a global power renowned for their military prowess, creative genius, and cultural enlightenment.

This chapter prepares the stage for dealing with America's woes in the Middle East by exploring the role of Islam in shaping the Arab psyche. That role is profound. Separating religion from the Arab psyche may be as difficult as separating Judaism from the Israeli psyche. Islam, like Judaism and Christianity, is more than a faith. It is a culture, a historical memory, and a way of looking at the world.

The chapter begins with a few words about the Islamic faith and then examines how Islam changed the Arab environment, altered the Arab psyche, and inevitably, shaped the way Arabs of the era behaved. In the process, the discussion touches on the glories of the Islamic era, the causes of its decline, and the role of Islam in shaping the red-flag issues of extremism, violence, unity, effective governance, democracy, equity, and development that frustrate both the Arabs and the Americans today.

A FEW WORDS ABOUT ISLAM

Islam, the religion of the world's 1.5 million Muslims, views itself as an extension of Judaism and Christianity. God, according to Islam, revealed the true faith to the Hebrews. Displeased by their lapses of faith, God revealed the true faith to Christ and charged Him with returning believers to the path of righteousness and salvation. Again displeased, God made his third and final revelation of the true faith to the Prophet Mohammed. Christians originally viewed Islam as a radical variation of Christianity, much as Jews originally considered Christianity to be yet another sect of Judaism.

All three faiths worship the same God, the one God, and Islam incorporates all of the major prophets of Judaism and Christianity, including Noah, Abraham, and Moses. Jesus is recognized as a major prophet, but not the son of God. This said, the Koran devotes an entire chapter to the Virgin Mary and prophesizes that the second coming of Christ will herald the approach of the end of time (Filiu, 2008). So close was the Koran to the Bible that critics at the time accused the Prophet Mohammed of using trickery to spread Jewish and Christian theology in the region (Raouf, 2005, 30).

Much like Christ before him, the Prophet Mohammed was a revolutionary reformer intent on leading the Arabs and all humanity to a world of peace, unity, hope, development, enlightenment, and salvation. Few features of tribal life were spared the Prophet's wrath, including the tribal psyche.

Also in common with Christianity and Judaism, the Koran (the revealed word of God) and the Sunna (the actions and sayings of the Prophet Mohammed) start with a clear list of commandments, buttressed by passages that submit to multiple interpretations.

The key commands of the Koran of which there is no ambiguity are the five pillars of Islam. First, Muslims must witness that, "There in no God but God and Mohammed is his Prophet." To become a Muslim requires no more than accepting this basic contract with God. This brief phrase, as Armajani writes, is the most oft-repeated sentence in the world of Islam:

It is whispered in the ear of the newborn child, it is repeated throughout life, and it is the last sentence uttered when he is laid in the grave. It

*is used to call the faithful to prayer and it has served as the battle
cry of Muslim soldiers in all of the wars of Islam* (Armajani, 1970, 4).

In addition to the basic submission to God, all Muslims are required
to pray five times a day, give generously of their wealth, fast during the
holy month of Ramadan, and baring insurmountable adversity, to make
at least one pilgrimage to Mecca during their lifetime.

Immediately after the five pillars of Islam come the cardinal prohibitions. Muslims are not to drink, fornicate, gamble, worship idols, charge
interest on loans, or eat pork and other impure foods. Worshiping idols
was a denial of the oneness of God, and food restrictions were borrowed from Judaism, although Christians often ignored them. The other
prohibitions address the main sources of social conflict in Arab society,
including the coveting of women, economic exploitation, alcoholism,
and honor feuds.

In addition to the prohibitions, Islam also preaches tolerance and
moderation. Muslims are not to kill other Muslims or People of the
Book, a special status granted to Christians and Jews who are allowed
to live in peace among Muslims in compensation for a tax. At a more
mundane level, Muslims are urged to be patient with their troubles,
avoid excess, and behave like reasonable and rational people. Or, as a
forgotten television cleric expressed, "Muslims were not to bray like an
ass or run around like a chicken with its head cut off."

Other passages in the Koran and Sunna, by contrast, are fiery calls
for believers to defend their faith. The contradiction between calls for
tolerance and fiery calls for the defense of the faith are not a matter of
great concern to most Muslims. They, like Christians and Jews, believe
that God's word is pure and free of contradictions. If contradictions
appear to exist, the problem lies with humans and their inability to
understand the wisdom of God.

The overall tone of the Koran and Sunna is one of moderation, but
extremists find little difficulty in twisting the words of the Koran and
Sunna to suit their own purposes. Of these, perhaps the most important to America's frustrations in the Middle East is the discussion of
jihad.

Jihad, the struggle against evil, is now widely viewed as a sixth pil-
lar of Islam among fundamentalists, but the trend is far from universal.
In reality, there are two jihads. The first requires Muslims to defend

their faith. If believers didn't defend their faith, there would be no faith. Ambiguity enters the picture when people attempt to define what it means to defend the faith. Does it mean resisting the occupation of Islamic lands, or does it also include preemptive attacks on suspected sources of evil, such as the United States?

The enemies of Islam are evil, but so are the temptations of the devil who leads Muslims from the path of righteousness. Indeed, the latter is often referred to as the "great" jihad. As explained by Sheikh Atiyyah Saqr, an eminent Muslim scholar long associated with Cairo's venerable Al-Azhar Mosque:

> The word "jihad" means exerting effort to achieve a desired thing or prevent an undesired one.... Among the types of Jihad are struggling against one's desires, the accursed Satan, poverty, illiteracy, disease, and all evil forces in the world.... Jihad is also done to avert aggression on the home countries and on all that is held sacred, or in order to face those who try to hinder the march of the call of truth (Islam Online, April 10, 2002).

Putting Theory into Practice

As might be expected, the people of Mecca, a center of idolatry, commerce, and debauchery, were hostile to the Prophet Mohammed's reforms. He was forced to flee to the city of Medina, then in a state of civil war, where he was invited to form a government based upon the divinely inspired principles of Islam.

The Medina period is particularly important in the practice of Islam because it forced the Prophet Mohammed to apply God's commandants to the nitty-gritty problems of running a county. Religion and state had become one, and are treated as such in the Koran. There is no separation of religion and state in Islam, nor do most Muslims see a need for one. Why, they ask, should morality be stripped from government?

When Muslim fundamentalists dream of a return to pure Islam, it is to Medina ruled by the Prophet Mohammed that they yearn to return. His rule, by all accounts, was fair, democratic in the consultative sense, humane, and innovative. In a curious irony, the humanitarian radicalism of the past has become the ultraconservatism of the present.

The picture, however, isn't quite that simple. The most fiery verses of the Koran were also those of the Medina period. This doesn't contradict the moderation of the Prophet's rule, but it does reflect his need to protect Islam from its enemies, whoever they might be (Elhadj, 2007). It is these verses that the jihadists magnify to justify their extremism and violence.

CONSOLIDATING ISLAM IN A TRIBAL ENVIRONMENT

In addition to being a reformer, the Prophet Mohammed was also a realist. Centuries of tribalism were not to be abolished with a wave of the hand. Compromises had to be made with the tribal values deeply ingrained in the Arab psyche. Practices that couldn't be abolished were restricted to make them palatable in a tribal culture of the time. Polygamy couldn't be eliminated, so men were restricted to four wives on the provision that all were treated equally. Ironically, this places the Prophet Mohammed among the world's first advocates of woman's liberation. He also understood that men found it difficult to control their emotions, and he requested that women do their part by dressing in a prudent manner. No mention was made of veiling the face. That would come later.

Islam similarly incorporated the tribal values of pride, hospitality, courage, and conformity. All, however, acquired an Islamic hue and were bent to the service of God. Pride in being an Arab, one of God's chosen people, fueled the expansion of the Islamic empire, as did the tribal emphasis on courage and bravery. The tribal virtues of generosity and hospitality gave substance to the notion of an Islamic state by encouraging Muslims to cooperate as they ventured throughout the world in search of conquest, trade, and knowledge. Brothers all, it was their obligation to share with other Muslims as they shared with their families.

The Prophet's pragmatism also involved a touch of political economy. Mecca had long been a spiritual center for the tribes of the region that made pilgrimages to the idols of the holy city and filled the coffers of its merchants, the foremost of whom were members of Prophet's tribe, the Kuraysh. How was he to win the support of his tribe at the same time that he destroyed its wealth by abolishing idols? The answer was simple. He abolished the idols but retained the pilgrimage. The merchants were appeased, and Islam established a procedure for bringing Muslims together, intensifying their zeal, and spreading the faith via Mecca's ever-expanding trade routes.

Charity giving, a basic requirement of Islam, found support in tribal notions of collective sharing and was used to ease the gap between rich and poor. The Islamic Umma, or nation, had merely become the tribe of all Muslims. The rich were to give freely of their wealth, and the poor were to avoid envy and accept reasonable inequalities in wealth as God's will. You know, the golden mean preached by both Judaism and Christianity. Capitalism was served, but so was the need to avoid excessive gaps in income.

Not only was the Prophet a leader in woman's rights, he was also among the world's earliest economic reformers. Women's rights were a hard sell, but not so the income leveling that gave Islam a strong populist appeal among the masses. Much the same was true of Islam's elimination of interest on loans, an excess that had been a scourge of Judaism, symbolized by Christ's chasing the money lenders from the temple. Commerce was promoted while a major source of social conflict was reduced. It is interesting to note that virtually all of the world's major banks have now opened Islamic branches that promote business while giving the banking trade a moral face, albeit not as moral as it might be. Religion and economics do mix in Islam.

It is doubtful that Islam would have survived if its message had been limited to the restrictions on the tribal practices outlined above. The genius of Islam was not its restrictions, but its incentives. Islam promised peace, prosperity, equality, and pride in being chosen to receive God's final message. Above all, Islam promised eternal salvation for those who believed. Did this mean seventy-two virgins? (Warraq, 2010). No, but the Muslim version of heaven is more sensuous than that of Christians or Jews.

For apostates who doubted the word of God, a burning sea of fire awaited. Dante could not have created a more heinous hell than that portrayed in Islam. Actually, Islamic thought on the subject appears to have inspired Dante (Hitti, 1956, 114). Yet, forgiveness awaited those who repented, but none more so than for those who died serving the faith.

Heaven and hell were essential to Islam, for as the Shia scholar Allalmah Sayid Muhammad Husayn Al Tabatabai writes with great candor, "And this is the truth of the matter because if there were to be no reckoning in God's actions and no reward or punishment, the religious message…would not have the least effect (Al Tabatabai, n.d., 165).

While dedicated to the reform of tribalism, the Prophet Mohammed also needed tribalism to spread the faith. This meant the use of tribal armies, for only the sword could convert infidels to Islam in this hostile environment. Thus it was decreed that 20 percent of the spoils of religious wars would go to Islam for education and good works. The rest went to the tribal warriors. Once again, religious zeal was blended with economic incentives, and both Islam and tribalism were served.

Alliances with tribes became an effective means of group conversion, as tribal leaders embraced Islam to awe their subjects. No longer ordinary mortals, they had become vicars of God. The tribal kings of Yemen became imams (divinely guided prayer leaders), while others proclaimed themselves to be the princes of believers. The sultans of the Ottoman Empire went one step better by proclaiming themselves to be the caliphs or successors to the Prophet Mohammed as the heads of the Islamic nation (Umma). The founder (Ibn Saud) of the Saudi dynasty, unable to claim direct linage to the Prophet Mohammed, formed a powerful alliance with Abdul Wahab, the dominant religious luminary of the region. The alliance remains today, and the Wahabi doctrine of Islam has become the official doctrine of Saudi Arabia.

THE GLORY OF ISLAM

The fusion of Islam and tribalism, however contradictory, unleashed an awesome force that would see Mecca capitulate to the Prophet's armies, and the rest is history. At its zenith, the conquests of the Prophet's successors extended from Spain to the gates of Vienna. Most of central Asia fell under Islam's sway, as did vast areas of the Indian subcontinent, East Asia, and Africa, many by proselytization rather than force.

A uniform moral and legal code, based upon the Koran, facilitated commerce, as did a broad knowledge of Koranic Arabic. Scholars traveled the width and breadth of the Islamic empire in search of knowledge. In the process, imperial cities such as Baghdad, Cairo, and Cordova became global centers of science and philosophy.

Those who adopted the Arab language as their own became naturalized Arabs. In the process, the Arab world was extended from the Atlantic to the Persian Gulf. Persians, Turks, Kurds, and other converts to Islam retained their own languages, but they often adopted the Arabic script as their own.

All, however, was not well. As in the case of Judaism and Christianity, the passing of God's chosen prophet saw simplicity give way to complexity as priests became the guardians of the faith, bickering over finer points of doctrine and preparing the way for eventual schisms.

In the case of Islam, the most devastating schism occurred in 656, when Muawiyah, the governor of Damascus, challenged Ali, the fourth and reigning caliph (successor to the Prophet Mohammed), for the leadership of Islam. Ali was assassinated, giving way to a bitter schism that has endured to the present time. The Sunni branch of Islam retained much of its desert purity, while the Shia, centered in Iraq, absorbed much of the mysticism of neighboring Persia.

In contrast to Sunni caliphs, who were mere mortals charged with managing the affairs of the Islamic nation, the Shia imams, the successors to the Prophet Mohammed in the Shia world, claimed powers similar to those of the pope, if not greater (Bill and Williams, 2002). Alas, the final imam/caliph despaired of the depravity of Muslims and went into occultation (spiritual withdrawal from earth) until the way is prepared for his return. Shia Muslims now await the return of the Hidden Imam, or Mahdi, much as Jews await the coming of the Messiah and Christians await the second coming of Christ.

In the meantime, the Shia were guided by profound religious scholars commonly referred to as ayatollahs (signs of God). Because of their superior piety and religious knowledge, ayatollahs were inspired by coded messages from the Hidden Imam that only they could understand. They, in turn served as sources of imitation and emulation for lesser scholars and the masses.

The Sunni and Shia versions of Islam have been at loggerheads since the assassination of the Caliph Ali, a schism that continues to serve as a major destabilizing force in the region. Some Sunni view the Shia as apostates who have wandered so far from the pale that they are no longer Muslims. For them, the Shia sect has become a separate religion. Other Sunni Muslims, by contrast, view the conflict as a historical event that invaders and dictators have used to weaken the Islamic faith and preclude the formation of an Islamic state (Al-Katab and Amaara, 2008). The Muslim Brotherhood, the world's largest Sunni fundamentalist organization, inclines toward this position. This is more than a theoretical issue for an American government that must decide whether it is dealing with one Islam or two.

There were other problems as well. Bedouin armies were suited to conquest but not to rule. Islam's ever-expanding empires required aristocracies to rule the peasants, bureaucracies to manage the affairs of state, clergies to interpret the faith to the masses, and armies to expand their glory and control the unruly tribes. All eclipsed the rudimentary organizational capacity of the Arabian tribes, and power soon passed from Mecca and Medina to Damascus, Baghdad, Cairo, Cordova, and eventually, to Istanbul, the Constantinople of old.

In the process, the purity of the Prophet's rule and the simple code of the Bedouin were overlaid with the corrupting influence of the Greeks, Persians, and Egyptians. Relatives of the sultan became aristocrats, as did many generals and tribal sheikhs.

Glory and Internal Decay

The empire soared, and great cities became centers of science, philosophy, and the arts. And glorious cities they were. Visitors to tenth-century Cairo were awed by a

> throne that took up the entire width of the room. Three of its sides were made of gold on which were hunting scenes depicting riders racing their horses.... A balustrade of golden latticework surrounded the throne, whose beauty defies all description. Behind the throne were steps of silver. I saw a tree that looked like an orange tree, whose branches, leaves, and fruits were made of sugar (Khusraw in Behrens-Abouseif, 1990, 7).

Another description of Cairo included the observation that

> Most of the houses are five or six stories high. The houses are separated from each other by orchards and garden and are sprinkled with well-water. They are built with such care and luxury that you would think that they were made of precious stones (Wiet, 1964, 19).

Alas, indulgence among the caliphs brought debauchery rather than faith, as they developed a taste for wine, sensuous music, and other perversions. The Byzantium practices of using eunuchs to guard ladies of the palace gave rise to elaborate harems and equally elaborate harem intrigues. Islam allowed only four wives, but concubines and slaves were acceptable, and it was possible for the son of a slave mother, if acknowledged by the father, to succeed him to the throne of Islam. It was the myth of Antar all over again, as pagan customs of the tribal era began to subvert the austerity of tribal Islam from within.

The simple piety of desert Islam began to erode with the shift of the caliphate from the austere environs of Mecca to the opulent luxury of Damascus. The decline in piety, however, did not slow the Islamic invasions. To the contrary, new conquests glorified the caliphs. Much as it was the wealth of conquest that fueled the opulence of Islam's imperial cities. Enlightenment followed as

> From Samarkand and Bukhara to Fez and Cordova, the entire Muslim empire was full of song: intellectual life was healthy and vigorous. Poetry, although it had lost the freshness of the desert, now took a wider range, and, no longer dwelling solely in the present, became reflective, and ultimately philosophical (Sacred Texts, 2011, 2).

The End of the Arab Enlightenment and the End of Arab Glory
Inevitably, time and debauchery took their toll. The internal decay of the Arab caliphates made them easy prey for the Crusaders of the West and barbarian tribes of the East, most of Turkish or Mongol (Tartar) origin. The story is too complex for easy telling, but suffice it to say that the twelfth and thirteenth centuries saw the Crusaders seize much of the Holy Land and surrounding regions, while Tartars overran what remained of the Abbasid caliphate in Baghdad. The royal family was put to death, and Baghdad was looted. Muslim rule in Spain followed suit and was largely broken by the end of the thirteenth century.

The Crusaders were driven from the Holy Lands by Salah-al-Din (Saladin), the son of a Kurdish general in the army of a Turkish warlord who controlled parts of Syria. Egypt was the crown jewel of Saladin's empire, and with his death, the reigns of power were passed on to his son. It was there that the legacy of Saladin, one of the pillars of Muslim history, would end. Aybak, originally a slave bodyguard of Saladin's son, seized power and initiated the reign of slave (Mamluk) sultans who would rule Egypt and Syria until the Ottoman Invasion of the early 1500s.

The slave bodyguards were originally of Turkish or Circassian origin, the latter having been more or less converted to Islam as youth. Hitti describes the Mamlukes, best known in the west for their conical hats and upturned slippers, as "uncultured, untutored, and bloodthirsty" (Hitti, 1961, 316). This said, he credits them with dazzling architecture, samples of which remain today. He also credits the Mamlukes with stemming the tide of the Mongol hoards that had destroyed Baghdad and what remained of the Abbasid caliphate. Mamluk sultans traditionally passed power to a former slave in their bodyguard. Many, it appears, inclined toward homosexuality.

The Ottoman Empire: A Return to Tribalism

About the same time that Mongol hoards were descending on Baghdad, waves of Turkish tribes were descending on Constantinople, the capital of the Byzantine Empire and Eastern Christendom. They failed to take Constantinople, but settled in the surrounding areas, where they converted to Sunni Islam.

A later wave of Turkish nomads headed by Osman descended on the region at the beginning of the fourteenth century. It was Osman's (Ottoman's) lineage, thirty-six sultans in all, who would rule Turkey and much of the Middle East until Turkey's defeat in WWI.

The Ottomans began their rise to glory as border raiders on the fringes of the Byzantine Empire. As in the time of the Prophet Mohammed, 20 percent of the spoils went to the sultan, and the rest to the raiding parties. The neighboring areas of Eastern Europe were favored because of their greater wealth and the reluctance of Muslim raiders to violate Islamic law by killing Muslims.

The Ottomans were more concerned with wealth than religion, and Christians were welcome to join the Ottoman raiding parties. Many became generals and admirals in the Ottoman army and were rewarded with landed estates (fiefdoms) in conquered Christian areas. Much as in feudal Europe, the new landed aristocracy kept the peace within their realm and provided knights to serve in the sultan's cavalry.

The spoils of war were counted in terms of gold, jewels, and human captives who served as slaves. The success of their raiding parties soon found the Ottomans awash in slaves. Always a practical people, they converted young Christian boys to Islam and forged them into an elite force loyal only to the sultan. This wasn't too difficult because the janissaries, as they were called, were not encumbered with local or family loyalties. What better way for the sultan to combat a disease deeply rooted in the aristocracy? By the middle of the sixteenth century, there were more than ten thousand janissaries, and it was they who formed the core of the sultan's army. Muslim boys couldn't join because Muslims couldn't become slaves. The janissaries were a slave army. Those with military ambition joined either the cavalry or infantry.

Iran had also been overrun by Turkish tribes, all of whom succumbed to the intoxication of Persian culture. Of these, the most famous were the Safavids, whose empire extended from the Tigris River in Iraq to northern India. It was the Safavids who converted Iran to Shia (Twelver) Islam, the main remnants of which are found in Iraq, Lebanon, and Yemen.

One way or another, the Islamic empire had fallen into non-Arab hands. The Arabs, so proud of their position as the chosen people of Islam, were now ruled by "shuoobi," the Arabic word for non-Muslim Arabs. Adding insult to injury, when the last Arab caliph died in Turkish custody, the reigning sultan added the title of caliph to the title of sultan. Religious and secular authority had again been reunited, and the new sultan-caliph was referred to in Europe as the Sublime Porte.

As caliph, the Ottoman sultan had the final word on Islamic affairs and maintained a large "Islamic institution" to parallel a massive palace bureaucracy that guided the affairs of state. Much like earlier empires, the caliph's Islamic institution included a vast array of religious scholars, referred to as the ulema. It was they, headed by a grand mufti, who served as judges, teachers, and interpreters of Islamic law in consultation with the caliph, at whose pleasure they served. Lest there be any doubt about the power of the grand mufti (senior religious judge), his official title was sheikh al-Islam.

This is not to suggest that Turkish caliphs were unduly religious. At the empire's peak, powerful sultans entertained thoughts of creating a grand religion that incorporated Islam, Christianity, and Judaism. This didn't happen, but Catholics, Protestants, Orthodox Christians, and Jews were all governed by the religious laws of their own faith (or millet).

On the secular side, the affairs of the palace (government) were managed by a grand vizier (prime minister) who reigned over a council (diwan) of lesser viziers. As in religious affairs, viziers served at the pleasure of the sultan, and their tenure was subject to his whim.

The wealthier the empire became, the more sultan-caliphs succumbed to the pleasures of the harem and the grape. While supreme in title, the power of the sultan-caliph was often rivaled by that of the grand vizier, the grand mufti, and the chief eunuch, officially referred to as "His Highness the Guardian of the Gate of the Imperial Felicity and Repose" (Cox, 1887, 530–537).

It was the story of the Arab caliphs all over again. Power led to wealth and indulgence, and indulgence led to decay and defeat. The weaker the sultan-caliphs became, the more the governors of distant provinces established their own petty dynasties. The most famous of these was Mohammed Ali, the pasha of Egypt, whose troops twice reached the walls of Istanbul in the nineteenth century.

The Environment of the Common Folk

Over the course of more than a thousand years, the spark of empire ignited by the Prophet Mohammed had evolved from the simple purity of the desert into the dominant global power of the Middle Ages. Like the Christian and Jewish empires that preceded it, the Islamic empire was a blend of contradictions and stark contrasts—of brutal tyranny and enlightened rule; of dazzling cities and rural poverty; of brilliant science and stifling conservatism; of innovation and rigid conformity; of religious unity and sectarian fragmentation; of expansion and decay; of glory and shame.

With each expansion of the faith came new embellishments far removed from the simple truths of the Koran. The Muslim clergy, for its part, became so enthralled with the finer points of doctrine that the simplicity of the Koran gave way to a stultifying rigidity that isolated the masses from their God. Islam also suffered from the inherent defects of beni Adam, from which there was no escape. Greed, jealously, fear, distrust, and nepotism sapped the empire of its strength and turned Muslim against Muslim. Emperors couldn't trust their own people, and so they surrounded themselves with slaves. While the Europeans were devising new ways to channel human energies into nation building, industrialization, and conquest, the Arabs clung to the past and glorified their tribal traditions. Islam was worshiped and honored, but it was the gut instincts of tribalism that came to the fore.

Did the glories of empire matter much to the common people? Yes and no. Most people during the era of empire remained either nomadic or agrarian, and life continued its dull routine much as it always had. Tribes, clans, and families remained the basic units of society, and most people worked their fingers to the bone in a constant struggle to survive.

The main difference, at least to the average person, was that tribal culture had been melded with Islamic law and religious obligations. Gone were the idols, and the pressures of society forced conformity with the faith, including prayer and prudent dress. Survival had become more difficult, as a feudal aristocracy used tax collectors to beat the last penny from the helpless peasants. The Bedouin, at least, could flee to the remote stretches of the desert after raiding the sultan's convoys.

It was in the glorious cities of empire that life had changed. A new strata of clergy, bureaucrats, soldiers, slaves, merchants, artisans, professionals, and beggars emerged to serve the palace, steal its wealth, and use positions of influence to exploit the masses. Organizations such as guilds and brotherhoods had emerged to offer artisans a modicum of protection from rapacious officials, but beneath it all, the core of society remained the family, clan, and tribe. Remember, the Ottomans were a tribe, much like the Saudis of the modern era.

THE SEARCH FOR THE ARABO-MUSLIM PSYCHE

Arabo-Muslim is a term that Arab scholars tend to use when they refer to Arabs of the Muslim faith, as opposed to Arabs in general. This, of itself, suggests that the psyche of the Arab Muslim differs in some degree from the psyche of Christian Arabs, who constitute about 10 percent of the Arab population. Just how much the two psyches differ is a matter of debate. The observations that follow are limited to Arab Muslims, but the line between the Arabo-Muslim psyche and the Christian-Arab psyche is often fine.

The search for the Arabo-Muslim psyche begins by examining how Muslim scholars view the Arab psyche and then seeing how their views fit into the view of the human psyche outlined in Chapter 1. Three distinct areas of difference are examined: faith as a human need, free will, and the role of child rearing in shaping the Arab psyche.

Is Faith a Human Need?

The divergence between Muslim and Western psychology, according to Malik Badri, a leading Arab psychologist, begins with the observation that Western psychology is secular and views religion as a belief system acquired by individuals as part of their cultural environment. It is an acquired need, but not a biologic need. Some people in the West are deeply religious by choice, while others ignore it altogether without feelings of pain or deprivation. Most simply take it or leave it as it suits their mood. They get religious when it makes them feel good, and they ignore it when it is inconvenient or stands in the way of their pursuit of pleasure (Badri, 2010). Similar views, albeit with an Islamic hue, are found in Boustani's two-volume *Islamic Psychology* (Boustani, 2000).

This is not so with Islamic psychology. According to Badri, Islam views religion as an innate human need that cannot be ignored. Just as a deprivation of food brings pain and stunts growth, so it is with the need for faith. Human beings, in the Islamic view, cannot live without faith, and the pain of deprivation will always drive those who have strayed back to their faith.

Badri is not talking here about a conscience or superego planted in the psyche by parents, peers, preachers, and prophets. He is talking about something far more fundamental, a religious gene if you like, that will always drive Muslims to return to their faith, regardless of the lure of secular modernity. This view may not be scientifically accurate, but it sure gives encouragement to an Islamic movement faced with the onslaught of westernization.

Soul Versus Psyche: Free Will, Fatalism, and the Appeal of Islam

Western psychology has great difficulty dealing with terms such as soul and psyche. The definitions of each in the official dictionary of the American Psychological Association lead to the conclusion that the psyche is the soul and the soul is the psyche.

This is not the case in Islamic psychology. According to Badri, Boustani, and others, Islam makes a clear distinction between the soul, the everlasting life force breathed into human beings at birth, and the psyche which controls the individual's relentless search to avoid pain and maximize pleasure. If the psyche chooses to nurture the soul, it will find tranquility on earth and everlasting joy in heaven. But if the psyche chooses to pursue the momentary pleasures of the flesh, it will be doomed to a life of worry and an eternity of pain.

This point is important because it stresses the notion of free will in Islam. People do play a role in shaping their lives and will pay for the consequences of their choices. Individuals are far from being robots and must struggle against the appetites of the flesh, the great jihad, much as they struggle against the foes of Islam.

Things, however, aren't quite that simple. While the Koran embraces free will, it also teaches that God is all powerful, all knowing, and controls all events that transpire on earth and in the heavens. Nothing escapes God's view, not even the wiles of the devil and his minions. This suggests predestination rather than free will. God, beyond question, could prevent people from straying from the path of righteousness if He so chose. Does God want people to sin? Isn't this a contradiction?

Not really. God could predestine all Muslims to spend an eternity in heaven if he so chose, but as the story of Adam and Eve makes clear, he preferred that his favored creatures be tested and prove their worth before being admitted to paradise. Redemption and forgiveness, yes, but Islam, like Christianity and Judaism, has little compassion for those who willingly chose the path of evil. Their souls will spend eternity in a sea of fire.

This script is virtually identical to that of Christianity and Judaism and once again reflects the similarity of the three faiths. If differences occur, it is in the greater leniency of Islam. Islam, Badri stresses, is the most forgiving of religions. God's plan is not to condemn people to an eternity in hell, but to encourage them to regret and repent.

Not only does Islam encourage repentance, but it goes one step farther by assuring a future in paradise for those who suffer in the name or the faith, a jihad if you like. This provision played a role in stimulating

THE ARAB PSYCHE FROM TRIBALISM TO ISLAM

the Islamic invasions of yore and is an important factor in understanding the terror that Islamic extremists perpetrate today. Most of the jihadists of today, it is interesting to note, were secularists who had fallen prey to the temptations of the West.

"If God controls everything," the moderator of the Al Jazeera program, cited above, baited Badri, "what did he hope to achieve by taking Moses, a major prophet in all three faiths, away from his parents as an infant and placing him in the palace of the pharaoh, a most evil of tyrants who claimed to be the true God?"

Moses' parents, Badri explained, were slaves of humble origin who lived in awe of the god-pharaoh. Had Moses been raised by his natural parents, he would have absorbed their humiliation and lived in awe of the false god, hardly the traits suited for a child predestined to receive the word of God and lead the Jews to the Promised Land. Thus it was, according to Badri, that Moses was placed in the household of the pharaoh, where he could observe the false god in all of his human filth and failings. Awed, Moses wasn't.

The moral of this story is don't try to second guess God by dwelling on contradictions that are beyond the comprehension of humans. Humans can do great things, but only with the inspiration and will of God. This may force them to break with their family and other groups on whom they rely for protection and the realization of their most basic needs. The Prophet Mohammed, it will be recalled, broke with members of his tribe when he was ordered to reveal the final message of God. The Koran recognizes and encourages the role of groups in providing for human needs, but only to the extent that they support the faith and the creation of a unified Muslim nation, the Umma.

Child Rearing: The Lactation Versus Indoctrination Debate

For the Freudians, Arab child-rearing practices during the early years of life doomed the Arabs to a flawed psyche. Arab attitudes toward women, as Raphael Patai explains in his *Arab Mind*, begin with the duration of breast feeding:

> *Local variations, of which there are many, aside, in general a boy is suckled twice as long as a girl.... Thus the verbalization of the one major childhood desire, that for the mother's breast, is followed, in most cases as least, by instant gratification. And what is psychologically*

equally important, the emphatic verbal formulation of the wish carries in itself, almost automatically, the guarantee of its fulfillment without the need for any additional action on the part of the child.... The only thing required is the word; the utterer can then relax and let the word bring about its own realization (Patai, 2002, 31–33).

The kindly and exploitable world of women, Patai elaborates, leads to psychological shock when the young boy is forced to enter the harsh world of men around age four. It is in the world of men that the young boy "learns who his superiors are, in addition to his father: all men older than he, including a brother or cousin who is his senior by only a year or so. On the other hand, he learns that he can treat boys younger than he as his inferiors, although not quite as inferior as the women" (Patai, 2002, 36).

Islamic child-rearing theories, by contrast, focus on religious indoctrination designed to produce a sound mind rooted in faith. By and large, religious indoctrination is divided into three clearly defined stages: early childhood (one to seven), later childhood (seven to fourteen), and pre-adulthood (fourteen to twenty-one).

In contrast to Freudians, Muslim psychologists attach little significance to the early years of childhood and allow children to develop their minds through play. Some religious instruction does occur, but it is limited. At age three, for example, parents are encouraged to say to the child seven times "There is no God but Allah." At three years, seven months, and twenty days, they are to say to the child seven times, "Mohammed is the Messenger of Allah." Prayers for Mohammed and His family are then added, as are rudimentary prayer rituals (Boustani, 2000, 60, 62). No sexual content is assumed at this stage.

By the advent of the second seven years, the male child is deemed sufficiently developed to master memorization of the Koran. Sex is openly discussed during this stage to preclude it from becoming a latent form of deviance. Instruction during the era of Islam took place in schools, called madrasas, attached to the mosque. Much religious instruction continues to take place in these schools, and they have become a major concern in America's war on terror.

Far more frequent is religious instruction in the public school systems of the Arab world. In Saudi Arabia, for example, religion constitutes some 40 percent of the curriculum from kindergarten to twelfth grade. Egypt, while far more open to Western ideas, maintains a vast network of religious schools that stress the Koranic version of life. The Koranic vision of the psyche is also pervasive in prayers and sermons of the mosque, not to mention the charismatic orations of the Muslim tele-preachers who have achieved immense popularity throughout the Islamic world.

The seven pre-adulthood years are devoted to acquiring a firm knowledge of Islamic morality, with heavy emphasis on sexual taboos. Islam is very clear on what is allowed and what isn't. Sex outside of marriage is forbidden. So are homosexual activities.

Muslim psychologists reject psychoanalytical studies of the Arab psyche on the grounds that they are inherently secular and ignore the role of Islamic teaching in shaping Arab and Muslim behavior. They also note that psychoanalysis is based upon a Western experience that differs dramatically from that of the Arab reality. To prove this point, Badri points to an item in a leading personality index that asks, "Do you eat with your fingers when nobody is looking?" This question is one of several items of a "lie scale" that is used to tell if respondents are telling the truth or not. What good is this question in Saudi Arabia, Badri wonders, when people eat with their fingers even when people are looking? As a consequence, an innocent Saudi is accused of lying, and the results of examination are flawed and unreliable (Badri and Uthman, 2010).

Personally, I think that it is simpler to say that boys learn their roles by watching how parents, siblings, and peers act. There is certainly no lack of empirical information on the topic, especially when you add the effectiveness of Islamic indoctrination. Why make things unnecessarily difficult by bringing breast suckling to the picture when, as Patai candidly admits, there is scarce data on the topic?

I merely mention the psychoanalytical approach because it seems to have influenced American policymakers and added to their frustrations by making questionable assumptions that are difficult to substantiate.

THE CONTENT OF THE ARABO-ISLAMIC PSYCHE

The analytical categories used in describing the psyche are much the same in both Western and Islamic psychology, but the content differs markedly.

Identity

With the emergence of Islam, the Arab identity became increasingly complex. Much as in the past, individuals identified themselves as members of a particular family, clan, and tribe, while being Arab remained part of their broader ethnic-linguistic consciousness. Islam, however, now made Muslims members of a nation of believers bound by faith and guided by the sharia, or laws of Islam. Islam had become part of who they were, and its teachings were embedded in their psyches. God's law stressed family values, but no group or identity was to stand between individuals and their God.

Much as in the case of Christians and Jews, Muslims varied in the intensity of their faith. They also differed over the best way to serve God. Few Muslims, however, were willing to sacrifice an eternity in paradise or risk the sea of fire by denying the supremacy of God and role of Mohammed as His prophet. Life for most people remained brutally hard, and their new identity offered them a sense of inner peace that came only from standing at the side of God. As harsh as their present was, an eternity in paradise beaconed.

What Motivated Beni-Islam?

Islamic psychology, like that of the secular West, embraces the pain-and-pleasure principle as the primary motivator of human behavior (Boustani, 2000). As always, the innate human needs for survival, sustenance, and sex remain part of the story. So too, do the appetites of greed, lust, power, and belonging. The search for God is considered a basic need in Islam and is increasingly debated as such in the West.

Learned wants were also pretty much as they had been during the tribal era, except when it came to religion. A reputation for piety was prized as a badge of honor and purity. Beyond this, it was a sign of baraka, best translated as God's special blessing or even the gift of grace. What better way to fight the jinn and evil spirits or to intimidate enemies with hints of mystical retribution? Rectitude also served as a source of power, for who was to question the word of a man blessed by the Holy Spirit? Pre-Islamic Bedouins had their witches and their demons, but none possessed the awe of Islam's men of religion cloaked in the blessing of the all-powerful God.

Conscience Versus Shame

Do Muslims have a conscience? I ask the question because many American talk shows give the impression that they don't. This impression is also conveyed by anthropological studies that classify the West as a guilt society while typifying Arabs as a shame society (Patai, 2002, 113; Hamady, 1960, 35).

All Abrahamic religions are guilt based and go to extreme lengths to implant a conscience in their adherents. This is even more the case in Islam, because Islam views faith as basic human need that will always drive Muslims who have strayed back into the fold (Badri, 2010). More to the point, how could Muslims have endured all of the religious indoctrination discussed earlier without having a conscience? Indoctrination, after all, is where the Christian conscience originated.

This said, there is not a single word in the Koran that expresses the precise meaning of the Christian concept of conscience. Rather, the Koran speaks of the self-accusing soul, the soul prone to evil, the peaceful soul, and the soul prone to good and evil (Hughes, 1886, 60). The Sunna (way of the Prophet) also urges Muslims to avoid anything that pricks their soul (ibid).

How, then, does one reconcile the existence of a Muslim conscience with the manifest evidence that Arabs are overwhelmingly influenced by fear of shame? Another contradiction?

Not at all. Muslims associate conscience with pleasing God. This doesn't mean that they don't stray, but it does mean that they experience the pain of a guilty conscience. Secular Muslims may resist for some time, but most will make their peace with God.

Shame, by contrast, regulates affairs between individuals. This is especially true of relations with people outside of the family, most of whom are treated with suspicion and fall beyond the pale of either religious or family morality. As later chapters will elaborate, most Arab scholars find little morality beyond the family. Even within the family, shame and peering eyes are the primary form of social control. Honor and the fear of conflict are too pressing to trust to free will. While God allows people time to repent, jealous neighbors do not.

Let me illustrate the overlap between conscience and guilt with the story of Ahmed the Prayerful. Ahmed the Prayerful isn't one individual, but a composite of several Arabo-Muslims who shared their lives with me over time. Ahmed the Prayerful and I were having a nightcap at the Nile Hilton in Cairo when I chided him for drinking alcohol, especially in public. He shrugged his shoulders with a laugh, saying, "I wouldn't drink in front of family, but it is all right at tourist hotels. Besides, I like a drink now and then."

A few years later, we were at the same hotel, and Ahmed the Prayerful, having a change of heart, refused my offer of a drink. I didn't press the point, but he volunteered that he was returning to his faith. The moral of the story is clear. Despite appearances, secularized Muslims do worry about their faith. Hard-core nonbelievers in the Arab world are few, and the power of the Islamic conscience is not to be ignored.

Badri supports this observation by lamenting that too much Islamic preaching stresses the horrors of hell rather than Islam's willingness to forgive those who repent their sins. By stressing the horrors of hell, according to Badri, misguided preachers place so much stress on sin that it drives some Muslims crazy and makes them easy prey for extremist organizers. This, he stresses, is not the fault of Islam, a most moderate of religions, but of a perversion of Islam inspired by the devil to destroy Islam (Badri, 2010).

Emotions

The story was much the same in the area of emotions, few of which escaped the influence of the new faith (Corrigan, 2004). But where to start? How about with the thrill of victory? Islam, led by the Bedouin tribes, had become the most powerful force in the known world. They were number one. The thrill of victory was accompanied by feelings of superiority and dominance, not to mention the sure knowledge of God's blessing. Contentment followed apace as wealth and slaves flooded the empire. Let the good times roll.

The thrill of victory was intensified by other emotions, including a profound sense of righteousness and hate of the infidel. It would also be naive to suggest that greed and avarice didn't play a role in the Islamic conquests. As mentioned earlier, the tribes did get 80 percent of the bounty. All in all, it was a matter of doing well for yourself by doing good for the faith.

Some people simply consider greed, lust, and other appetites to be emotions, but there is a difference. While both trigger behavior, appetites are part of the human condition and remain constant. Emotions, by contrast, are temporary and come and go according to the circumstances.

The thrill of victory for the Bedouin faded with the shift of power to the great cities of empire and the emergence of standing armies. Standing armies limited the power of the tribes and paved the way for rapacious governors and tax collectors. Invariably, fear, resignation, and other emotions of the tribal era reasserted themselves.

This was not the case among the educated elite of Baghdad and other cities of empire. Grand mosques became centers of learning in which the emotions of skepticism and curiosity triumphed over resignation and fatalism. Faith and science merged as the joy of enlightenment flourished, and wealthy aristocrats became patrons of the arts. For the poor and oppressed, and there were many, an endless array of mystics opened the secrets of heaven.

From Motivation to Action

Motivators push people to act, but the course of those actions is often unpredictable. Sometimes insults trigger violence, while in others they simmer unnoticed until an appropriate opportunity for revenge presents itself. The era of Islam even urged people to gain God's blessing by turning the other cheek.

In reality, beni Islam did all three as circumstances and the intensity of emotions dictated. His ego tried to be rational in its efforts to maximize pleasure with minimal pain, but the advent of Islam had made the reasoning process increasingly complex. Unlike the simple days of yore, one now had to be ever alert to the demands of God and the wiles of the devil, the minions of whom often took the guise of corrupt bureaucrats and false men of religion purveying conflicting versions of the true faith. How were simple folk to distinguish between the true faith and the beguiling intrigues of the devil?

Just when the rigors of pleasing God had taxed the reasoning process to the limit, along came the enlightenment and the contest between faith and science. This debate didn't trouble the masses, but it had a profound influence on the intellectual course of the Islamic empire as gifted astronomers, physicians, engineers, and philosophers began to chart the order of a universe that was at odds with popular beliefs. A few, such as Omar Khayam, famous for his poetry but also a gifted astronomer, became openly secular. Imagine, if you will, the impact of poems that glorified the flesh with tributes to "bread, wine, and thou" and questioned the hereafter by noting that none had returned to tell about it. From witchcraft to secular science, it was all there and had to be dealt with.

To make matters worse, many of the most gifted scientists, Omar Khayam included, weren't Arabs. Not only had control of the Islamic empire shifted to non-Arabs, but they also had begun to dominate the intellectual world of the Arabs.

Invariably, efforts to deal with the complexity and painful decline of the Islamic empire allowed the ego to be beguiled by the defense mechanisms of which we spoke earlier. More than ever, people saw what they wanted to see and heard what they wanted to hear. Rationalization eased their consciences, and if the pain of guilt became too great, it could always be displaced on witches, wives, and slaves. The era of seclusion had arrived, and Islam allowed wife beating with proper justification. The beating of slaves and witches required no justification.

When the era of enlightenment ended, the Arab psyche closed its mind to reality and looked to the past rather than the future. The practice of allowing gifted scholars to keep Islamic doctrine in touch with changing times was cancelled, and Sunni Islam became rigid and impervious to change. Key Shia luminaries continue to adjust Islam doctrine, a practice that further divides the two major sects of Islam.

Others blame the Turks for crushing the emergence of Arab enlightenment and returning the Arab world to an era of backwardness. The Turks were tribal, and they saw enlightenment as a threat to their power.

As the empire declined, the tribal traits of authoritarianism, collectivism, mysticism, and a craving for a strong leader, never far from the surface, reasserted themselves. For many people of the era, mysticism and the craving for a strong leader merged into the longing for a return of the Mahdi. An ordinary man on horseback wouldn't do. He had to possess the gift of grace.

Language as the Soul of the Arabs

The Arab fixation with their language during the tribal era paled in comparison with the psychological role of the Arabic language during the era of Islam. Far from being merely a language of great beauty and emotion, it had become the language of God.

Alas, speaking the language of God also had its drawbacks. Because Arabic was the language of God, it could not be changed. By and large, this made Koranic Arabic the preserve of religious scholars and poets. This posed little problem to the Bedouin Arabs of the seventh century, but it became problematic for the Arabs of empire. Settled populations stretching from Morocco to Mesopotamia found the complexities of formal Arabic poorly suited to the mundane tasks of their daily life, and they invented their own dialects, many distinct from the dialects of people even a few miles away. Intellectuals could communicate in Koranic Arabic, but the illiterate masses could not.

Add to this the problems of empire that brought millions of non-Arabs under Islamic rule. The Koran was studied in Arabic, but it was discussed in foreign languages devoid of Arabic's subtleties. Again, the learned scholars of empire could debate in Arabic, but not ordinary Turks, Persians, and others who, presumably, viewed Islam through the lenses of their own languages. The Turkish language was harsh and direct; Persian was soft and mystical. Neither were Semitic languages. Words of both found their way into colloquial Arabic as Persians and Turks seized control of the Islamic empire.

The vagaries of the Arabic language also led to bitter disputes over the precise meaning of key phrases of the Koran and the sayings of the Prophet. This was all the more the case because vowel markings, the key to precision in the Arabic language, were often assumed rather than written. Rare, indeed, is a book written in Arabic today that contains more than an occasional vowel marking. Be warned, that includes studies of the Arab psyche included in this book.

This, in turn, returns us to the earlier argument that communication in Arabic is influenced as much by pronunciation as it is by content. By way of example, the words "break" and "smash" in Arabic use precisely the same letters, the differences coming in vowel markings pronounced and embellished, but not written. What you read, accordingly, may only give a hint of the meaning intended. Far worse, each reader or poet added marks of emphasis to suit his own purposes. The charm of Arabic is in its flourishes.

These may seem like minor issues, but they are not. The more Islam fragmented into two basic sects, and they into a multitude of schools and doctrines, the more Muslims interpreted the Koran and Sunna in a manner that supported their unique theological positions. Each sect and sub-sect became convinced that its interpretation of the Koran and Sunna was God's will, and compromise became impossible. After all, how can you compromise with the will of God?

The plot thickens as you add Sufis to the mix, each Sufi way (branch) attempting to find oneness with God by discovering hidden meanings in the Koran and Sunna. The missing vowels, if properly interpreted, made everything remotely believable. If this trickery were inadequate, they invented new Hadith (traditions of the Prophet) to justify their position.

What this means, in effect, is that Muslims spend even more time talking past each other than Christians, a challenge indeed.

Such, then, was the Arabo-Islamic psyche that gave birth to one of the world's great religions and dazzled the world with its science and philosophy. Sadly, it was also a psyche that turned inward and closed its mind to enlightenment. Rather than using the enlightened passages of the Koran and Sunna to navigate the challenges of the future, it chose a roadmap that led to the past and recoiled in the face of reform and change. This decay would be reflected in all phases of Arabo-Muslim behavior during the declining years of the Islamic empire. Arabs began to bet on the past rather than the future.

EVOLVING BEHAVIOR PATTERNS DURING
THE ERA OF ISLAM

Both the environmental changes produced by the Islamic era and the growing complexity of the Arabo-Islamic psyche dictated that the Arabs of the era would have to work harder to strike an acceptable balance between pain and pleasure. This was particularly the case in the ruling cities of the empires, where opportunities for wealth and power soared. However, so did the risks of betrayal and defeat. Most of the skills for dealing with tyrants and circumventing authority that haunt the Arab world today were forged during the Islamic era.

The discussion begins with political behavior and then turns to social and economic behavior. Lines between the three categories are blurred because Islam does not draw a sharp distinction between politics, society, and economics. All are coordinated to serve the faith.

Political Behavior

Expressing Nationalism, Ethnicity, and Tribalism

For the most part, Arabs handled the tension between their tribal and Islamic identities quite well. Kinship regulated daily life, while Islam provided for the hereafter. People followed the rules of Islam to the best of their abilities and otherwise played the social roles fate had assigned to them.

Arabism soared as the Arabs relished their role as the vanguard of Islam. Even when power shifted to Iran and Turkey, the Arabs were sustained by the sense that they were the purest of all Muslims. And well they should, for the word of God was written in Arabic.

Caliphs, the successors to the Prophet Mohammed as the head of the Islamic nation, evoked awe among the faithful. The early prophets were selected from among the Prophet's inner circle. Most were related to the Prophet by marriage. Court intrigues had much to do with the selection of later caliphs.

Whatever their glory, caliphs were mortal humans and possessed no special powers to intervene with God and bring people closer to their maker. As the empire expanded, the caliph became a remote figure who ruled through legions of landed aristocracy, bureaucrats, soldiers, and tax collectors. Awe of the caliph was muted by fear of his security forces and tax collectors.

If one is to judge by the stories of *The Arabian Nights*, fear and awe did not translate into loyalty. Why else would the later caliphs have to place their security in the hands of slave guards? The Turks abolished the caliphate in 1924 with hardly a whimper throughout the Sunni world. The position remains empty today, but pressure is mounting among Muslim fundamentalists to have it restored. This is particularly the case among Arab Muslims who yearn to see the caliphate return to the Arab fold.

The Shia, in contrast to the Sunni, accorded mystical powers to Ali, the fourth Caliph. Ali, in their view, should have been the successor to the Prophet Mohammed, and they refuse to recognize the legitimacy of caliphs other than Ali, much as Protestants refuse to acknowledge the pope as the leader of the Christian Church. Far worse, the Shia reject all of the later caliphs as imposters and usurpers to the throne of Islam. Until the Hidden Imam returns to bring peace on earth, it is the ayatollahs who interpret his wishes. This provides them with supernatural powers, and they are held in awe by their followers, who view them as objects of emulation.

Awe does translate into loyalty among Shia populations, and ayatollahs have become major powerbrokers among Shia populations in Iraq, Lebanon, Syria, Yemen, Iran, Pakistan, and Afghanistan. Rare Shia sects, such as the Alawi of Syria, suggest that Ali was intended to be the Messenger of God, but that God happened upon Mohammed by mistake. Heretical stuff, indeed.

Most Shia reject this position, and I only mention it because the Alawi controlled the government of Syria for more than three decades, leading up to the 2011 populist revolutions.

This said, both the Sunni and Shia have steadfastly identified themselves as Muslims and called for the unity of the faith. Such calls, while frequent, have been in vain, as the strength of sectarian loyalties has precluded compromise. No one dare say that being Sunni or Shia is more important than being Muslim, but each sect continues to maintain that its version of Islam alone is the true faith.

Expressing Spiritualism

Islam's message of one God, while indelibly stamped on the Arab psyche, did not eliminate the Bedouins' healthy skepticism of any form of authority, religious or otherwise. The early years of Islam had even seen other tribes proclaim their own prophets to counter the influence of the Prophet Mohammed and the power of the Kuraysh. Little wonder that the Koran had harsh words for the Bedouin.

Nor did the advent of Islam reduce the superstition so common in the pre-Islamic era. Belief in jinn was incorporated into Islam, and they were much feared by the people of the era, who viewed them as evil. This, as the noted Shia scholar Sayeed Hossein Nasr explains, was a mistake. They could be either good or evil.

The jinn in Islamic doctrines are that group of creatures which was made of fire rather than earth, and into which God also breathed His spirit.... This means that they are essentially creatures of the psychic rather than the physical world and that they can appear to man in different forms and shapes.... Some are "religious" and "Muslim." These are intermediate angels, the psychic forces that can lead Man from the physical world to the spiritual world.... Others are malefic forces that have rebelled against God...[and] lead man away from the Truth (Nasr, 1971, 235–236).

If you are having trouble following this, recall that apparent con-tradictions within the world of God are merely a reflection of human shortcomings. As Nasr explains, "To understand the meaning of jinn one must therefore go beyond a conception of reality which includes only the world of matter and the mind (this paralyzing dualism that makes an understanding of traditional doctrines impossible) to an awareness of a hierarchic reality made up of the three worlds of spirit, psyche, and matter" (Nasr, 1971, 235–236).

Witchcraft was more mundane than the jinn and played a greater role in interpersonal relations and dealing with life's little problems. It wasn't proper, after all, to use prayer in the pursuit of greed or for the destruction of another Muslim, both practices being forbidden by the Koran. Witches promised both, as well as protection from other witches and the evil jinn. In a curious irony, witches often protected clients from the spells of other witches by having their clients repeat the appropriate verses of the Koran, a practice that remains prevalent in Saudi Arabia. Women were among their foremost clients, for an evil spell by an envious rival remained the most acceptable explanation of a woman's inability to give birth.

Nor was witchcraft limited to common folk. Leaders routinely con-sulted astrologers or other seers before embarking on a journey or launching a battle. Even during the early years of the twentieth century, the imams (religious kings) of Yemen wouldn't travel without checking with the stargazer and taking trunks of gold to bribe the tribes in case of a revolt in their absence (Shamees, 1958).

The more the empire declined, the more people prayed for the appearance of the Mahdi, a Messiah-like figure, to bring an end to their suffering and lead them to eternal peace (Filiu, 2008). Alas, the Mahdi was distant and their suffering great, so the dispossessed sought salvation in mystical Sufi orders led by holy men who promised oneness with God.

One way or another, the people of the era had crafted a spiritual universe of multiple layers headed by Islam and descending through layers of angels, jinn, Sufi leaders, saintly shrines, and holy men until they reached the forbidden world of witches and sorcery. Each guided their behavior, one often overlapping with the other, as witches chanted Koranic verses to purge evil spirits.

Searching for a Strong Basis of Group Support

For all of Islam's preaching of brotherhood, it was the family, clan, and tribe that formed the core of the individual's support base.

This was fine for the nomadic tribes who continued to be a world unto themselves, but not for people who flocked to the grand cities of empire. While families and clans remained the core or urban society, both security and getting one's share of the cake required connections that exceeded the family.

The cities of empire, moreover, weren't cities in the modern sense of the word. Rather, they were collections of ethnic, tribal, and religious quarters in which families and clans were of similar backgrounds and sought protection from rapacious officials and hostile sects, tribes, and ethnic groups. People did not migrate to a city. They migrated to a specific quarter of a city in which there were relatives and co-sectarians to welcome them. Merchants and craftsmen clustered in guilds, the precursors to the modern chambers of commerce. The bazaar became a source of financial power that was able to protect itself by buying influence in the court. Religious societies also emerged to provide mutual support and protection. Their leaders often became powerful individuals and were perhaps a source of worry to the tyrant. In addition to offering protection, the guilds and religious associations served as platforms for trading favors and influence in a society in which laws depended on the whim of the tyrant or swelling aristocracy of landowners and generals, often one in the same.

Expressing Loyalty

This didn't mean that the family and clan decreased in importance. To the contrary, the clever family had a representative in all of the key centers of power, including the palace, the military, the bazaar, the religious establishment, the landed aristocracy, and the tribes. It was there that loyalty lay, not with the state or caliph.

Among those in the service of the sultan was a vast fabric of superior-subordinate relationships stretching from the sultan to the lowest clerk. Lower officials needed a patron to protect their interests, and more powerful officials needed a powerbase of lower officials on whom they could count to carry out their orders, legal and otherwise. Relatives were prevalent in the networks. Who else could you trust? Not that relatives were always that reliable.

Patron-client networks were a mutual relationship in which each member was dependent on the other. Lower officials couldn't advance or get their share of the illicit gains without the support of a patron, and a patron couldn't survive without his mafia inside the governmental hierarchy. Everyone was a patron to someone, and if a patron fell, which was often, the clients ran for cover. Actually, they would run for cover at the first signs of a patron's weakness. Appearances were everything, and it was vital that patrons retain an image of power at all costs.

An Obsession for Control

Much as in the tribal era, most people during the era of Islam continued to live within the iron frame of the family and clan in which everyone was locked into a dominant-subordinate relationship based on age, sex, and social status. It was much the same within the bureaucracies of empire, with the exception that dominant-subordinate relationships were based on access to power and wealth. As always, the ever-peering eyes noted the slightest infraction and invented those they couldn't see. Envy and innuendo were pervasive, and just to add spice to the mix, heretics were hanged.

In addition to the social pressures of the earlier era, the Islamic faith demanded submission to political authority, be it the tribal chief or the reigning caliph. God did not condone tyranny and had no illusions about the frailty of His human agents. Order, however, was essential to the survival of the faith, and the Koran made it clear that it would be God, not humans, who judged the sinners. "Obey God, and obey God's messenger, and obey those of authority among you" (Koran, 4:59). The devout were to obey and receive their reward in heaven.

Nor did the masses have any doubt about the quality of their leaders, religious or otherwise. I recall listening to a radio drama during the thousandth anniversary of Al-Azhar University. In the drama, a wealthy merchant admonished his son for wanting to become an Islamic judge. "For every judge in heaven," the father lamented, "there are two in hell." The son persisted, saying that it was the obligation of the pious to enter the clergy if the faith were to be rescued from the hands of knaves.

So it was with expressions of satisfaction and discontent. Everyone belonged to a group of some sort, be it a tribe, sect, guild, or patron-client network. Many belonged to several, beginning with the family and branching out to a sect and professional guild. People communicated with the person above them, and they with their superior, and so forth up the chain of command. Communications may not have been free and direct, but the later caliphs got the message. Why else would they have surrounded themselves with legions of mercenaries?

The key point to be made is that everything was personalized, and formal rules counted for little if you knew somebody in a position in authority. Influence peddling (wasta) reigned, and the more powerful your patron, the greater your ability to trade favors with others. Patron-client relationships remain the core of the political process in the Arab world today.

Social Behavior
Social behavior during the era reflected a constant struggle between conforming to the pressures of culture and tradition, and attempts to circumvent those pressures stimulated by an enlightened atmosphere and the opulence of the royal courts.

Conforming to the Pressures of Culture and Tradition
This is not to say that Arabs of the Islamic era didn't cheat on the margins. After all, they were only human. Lust, greed, cravings for power, and all of the rest just wouldn't go away. While shame remained a key element of control, the greater mobility and temptations of the Islamic

era required more than shame. The eyes continued to peer, but even the eyes of the security police couldn't see everything.

As a result, an ever greater emphasis was placed on guilt and moral teachings as a means of controlling human appetites. Guilt was inherent in the Koran, but knowing right from wrong wasn't enough. The pangs of conscience had to accompany sin.

Of these efforts, perhaps the most famous were those of Imam Ghazali (1058–1111), who preached moral intelligence and self-purification as the surest path to inner peace and salvation.

Moral intelligence and self-purification began with the cardinal virtues of wisdom, courage, temperance, and justice. These, all grounded in the Koran and the teachings of the Prophet, led to the primary moral virtues of patience, modesty, gentleness, humility, forgiveness, gratitude, kindness, honesty, and generosity. Finally came the secondary qualities of orderliness, responsibility, prudence, lucidity, optimism, perseverance, industriousness, steadfastness, shyness, flexibility, obedience, simplicity, moderation, self-control, friendship, contentedness, sincerity, integrity, loyalty, and respect (Hussain, 2009, 7).

Ghazali's personal journey of self-discovery took him from regional schools in Iran to Baghdad, Damascus, and eventually Jerusalem. At the tomb of the Prophet Ibrahim he made three pledges to himself. He would:

1. Never visit a royal court.
2. Never accept royal gifts.
3. Never debate with anyone (Hussain, 2009, 96).

Did people listen? Do people ever listen? As always, the culprits were our old friends: greed, lust, power, and the rest of the appetites common to the human race. Ghazali added arrogance, anger, and envy to the list just for good measure.

Lust appeared to be the most daunting of problems. Islam was well aware of the inability of men to control their appetites, and it had done its best to keep order by requiring women to be prudent and allowing polygamy and early marriages.

Alas, it was to no avail. Multiple marriages could satisfy the raw sexual urge of males but couldn't accommodate their predatory curiosity or the pride of conquest. Such, after all, is the nature of the beast. The more women covered their bodies, the crazier men became. Who knew what joys lay hidden beneath those robes of mystery, not that hints on the topic were lacking?

The Shia added temporary marriage to ease the pain, and many Sunni followed suit, although Sunni doctrine finds the practice abhorrent. The Koran says nothing about temporary marriages, but marrying a woman for a night or two did skirt Koranic prohibitions against sex outside of marriage. The Egyptian press continues to attack the practice as a travesty against human rights, but the issue is more economic than moral as poor families struggle to survive.

This, according to Abdelwahab Bouhdiba, a professor of Islamic sociology at the University of Tunis, does not mean that moral teaching has not taken root. Rather, he sees the struggle between lust and conscience as the bane of the Muslim man whose

> energy is literally caught up in a permanent experience of his own body. Islam teaches the art of remaining pure as long as possible and of expelling impurity as soon as one becomes aware of it. The life of the Muslim is a succession of states of purity acquired then lost and of impurity removed and then found again. Man is never ultimately purified. Nor is he condemned to permanent impurity (Bouhdiba, 2004, 43).

Nor were women as passive as they might have been. The more purdah (covering) was imposed, the more skilled women became in beguiling men with their eyes. It was ever thus. They knew their prey well. If the poetry of the era is any guide, there were no eyes more sensuous than those of an Arab maiden.

According to the Koran, Allah was aware of the danger of female eyes and thus the command to women:

> And say to the believing women, that thy cast down their eyes and guard their private parts, and reveal not their adornment save such as is outward; and let them cast their veils over their bosoms, and not reveal their adornments save to their husbands (Koran, Light XXIV 30–1).

Note that the Koran requires women to cast their eyes down in the presence of a man outside of her family, but does not require that they be veiled. Veiling came with Omar (the third caliph or successor to the Prophet Mohammed), lest pride be sullied and revenge plotted.

Earthly women could also be vindictive if need be. This, after all, is the major theme of *The Arabian Nights*, one of the most fascinating stories of which is that of the beautiful princess who took the poorest beggar in the realm as a lover to punish an unfaithful husband.

Social Deviance: Enter the Fox

The more superiors attempted to control the behavior of their subordinates, the more creative people had to become if they were to outsmart the peering eyes, the security forces, and for that matter, their own conscience. Thus the wily skills of the fox, while not unknown during the era of ignorance, evolved dramatically during the era of empire. The truly clever individual played the lion to intimidate his subordinates while playing the fox to evade his superior.

While revered throughout society, it was in the courts of Damascus, Cairo, Baghdad, and Constantinople that the fox reigned supreme. The powerful ruled with cruelty and caprice while their wives schemed from the harem. Great feats of science and philosophy were achieved during the reign of Haram Rashid of *The Arabian Nights* fame, and other enlightened caliphs, but their reign was short and their progeny weak. The more the empire decayed, the worse things became.

People did what they had to do to take care of themselves and outshine their neighbors. Among other things, this meant evading the law, bribing government officials, double-crossing allies, spreading rumors, and shaming others caught in minor transgressions. What choice did they have? These were the rules of the game.

For those in official positions, however menial, the road was well trodden. Subordinates sucked up to superiors while undermining their authority, tore down other officials, stole from the government, favored relatives and co-sectarians, placed them in positions of authority when the opportunity presented itself, extracted bribes from supplicants, punished opposing families and sects, and traded wasta (influence peddling) whenever the price was right.

Superiors countered by acquiring as much power as possible, intimidating subordinates, hoarding bribes, avoiding sedition by micromanaging everything, and delegating as little authority as possible. Few officials shared much information with subordinates, and when they did, it was trickled out to different subordinates a piece at a time to ensure that only the patron had a complete picture of what was going on. It was always possible that subordinates would compare notes, but the risk was small. They didn't trust each other. Just to be on the safe side, life was spiced with false information and occasional hints of treachery among the plotters.

Rule by fear and force were essential, for the foxes preyed from within and jackals lurked without. The very hint of weakness was a death warrant. Yet, force was often tempered with acts of compassion and generosity granted by a wise sultan to beguile the masses and please God. Force came first, and then generosity. Don't forget, the wise sultan was also a fox.

At the personal level, the daily struggle to get along often found defense to be the best offense. Admitting error invited shame and retribution, so people blamed others, stonewalled, denied, angered quickly, and attacked critics with a vengeance. Officials, for their part, added the cloak of infallibility. To question one in authority was to invite disaster.

Appearances were vital to playing the fox, for how could he mingle with the sheep without pretending to be one of them? The appearance of strength gave adversaries pause while the appearance of wealth tempted them. If adversaries demanded flattery and subservience, so be it. Hypocrisy was the fox's stock and trade.

Was this a problem? Yes, so much so that Imam Ali, the fourth caliph and intellectual interpreter of Islam, classified behavior into three basic categories: Faith, hypocrisy, and apostasy. Apostates were visible and could either be killed or converted. But what to do with the fox, that inveterate hypocrite, who destroyed both faith and society from within?

The fox was all the more lethal because this master of disguises was equally a master of positioning. Then as now, the fox hovered on the fringes of power, hand in the till, but never close enough to be caught.

The high rollers were willing to risk all for moments of glory. It was they who became the viziers, grand muftis, princes, generals, and aristocrats who ruled in the name of the sultan. Alas, their greed and lust for power made them as visible as they were threatening and, therefore, short lived. No wonder the sultans and caliphs relied on slave troops to protect themselves. But how could the slave guards protect themselves from the fox?

Time and space during the Islamic era took on both earthy and spiritual dimensions. At the spiritual level, concerns of time included salvation and the end of time, when the Mahdi would return and unite heaven and earth. For the destitute and disinherited, thoughts of the return of the Mahdi inspired visions of paradise and revenge on their oppressors. Fanatics seemed to court death, and even for lesser believers, notions of the Day of Judgment strengthened their resolve to struggle against the temptations of the devil and protect Islam from it enemies. Perhaps this was to be expected for, as Al-Tabatabai writes,

> Among the sacred texts the Quran is the only one to have spoken in detail about the Day of Judgment. Although the Torah has not mentioned this day and the Gospels have only alluded to it, the Quran has mentioned the Day of Judgment in hundreds of places using different names.... [The] Day of Recompense (Day of Judgment) is on the same scale of importance as faith in God and is one of the three principles of Islam.... [H]e who lacks this faith, that is, who denies resurrection, is outside the pale of Islam and has not destiny other than internal perdition (165).

As a result, Islamic space became sacred and had to be defended, a drama played out in the Crusades that pitted Islam against Christianity. Both concepts play a key role in America's dealing with the Islamic world today.

Time and space also shaped most earthly behaviors. Much as during the tribal era, land represented wealth and security. Space, however, became scarcer during the era of Islam, as the collective land of the tribes was increasingly parceled out as aristocratic fiefdoms. With time and the gradual settlement of the tribes, proud nomads were reduced to peasant sharecroppers. Their fears and frustrations increased apace, as did their mystical search for God. Sunni tribes in southern Iraq defied sheiks-cum-aristocrats by embracing Shia Islam and its user-friendly approach to unity with God. In Egypt, a similar process was happening as the dispossessed embraced the popular religion of the Sufi and mystical preachers.

Economic Behavior

The greed and avarice of the elite contradicted the economic spirit of Islam which called upon the rich to be generous and the poor to accept their position and avoid envy. Most believers, if today's practice is any indication, paid the 2.5 percent religious tax required by Islam to fund good deeds and help the poor. The Shia paid 20 percent of their income to the preferred ayatollah to promote his mission. Begging was allowed for those in need, but often became a profession.

The collection of interest was forbidden because it caused conflict, promoted greed, and did little to benefit the welfare of the Islamic nation. Commerce was promoted and swelled the coffers of Islam, while simultaneously promoting Islam as a faith. Most of the Muslims in Africa and East Asia were introduced to Islam by merchants rather than by the sword. Hard work continued to be the norm among Bedouin and peasants struggling to survive, but sloth and venality corrupted the bureaucracies. It would never be eradicated.

RED-FLAG ISSUES: FROM ENLIGHTENMENT TO DECAY

Extremism, violence, unity, democracy, equity, and development are all complex phenomena that embrace the full range of environmental, psychological, and behavioral issues discussed above. Each had its origins in the tribal era, and each was dramatically modified by the forces of the Islamic era.

Religious Extremism Versus Religious Moderation

The Koran and the Sunna (way of the Prophet), much like the holy books of Judaism and Christianity, lend themselves to both moderation and extremism. Eras of Islamic enlightenment produced great feats of science, literature, and philosophy. There is no reason that enlightened Islamic rule could not do the same today. Eras of extremism, by contrast, produced nothing but darkness.

The most vivid picture of this situation was the 1912 Saudi experiment on settling tribes by integrating them into Islamic cooperatives guided by the ultraconservative and close-minded Wahabi interpretation of Islam. The story is presented here because the Saudi kingdom remained very much a medieval kingdom at the dawn of the twentieth century.

> *The Prophet condemned personal ostentation, so the Ikwan (brothers in Islam) shunned silk, gold, jewelry and…cut their robes short above the ankles. This was because the Prophet had declared that clothes that brushed the ground to be an affectation, and the same went for luxuriant moustaches. So the Ikwan clipped the hair on their upper lip to a mere shadow of stubbiness—while adopting a different rule for hair on the chin. In this case, they argued, it would be an affectation to trim and shape, so beards must be left to grow as long and to straggle as far as God might will them* (Lacy, 1981, 142–143).

The prevailing emotions of fear, suspicion, and closed mindedness also played their roles in the Ikwan's zealousness. It couldn't be otherwise, for the Ikwan camps were pressure cookers that abided no deviance. Conformity was expected, and even the hint of moderation was a sin. Nothing escaped the watchful eyes of prayer leaders and peers.

Anger, frustration, and humiliation must also have contributed to the ferocity of proud Bedouins uprooted from their tribe and forcibly settled in agricultural cooperatives by the king of a conquering tribe. They were searching for a new identity, and they found it in their faith and visions of a glorious hereafter.

Aside from the stringent nature of Wahabi preaching, other factors also led to extremism, not the least of which were a lack of exposure to a more liberal environment and an unwillingness to accept new ideas. The founder of the Saudi dynasty, for example, could only fight the belief that radio broadcasts were the work of the devil by using his radio station to broadcast readings from the Koran.

The Ikwan soon had more than ten thousand members. Their tribal spirit, as Lacy notes, was redirected from raiding to the glorification of Islam. They helped the Saudi king expand his conquest of the Arabian Peninsula but soon turned on him and had to be disbanded. Loyalty to God, it seems, did not extend to the king.

While the story of Saud Ikwan is but a curious footnote in history, it is not far different from life in the Taliban-controlled areas of Afghanistan and Pakistan today. If anything, the Deobandi doctrine of the Taliban is more extreme than the Wahabi doctrine of Saudi Arabia.

Both look to the past rather than the future, and both have a great deal in common with jihadist movements such as al-Qaeda.

To put it simply, the enemy of the Unites States and its allies is not Islam, but Islamic extremism.

The Evolution of Violence during the Islamic Era

Religious conflicts and violence during the era of Islam were frequent and born of the same causes as religious extremism, and they operated at all levels of society. Virtually all of the emotions discussed earlier were at play, including our old friends: frustration, anger, fear, suspicion, hopelessness, righteousness, and wounded pride. None guaranteed violence, but the more they stacked up, there was a greater likelihood of violence.

Religious extremism, while not violent when it looked inward, often turned violent, as schism after schism resorted to violence during the Islamic era to either impose its view on others or escape the wrath of the majority. The first example of this occurrence, as we have seen, was the splintering of Islam into warring sects and the subsequent wars of religion to capture the soul of the Muslim world.

Hardly had this rift between Sunni and Shia been unleashed than a contrary movement, the Kharijites, emerged to demand that Islam abandon its growing emphasis on moderation and consensus and return to its basic focus of "commanding the good and forbidding evil" (Rahman, 1966, 205).

Much like modern fundamentalists, the Kharijites focused on simple truths and the abolition of the priestly class. They even advocated abolishing the link between the caliphate and the Prophet's family, arguing that the Prophet Mohammed had not designated a successor and had said nothing about the matter. In their view, maintaining the line of the Prophet was an unfortunate mixture of tribalism and mysticism, neither of which were advocated by the Prophet. The caliphate was essential to Islam, and so the Kharijites urged that each new caliph be selected on the basis of merit and piety. In many ways, their views contained the seeds of democracy. If a slave emerged as the most qualified person to lead the faith, so be it.

Unfortunately, the Kharijites were so obsessed with the righteousness of their view of Islam that they killed anyone who disagreed with them, including the Caliph Ali. Why should a vision of merit and democracy spawn violence? Probably because the Kharijites also believed that behavior was a reflection of faith. Those who strayed from the path of purity were weak on faith and had to be destroyed (Rahman, 1966, 156). In the final analysis, Kharijite violence became so brutal that people who may have sympathized with their beliefs recoiled and returned to the prevailing view of moderation and consensus.

How similar are the Kharijites to the jihadists of today in their rejection of mysticism and their resort to violence as the only way to purify a corrupt society? The comparison is not perfect, but Kharijite ideas are clearly present in the extremist ideas of the Wahabi and other advocates of simple purity of faith (Rahman, 1966, 206).

Toward the last quarter of the ninth century, Hamdan Qarmat, a Shia religious student of peasant stock, led a socioeconomic revolt against the Sunni Abbasid caliph in Iraq and established something close to a communist order in which all things, including wives, were shared in the name of Islamic love and equality.

As in the case of the Kharijites, the Qarmatians, or "Islamic communists" as they were later referred to, unleashed a torrent of violence against those who rejected their doctrines (Hitti, 1956, 445). Again, potential supporters recoiled in fear. The movement was eventually crushed, but not before the Qarmatians had established their own mini-state on the Persian Gulf and, in 930, seized the sacred Black Stone from the Kabba in Mecca (Rahman, 1966).

Unlike the Kharijites who sought to break Islam from the grip of the ulema by focusing mass emotions on the simple issues of good and evil, the Qarmatians blended religious zeal with the intense mysticism of the Shia. Even the Koran, they claimed, was not what it appeared to be. Every word and every passage, they preached, had two or three hidden meanings that could only be understood by learned scholars who had studied the holy texts with such intensity that God, via the Hidden Imam, rewarded them with the gift of perfect knowledge.

Underlying the religious doctrine of the Qarmatians was Arab hostility toward the Iranians, peasant hostility toward the ruling elite, and the ever-present tension between the Bedouin and the more cultured settled populations. While it is premature to speak of class conflict, most of the sect's members were peasants and the urban poor. The movement was also embraced by the emerging guilds, the craftsmen of which saw it as a refuge from the arbitrariness of the ruling elite.

Even further removed from Koranic doctrine were the Assassins, a corrupted pronunciation of the Arabic word for those who use hashish. Their doctrine was a distant Shia offshoot that centered on achieving spiritual emancipation by believing in nothing and daring everything (Hitti, 1956, 446). The intensity of their violence, much of it directed against the Sunni Turks and Christian Crusaders, now lives forever in the world's vocabulary.

Again, poverty, despair, fear, frustration, revenge against oppressive elites, escape from the social turmoil swirling around them, the need for belonging, and the search for inner peace by serving God are all suggested as possible reasons for why people joined the Assassins.

The search for inner peace is of particular importance in explaining why members of the ruling classes and intellectuals joined the Assassins. Their numbers were not large, but they stand in testimony to the power of faith and mysticism on people from all backgrounds and classes. The Assassins, at least as far as one can tell from the chronicles of Marco Polo, who had visited the region at the time, were much like the jihadists of today. They were individual seekers who entered a most dangerous of secret societies at great personal risk. There is not enough information to sort things out at this point, but the topic will be rejoined in the later examination of the jihadists of today.

Personal motivations for joining the Assassins, and their curious doctrine of seeking internal peace by believing in nothing, remain vague, but one can only be awed by the effectiveness of their organizational structure and their capacity to indoctrinate adherents to commit the most atrocious acts of violence. Of particular interest was the process of indoctrinating the candidate members along the path of learning and violence. As described by Marco Polo,

> Now no man was allowed to enter the Garden (of the grand master) save those whom he intended to be his Ashishin. There was a fortress at the entrance to the Garden, strong enough to resist all the world, and there was no other way to get in. He kept at his Court a number of youths of the country, from twelve to twenty years of age, such as had a taste for soldiering…then he would introduce them into his Garden, some four, or six, or ten at a time, having first made them

drink a certain potion which cast them into a deep sleep, and then causing them to be lifted and carried in. So when they awoke they found themselves in the Garden.

When therefore they awoke, and found themselves in a place so charming, they deemed that it was Paradise in very truth. And the ladies and damsels dallied with them to their heart's content.

So when the Old Man would have any Prince slain, he would say to such a youth: "Go thou and slay So and So; and when thou returnest my Angels shall bear thee into Paradise. And shouldst thou die, nonetheless even so will I send my Angels to carry thee back into Paradise (Yule, 1875).

At every stage of Islam's evolution, or so it seems, the efforts to free Islam from the oppression of tyrants and the stifling rigidity of clerical legalisms has spawned a violent reaction, the latest manifestation of which are the jihadists of today. Then, like today, oppressive tyrants ruled without mercy. Their official clergy (ulema) were isolated from the masses by imponderable legalism. Poverty and insecurity were rife, and the masses were desperate for a solution, any solution, however extreme.

Again, the link between religious extremism and violence should not lead us to conclude that religious extremism must inevitably result in violence. Different forms of extremism didn't necessarily lead to violence during the Islamic era. But if they did lead to violence, their targets and triggers often differed.

Much Shia violence, as the following description illustrates, was self-directed, as the faithful engaged in self-flagellation to commemorate the assassination of Ali's son and successor in the Shia religious hierarchy. From a psychological point of view, it also provided a form of catharsis, releasing frustrations that might otherwise have been directed toward the ruling elite.

Under the guidance of this leader, the circle will begin to move round, ever faster and faster. He watches for the psychological moment; and suddenly with a shriek of "Shikhasn" he brings his sword down on his own head. The blood spurts up and falls, covering his white robe with a crimson stain. The sight of blood removes all restraint and all order. Shouts of "Hasan, Hussein, Ali!" and the dull blow of the swords mingle with the shrieks, groans, and sobs of the onlookers.... [The] band leaves the mosque and proceeds around the town, slashing themselves every few yards (Lyell, 1923, 68–70).

Aside from the violent exceptions reviewed above, most Sufi orders and other forms of popular Islam that evolved during the era looked inward in their search for God, although many holy men were often associated with peasant revolts and mass despair.

As in the case of the Assassins, much depended on the views of the sheikh or master, who assumed mystical proportions and claimed a special baraka, or gift of grace from God. As such, he was infallible and immune from error. Miracles abounded, as did mystical states of ecstasy inspired by the love of God. Sufi sheikhs attracted mass followings, and with their passing, they often became saints, and their tombs were worshiped. All of this was abhorrent to Islamic doctrine, but the ulema eventually accepted minor miracles in an effort to keep in touch with the masses.

Hitti cites the following exchange between a woman mystic of noble background who, when asked by the Prophet Mohammed in a dream if she loved him, her reply was that "My love for God has so possessed me that no place remains for hating aught loving any save Him (Hitti, 1956, 439).

By the end of the Islamic era, Sufi orders had taken on the characteristics of monastic societies, never a part of Islam. Their members, frequently referred to as dervishes, clustered in special quarters to gain fellowship and confidence in God's blessing beyond that provided by the mosque. Below them were the affiliate members and supporters who sought grace by their association with the order.

Fragmentation Versus Solidarity

Islam calls for a nation of believers, the Umma. This union was achieved during the Islamic era and remained intact as long as a caliph reigned as the symbolic head of the faithful. The long chain of Arab caliphs who claimed the bloodline of the Prophet Mohammed had given way to Turkish sultans by the middle of the Islamic era, but at least Muslims were ruling Muslims.

It was a much flawed unity torn by extremism, violence, sectarian schisms, immoral behavior, greed, and all the rest, but Islam was whole. Even that pretense of unity was destroyed by the advent of colonialism, but it lives on as a dream in the heart of many Muslims who believe that God's will demands the re-creation of a nation lost. Just how relevant is this dream to America's frustration in the Middle East? This question is pondered throughout the remainder of the book, but it is clearly part of the puzzle.

Tyranny versus Democracy

Imagine, if you will, the problems of governing a vast empire embracing multiple ethnic, linguistic, and religious groups, all pulling in different directions, demanding greater autonomy, and rebelling whenever the opportunity presented itself. Add to the mix the fierce independence of the Bedouin who roamed the vast deserts, the peasant who was hostile to authority, and the fox who lurked in the cities.

The most serious problem, however, appeared to be the disconnect between the masses and a palace elite that was isolated from the masses by legions of bureaucrats, tax collectors, and landed aristocrats. While the elite lived in oriental splendor, the masses lived in oriental squalor. It were almost as if the two sides were on different planets. No wonder there was so little cohesion within the Islamic nation.

The seeds for democracy existed in both tribalism and Islam, but they soon withered under the oppression of remote caliphs and the obtuse religious legalisms of the ulema (clergy.) What the elite didn't crush was washed away by the violence of extremist groups. Authoritarianism prevailed, as hopes for democracy faded with the passing of enlightenment.

Inequality Versus Equity

The seeds of human rights were firmly established in the Koran which states, "Whoever works righteousness, man or women, and has faith, verily, to him will We give a new Life, a life that is good and pure" (16–97). And "Whoever does right, whether man or woman, and is a believer, will enter Paradise" (Koran, 40:40).

This didn't mean equality between the sexes. Islam, like its sister faiths on which it drew so heavily, embraced the biblical practice of establishing men as the masters and guardians of women. The Koran states that women are to be devoutly obedient. Those who are not obedient "are to be left alone in their beds and may be beaten" (Koran,

4:34). In legal matters, the word of one male was the equivalent to that of two women.

While retrogressive by today's standards, Islam's view of gender equality paralleled Christian and Jewish practice of the era. This didn't mean that practice always followed theory. The emotions of dominance, fear, and honor led to the seclusion and veiling of women, not to mention intentional efforts to destroy their self-esteem through ignorance and oppression. You can blame this on males, but not on Islam.

The same duality exists in Islam's treatment of the rights of Jews and Christians, the People of the Book. On one hand, the Koran stresses tolerance of Christians and Jews in unequivocal terms. "Those who believe, and those who follow the Jewish (Torah) and the Christians and Sabians—any who believe in Allah and the Last Day, and work righteousness, shall have their reward with their Lord; on them shall be no fear, nor shall they grieve" (Koran, 2:62).

Other verses, by contrast, are openly hostile to other faiths. "Never will the Jews or the Christians be satisfied with you unless you follow their form of religion" (Koran, 2:120). And "Take not the Jews and the Christians for your friends and protectors: they are but friends and protectors to each other" (Koran, 5:51).

As in most areas of life, then, Muslims are presented with both tolerant and extremist options for dealing with minorities and human rights. As a general principle, Jews and Christians lived in peace with Muslims during the era of Islam, many rising to high positions in the court of the caliph. The more extremism increased, the more tolerance declined. The same principle applies today.

Economic Stagnation Versus Economic Growth

The mission of Islam was to lead the Arabs from the era of ignorance into an era of religious and social enlightenment. Economic development was dazzling as long as Islam and its leaders remained open to enlightenment. When Islam turned inward, change went into reverse, and intellectual enlightenment and technological development stopped.

The glories of the era of Islam play a dual rule in the story of the Arabs. First, they illustrate that Islam as a faith can foster innovation and development if applied with wisdom. Second, the era of Islamic glory remains lodged in the psyche of the Arabs and other Muslims as the symbol of what could be if only they could find leaders of wisdom. But where to look?

Such, then, was the state of the Arab psyche as an awakened Europe, fired by nationalism and the desire for conquest, cast a covetous eye to its lands.

CHAPTER 4

COLONIALISM AND THE ARAB PSYCHE

The Western colonization of the Arab world began with Napoleon's invasion of Egypt in 1798. In addition to soldiers, his expeditionary force included a contingent of social scientists to study the psyche of his new conquests. A true military genius, Napoleon understood that the psyche of the enemy was vital to sustained conquest. British jealousies brought an end to Napoleon's occupation of Egypt three years later, but Egyptian scholars today often wonder if American social scientists intent on studying the Arab psyche haven't been sent on a similar mission.

The French were thwarted in Egypt but soon turned their attention to Algeria which they occupied in 1830. The British claimed Egypt as a protectorate in 1882, and established a few enclaves in the Persian Gulf about the same time. Aside from these early ventures, the sovereignty of the Ottoman Empire over the Arab world was respected. It wasn't Turkish power that kept the Europeans at bay, but the inability of Britain, France, and Russia, the major powers of the time, to agree on anything, including who should claim which possessions of the decaying Islamic Empire.

The "Eastern question," as it was referred to at the time, was brought to an end by the defeat of Germany in WWI. Turkey, an ally of Germany in the war, was stripped of its colonies, and the land grab began. The British claimed what are now Iraq, Jordan, and Israel, while the French made do with Syria, having earlier added Morocco and Tunisia to their North African empire. The Italians settled for Libya, then a barren stretch of the North African coast between Egypt and Tunisia.

It wasn't much, but Italy proclaimed it to be the first step in rebuilding the Roman Empire of old.

All that remained of the Arab world was the Arabian Peninsula, a desolate and inhospitable area of little interest to anyone. Even here, however, the British carved out a small colony on the tip of the Arabian Peninsula to guard the entrance to the Persian Gulf and the sea lanes to India, the crown jewel of the British Empire.

The areas seized from the Turks were technically mandates, a term implying that the territories were to be guided toward independence and democracy. The British and French went along with this quaint notion to please the Americans, but the result was the same.

The British and French redrew the boundaries of the Arab world in line with their national interests. Tribes, ethnic groups, and religious minorities, once cohesive units, were divided pell-mell between colonial possessions as if they were pawns in a global chess game, which of course, they were. Tiny Kuwait was spun off as a British protectorate while some twenty million Kurds, who had been promised an independent country, were scattered among Iraq, Turkey, Iran, Russia, and Syria. It wasn't big news at the time, but it is today.

Turkey and Persia (Iran) were not colonized, but their empires had started to collapse long before WWI, and both had turned to Germany to modernize their military establishments. A brisk commerce followed, and modernity was in the air.

The British, responding to wartime pressures, issued the Balfour Declaration in 1917, proclaiming that "His Majesty's Government views with favour the establishment in Palestine of a national home for the Jews…it being clearly understood that nothing shall be done which may prejudice the civil and religious rights of existing non-Jewish communities in Palestine, or the rights and political status enjoyed by Jews in any other country (Fraser, 1980, 18; Schneer, 2010). What precisely did this most confusing declaration mean? A century of bloodshed and terror have yet to resolve the issue.

ENTER THE KAWAGA: HOW THE EUROPEANS RULED

Kawaga, simply translated, means "mister" when referring to a Christian foreigner. It was that but so much more. Don't forget that it is the pronunciation and emotion that gives Arabic words their meaning. Seeing that most of the Christian foreigners during the era of colonialism were occupiers and exploiters, the definition of kawaga began to mean, "Hello, mister foreign occupier who has come to exploit us." On the surface, kawaga implies respect and submission. Lurking just beneath the surface is mockery, resistance, and the subtle hint of duplicity that the Arabs have always used to defeat their conquerors.

I first encountered the term while a student in Egypt during the early 1960s. To the people on the street, I was a kawaga. "Whatever you want, kawaga. Right away, kawaga. If God wills, kawaga."

It was a perfect arrangement. The colonial masters received the respect they demanded while the Arabs taunted them by establishing the higher power of God. God also became an excuse for delay, forgetfulness, duplicity, and a thousand and one other subtle forms of resistance. The Arabs had been conquered, but their psyche had not been defeated.

The British, French, and Italians were the main kawagas of the colonial era, but they relinquished that honor to the Americans and Soviets during the Cold War. The Americans now reign alone as the main kawaga, an open invitation to frustration. The Turks were never kawaga because they ruled as the head of the Muslim nation.

Some colonies were governed by a high commissioner supported by military garrisons and a phalanx of European civil servants. Others, and especially British mandates, were governed by kings or dictators put into place by the colonial power. European military garrisons occupied areas of strategic importance, while European bureaucrats managed matters of importance to the colonial power. King or no, it was the British or French ambassador who called most of the shots.

Lesser tasks were allocated to natives trained to serve the interests of the colonial power. This policy had been honed by the British in India and was designed "to form a class who may be the interpreters between us and the millions whom we govern, a class of persons Indian in blood and color, but English in taste, in opinions, in morals, and in intellect" (Tully and Mansani, 1988, 40).

In order to create this class of cooperative Arabs, the colonial powers created schools to teach the Arabs the colonial language, not to mention large doses of European culture and history. Arabic language and culture were seldom in the curriculum, and the French attempted to stamp out the teaching of Arabic in their North African colonies. What a curious irony that Arab revolutionaries in North Africa plotted in French rather than Arabic.

The French had some success in spreading French culture and values in Algeria, where they ruled for almost a century, but British ventures in the Arab world lasted but a few decades. Even then, the British preferred to rule through their puppet kings rather than doing the dirty work themselves. This didn't mean that the British were not unmindful of the psychological advantages of teaching the superiority of British culture to their colonial subjects. What better way to implant a subliminal message of inferiority into the Arab psyche? The Italians were far less subtle. Or as a Libyan friend put it, "The Italians taught us that we were toads."

There can also be little doubt that many diplomats looked down on the Arabs. A few became noted Arabists, but many others shared the views of a friend in the British Foreign Service who quipped, "The Persian Gulf is the asshole of the world, and Baghdad is up it." I wonder if the same attitude influenced the behavior of the American kawaga in Iraq, Afghanistan, and elsewhere?

The Problem with Puppets

Did it work? Not really. Puppets, then as now, were notoriously corrupt and unreliable. Actually, puppet is a misleading term. Puppets are toys attached to strings that can be manipulated at will. Puppet kings, by contrast, had their own agenda and used the shield provided by the colonial power to crush their opponents and feather their own nests. Seeing that many of America's frustrations in the Arab world stem from its infatuation with puppets, let me give a few British tales of woe from Egypt and Iraq.

In the lead-up to WWII, the British had converted Egypt into a staging center for their looming war with Germany in North Africa. The Egyptian king at the time was suspected of harboring Nazi sympathies and was deposed in favor of his son Farouk. The British weren't delighted with Farouk, who was addicted to gambling and consorted with belly dancers most of the night. But what choice did they have? Farouk was the best alternative available, and venality has its uses.

Alas, their fears were well founded, for aside from his profligate lifestyle and Albanian lineage, Farouk turned out to be an erratic, self-absorbed, and strong-willed autocrat who viewed his subjects with contempt. Gambling wasn't too much of a problem, for Farouk seldom lost. After all, it wasn't polite to embarrass the king, especially when he was more than generous with his cronies. Then, as now, the secret of power in the Arab world is having the ear of the tyrant.

The problem, according to Hassan Youssef Pasha, the head of the royal diwan (cabinet) with whom I shared an office at the Al-Ahram Center for Political and Strategic Studies, was that Farouk was the victim of bad advice. The king, it seemed, had two diwans or cabinets. An afternoon cabinet, headed by Hassan Youssef, urged Farouk to pursue policies that would strengthen his regime and build popular support. A nighttime cabinet, by contrast, consisted of knaves who pandered to the king's less-savory appetites. Unfortunately, the pasha lamented, the nighttime cabinet usually held sway.

By way of passing, I might note that Hassan Youssef Pasha was a man of exceptional talent who spoke four languages fluently. It wasn't his intelligence, however, that propelled the pasha to his exalted position as chief of the royal diwan. Rather, is was an accident of fate that saw the pasha, then a young diplomat in London, charged with providing then Prince Farouk with all the money required to carry out his studies in a royal manner. When I asked him how one got to be a pasha, a most exalted of titles, he smiled and replied, "By donating lots of money to the king's favorite charities." He didn't elaborate.

Why didn't the British just get rid of Farouk, much like they got rid of his father? Because Farouk was next in line for the throne, and WWII loomed. This made the British reluctant to further inflame an extremely popular independence movement which was demanding the immediate evacuation of British forces stationed in Egypt. For better or for worse, Egyptian politics had become a three-way struggle between the British, the king, and ultranationalist Wafd party. When the king attempted to build popular support by refusing British demands vital to the war effort, the British surrounded the palace with tanks, and Farouk capitulated. Hostility toward the British, already intense, reached crisis proportions, and respect for Farouk, never great, plummeted.

A similar scenario was playing itself out in Iraq when Nuri as-Said, the British-puppet strongman, was inflaming anti-British hostility by shifting land and wealth to his aristocratic friends. The British ambassador complained that the pro-British Iraqi monarchy was rapidly losing touch with reality, but to no avail. Angry mobs dragged the dismembered body of Nuri as-Said, disguised as a woman, through the streets of Baghdad in 1958. The monarchy was no more (Cornwallis, cited in Elliot, 1996).

Not only were colonial puppets unreliable, but native support personnel were drawn from the sons of influential notables or favored minorities less hostile to the occupation than the general population. Thus, the French relied heavily on Christians in Syria and Lebanon, while the British favored the Sunni in Iraq. In addition to providing a ready supply of cooperative natives, this policy had the advantage of turning tribe against tribe, religion against religion, sect against sect, and class against class. What is better than the policy of divide and rule to keep the natives quiescent?

The trouble with British divide-and-rule policies, now adopted by the Americans, was that the favored groups used their authority to exact revenge on their opponents, place friends and relatives in power, and rip off the wealth of the country while the getting was good. In the meanwhile, the dispossessed, usually the majority, turned on the colonial power and bided their time while they plotted revolution. This lesson is simple. Divide-and-rule tactics serve momentary goals but ultimately make a country ungovernable.

How Colonialism Changed the Arab World

While the colonial powers had little interest in riling the masses, their desire to exploit the economic and strategic advantages of the colonies often left them little choice. Creating an educated class of Arabs to serve the colonial enterprise required the establishment of educational institutions that soon served as the embryo of Arab nationalism.

Health reforms were essential to make the colonies safe for Europeans, but they soon spawned a population explosion, as people longing for large families found themselves with more children than they could support. Life expectancies soared, but economic opportunities couldn't keep pace. As a result, the rural poor were pushed to the cities in the vain hope of finding work. What they found were slums and despair. Violence and extremism followed in their wake.

The Europeans reshaped the colonial economies to supply raw materials to their home industries and serve as a dumping ground for their industrial exports. As a result, consumerism increased while industrialization of the Arab world was stunted. Peopled wanted more, but they didn't have the money to buy it. Frustration and political agitation followed.

Expanded transportation and communication networks served the commercial and strategic interests of the colonialists, but they also allowed extremist groups and nationalist agitators to communicate easily and reach an ever-larger population. What is the old adage? The knife that cuts can also spread.

Western legal systems were superimposed upon existing Turkish and Islamic law to make them compatible with the commercial laws of the colonial power. This resulted in a legal mishmash that saw the kawaga tried in European courts while Arabs remained subject to harsher codes of yore. In effect, Arabs had become second-class citizens in their own countries. Under no circumstances could they gain equality with the kawaga. Resentment simmered even among those who aped the ways of the kawaga. Perhaps I should say especially among those who copied the ways of the kawaga, for their sense of deprivation and humiliation was far deeper than that of the rural masses that constituted the vast majority of the Arab population during the colonial era.

An even more profound source of change was the influx of settler populations in North Africa and Palestine. Algeria, with some two million settlers, often referred to as black feet, was made a department of France, while Jewish settlements in Palestine constituted a virtual country within a country.

The impact of colonialism traced above was proportional to the intrusiveness of the colonial venture. Egypt, Algeria, Palestine, Syria, and Iraq bore the brunt of the colonial assault, while Saudi Arabia and Yemen remained largely unscathed. The countryside slumbered while the slums seethed with frustration, and the sons of the rich and influential yearned to seize the reins of power.

THE ARAB PSYCHE CONFRONTS COLONIALISM

Much as Islam had added a new layer of complexity to the tribal psyche, so colonialism added a new layer of complexity to the Arabo-Islamic psyche. In addition to dealing with all of the existing pressures of family, faith, and tyrants, the Arab colonial psyche now had to deal with the defeat of Islam and the humiliation of occupation by a Christian power. Perhaps more challenging was the need to adjust to the dominance of a secular worldview that was diametrically opposed to everything that the Arab psyche believed. Not only had the Arab psyche's world been turned upside down, it had been turned upside down virtually overnight.

Identity

The first issue to be confronted was that of identity. How could Arabs confront the pain that engulfed them without figuring out who they were and how they fit in the world around them? As J. Nehru, India's first prime minister, framed the issue, people had to choose whether they were forward looking or backward looking.

It was a cruel choice. The past was part of the Arab psyche, but of decreasing utility in meeting its needs in the ever-changing colonial environment. Western secularism, by contrast, offered a dazzling image of power and prosperity, but was never part of the Arab psyche. Most people, except for a narrow elite educated in Europe, weren't even quite sure of what it meant to be Western other than to dress European. That was certainly the case with the vast majority of people locked in the stifling ignorance of the rural areas.

Aside from family and faith, most people didn't seem to worry much about whom they were or what they were, and gradually evolved a transitional identity that clung to the past while sampling the pleasures of modernity, not the least of which were motion pictures and alcohol. Identities of family and faith were never in doubt, but how could one resist vicariously assuming the identities of the movie heroes, much as their ancestors had thrilled to the stories of Antar and *The Arabian Nights?* Their lives revolved around family and faith, but thoughts of becoming Western had etched a place in the Arab identity. It was a small window at first, but it kept expanding during the colonial era.

As a practical matter, Western identities were generally limited a small elite that had been educated in the West and exposed to the heady ideas of Arab nationalism and Marxism. It was they who formed the core of the Arab nationalist movement with its dreams of an Arab return to glory based on science and socialism.

The traditionalists, by contrast, were rooted in a religious community that condemned colonial secularism as a plot against Islam. Their standard bearer would be the Muslim Brotherhood, branches of which soon spread throughout the Arab world.

Between the two extremes was the broad mass of Muslim Arabs attempting to find a comfort zone between tradition and modernity. There was little cause for conflict between the two views, for both the secular nationalists and the Muslim Brotherhood were intent on driving the kawaga from the Arab world. Christian Arabs viewed the Brotherhood with suspicion but were strongly represented in the ranks of the Arab nationalists.

Motivations

The innate needs of beni Adam remained unchanged during the colonial era, as did the appetites of greed, lust, and the rest. The learned wants of pride, honor, Islamic morality, and family loyalty also remained intact.

This didn't mean that colonialism didn't change the Arab psyche. The dazzling lifestyle of the Europeans, now emulated by the elite and glamorized by the cinema, led to a dramatic increase in material wants. The new materialism, in turn, began to rival age, lineage, and other traditional symbols of status. This wasn't difficult, for even a little wealth went a long way in a culture of poverty.

Not even money was essential, for those who returned home with the castoffs of the kawaga invariably created a stir in the village. I recall having been stationed in French Morocco and watching the boys from the neighboring village return home laden with whatever castoffs they could lay their hands on, including everything from discarded shoes to fuel tins. It was a daily routine, and they wore their new importance on their sleeve. Cups of tea followed, for Americans at the time were the good kawaga who mixed with the Arabs far more freely than the French colonists (settlers), who despised them. Woe to the lone Moroccan female caught unawares by a truckload of French Legionaries. I could tell you about the women's prisons that the French built, but I won't.

While colonialism created new opportunities for those who played the colonial game, it also invited the hostility of those who didn't. There were new choices to be weighed as the old calculus of pain and pleasure began to fray at the edges. This, of itself, was painful, for choices did not come easy to an authoritarian psyche accustomed to obeying and emulating rather than innovating.

Displays of westernization may have been superficial, but the intense pain of wounded honor was not. The Arabs and Islam had been humiliated. Once rulers of the world, they had become despised subjects of Christian Europe. The humiliation of Islam was worse, for they had failed to defend their faith. The pain of humiliation rivaled the pain of poverty and despair. Perhaps they were linked. One way or another, something had to be done, but what?

How could the Arabs even think of regaining their power when most of their waking hours were devoted to the all-consuming task of surviving a colonial environment that had ignited a vortex of change and insecurity? The rules had changed. The power structure had changed. The culture was changing. It was changing slowly to be sure, but it was changing. On the other hand, given the Arab emphasis on dignity and faith, how could they not think about it? How long could they remain the defeated remnants of the most glorious of peoples? Psychologists call it relative deprivation. It was the memories of past glories that made the defeat of the present so difficult to bear.

Guilt and Conscience

Colonialism also introduced new issues of morality and conscience. Working for the colonial master served material wants and enhanced personal status, but was it moral? Could one serve those intent on destroying Arabism and desecrating Islam without rotting in hell?

God would judge, but what did God demand in dealing with the kawaga? Did morality demand defeating the kawaga by every means at their disposal, including deception, or did it mean learning from the kawaga in order to defeat him? Perhaps it meant learning from the kawaga in order to improve the quality of life in Muslim societies. For some, God demanded no more than keeping the faith alive by surviving periods of adversity. Colonialism spawned this debate, but it continues unabated today.

Emotion: The Mahdi Complex Meets the Kawaga Complex

This brings us to the dominant emotions of the era. We have already touched on fear, anger, humiliation, and guilt. Now, add self-doubt to the equation. In addition to humiliation, occupation saddled the Arab psyche with self-doubt and the kawaga complex. The Arab psyche didn't like the kawaga, but it was awed by him. So much so, in fact, that the Arab psyche attributed almost mystical powers to the kawaga. The kawaga knew everything and could do everything. He was invincible. The Arabs could never catch up, and trying was futile.

The kawaga complex, in turn, bred feelings of inferiority, low effectiveness, and defeatism. If this were not damaging enough, the kawaga complex also incorporated the profound feelings of resignation and fatalism already deeply rooted in the Arab psyche. Let me give you a modern example. I was visiting one of my Saudi graduate students a few years ago when he looked at me in despair and complained, "Now I know as much as you do, but the government officials won't listen to me. They only listen to the kawaga."

This, of course, was the mindset that the Europeans were attempting to instill in the Arabs. For the Arabs to be ruled effectively, physical defeat had to be accompanied by psychological defeat. The Israelis would soon play upon the kawaga complex to build a myth of invincibility.

How nicely the kawaga complex dovetails with the Mahdi complex, introduced in our review of the Arabo-Islamic psyche. If the kawaga were invincible, the only hope the Arabs had was to pray for the arrival of a superhero, if not the Mahdi sent by God, to lead them to victory.

But what form would the Mahdi take? Some believed that he would appear as a religious mystic bearing the signs of God's grace. Others envisioned a new Saladin sent to drive the crusaders from the Arab heart of Islam. Much to the dismay of the Arab nationalists of the era, resignation and passivism reigned while the masses waited for the arrival of the Mahdi. This didn't mean that the masses didn't seethe with frustration and hatred for the kawaga. It just meant that emotional pressure was building while they waited for the return of the Mahdi.

Thus, we had better add frustration to the discussion as well. In eras past, people pretty much accepted their lot as the fate of God, but the glitzy lifestyles of the colonials, native elites, and the advent of the cinema sent material wants soaring, especially in the large urban centers such as Cairo and Baghdad. The masses could look and dream, but they couldn't touch. Very frustrating, especially for the youth, and they were at least half of the population. Maybe more.

Navigating between Pain and Pleasure

The uncertainties and emotional tensions of the colonial era put a strain on even the most strenuous effort to make rational decisions in dealing with the kawaga. Without repeating all the complexities of the reasoning process, a few simple questions will illustrate our point. The answers to the questions will become apparent in the review of Arab behavior during the colonial era which follows.

Let's start with perception. How much did beni colonial's psyche really know about the events going on around it, especially the plans of the British, the curious kings of the era, the leaders of the independence movements, and the Muslim Brotherhood? Bear in mind, the mass media was rudimentary, and most people couldn't read. Did beni colonial suffer from an information overload or a shortage of information? Perhaps the colonial psyche suffered from both, too many emotional slogans and too little hard data.

This brings us to the question of evaluation. Was the colonial psyche really in position to evaluate much of the information, most of it confused and laden with emotion, which swirled around its head? Now add faith and science to the equation. Which standard was the colonial psyche to use in evaluating and categorizing the information that it did have? Was it better to bet on faith or science?

Next was the problem of balancing emotions. Arabs of the colonial era were frustrated, humiliated, and angry, but they were also fearful, distrustful, and resigned. They were full of self-doubt, haunted by the kawaga complex, and inclined to wait for a Mahdi to rescue them from the scourge of occupation. How were they to reconcile these conflicting emotions? The kawaga, for his part, knew that the pot was boiling, but was it in danger of boiling over?

We still have to deal with defense mechanisms. Whatever information the Arab psyche had at its disposal, did it want to see the truth? I ask the question because, as always, beni Adam's ego was adept at protecting the psyche from the painful realities of defeat, humiliation, and hopelessness. As we shall see in the following section, some denied their plight by closing their minds to the changes occurring around them or by longing ever more fervently for the arrival of the Mahdi. Others absolved themselves of personal responsibility for their plight by claiming it to be the will of God. Things would change when God wanted them to change, so what could they do? The defense mechanisms of substitution and avoidance thus transformed resignation into a virtue. This was especially the case for those who sought rapture of oneness with God promised by the Sufis.

Add the timeworn traits of authoritarianism, collectivism, mysticism, and reliance on a strong leader to the formula. Put them all together, and they add up to a longing for the return of the Mahdi.

If language shapes thought patterns, as the psycholinguistic theories suggest, then the Arabs and their colonial masters were on different planets. Even when they thought they were communicating, no one could be quite sure what had been agreed upon, if anything. The British are known for their reserved subtly and understatement, the Arabs for their exaggeration and embellishment. A simple statement suffices for the British, whereas in Arabic, sincerity requires emotion and endless repetition. Even a simple agreement in Arabic is couched in "tomorrow, if God wills." The Arabs learned English and French with great facility, but did this mean that they could think as the English and French thought? For that matter, were the British and French beguiling themselves when they thought that they could think like Arabs?

Colonial Poker Anyone?

So the game of colonial poker lumbered on, as the Arab psyche attempted to get along in a world dominated by foreigners. Unlike the roadmap of the Islamic era, the Arab psyche could no longer seek comfort by clinging to the past. It now had to face the hard reality of Western dominance if it were to achieve its needs and wants. Pretending wouldn't help. But where to place its bets—on a revitalized Islam or on secular modernization? Perhaps it was possible to combine the two. Unfortunately, the Arab psyche was so divided among itself that there was no agreement on the issue.

THE COLONIAL LION VERSUS THE ARAB FOX: ARAB RESPONSES TO COLONIALISM

How, then, did the Arabs of the era respond to the colonial environment? It depends which Arabs you are talking about. The people in the rural areas, and that was most of them, went about living their lives much as they had during the era of Islam. By and large, they remained wedded to the traditions of the past and viewed modernity with suspicion. In the view of the intellectuals of the era, they were asleep. The same was true of Saudi Arabia and Yemen, the two Arab countries to remain free of Western penetration.

Most Arabs simply adjusted as best they could by enjoying the material benefits of colonialism while clinging to the ways of tradition. By and large, they were bystanders in the drama unfolding around them.

This was not the case for a narrow layer of intellectuals, religious leaders, aristocrats, merchants, and politicians who found their aspirations constrained by the colonial powers. They wanted the kawaga gone. The same was true of cooperative natives drawn into the bureaucracy and security forces of the colonial power. Natives could rise to middle positions only, at best. Even then, they only commanded Arabs. Quality didn't matter. The Europeans ruled. It was the same in social life. Arabs, regardless of how cultured or westernized, entered elite hotels and sporting clubs through the servant's entrance. That was their role.

Because this native elite felt the humiliation of colonization so intensely, it was they who would lead the charge against colonial domination. It would not be easy, for their numbers were few. The sleepers had to be awakened and the bystanders energized.

Also problematic were the deep divisions within the Arab elite itself. Popular religious leaders vowed to resist westernization, viewing it as an attack on their faith. Enlightened religious leaders, by contrast, argued that only a fusion of modern science and Islamic morality could revive the Arab and Islamic worlds. In their view, nothing was to be gained by Arabs and Muslims sticking their collective heads in the sand. A third current condemned Islamic and Arab traditions as a negative force that doomed the Arabs to perpetual backwardness and subservience. In their view, one could only fight European domination by becoming European. There was no middle ground. This view

116

was particularly strong among Arabs and Muslims who had studied in Europe and absorbed a large dose of Marxist ideology.

It would be these three positions that struggled for control of the Arab psyche during the colonial era. The struggle continues in one guise or another today. For the moment, however, the behavior of most people continued to be driven by the mundane tasks of getting along in a most uncertain world. They didn't care for their foreign masters, the kawaga, but they were part of life and had to be dealt with. Not everyone behaved as described, but the behaviors described below were common enough to drive the kawaga crazy.

What this meant, in practical terms, was that the colonial era would become a struggle between the lion and the fox. Oh, how the British and the French adored the lion, that revered symbol of power, order, organization, and self-discipline. That most noble of beasts adorned the palaces and bridges of London and Paris, much as they adorned the imperial embassies and bridges that symbolized European rule in the Middle East.

I have seen no statutes of the fox in the Arab world, which is curious, for it was the fox who liberated the Arabs from the scourge of the lion and bequeathed to them a society that longs in vain for power, order, organization and self-discipline.

Like the fox, the Arabs were most versatile, shifting their guise to fit the needs of the moment. They could play the lion when it suited their purposes, but more often than not, they pretended to obey, their masks of docility hiding what they chose not to say.

Some used their masks to avoid confronting the kawaga while they bided their time. Others used their masks to beguile him while they pursued their hidden agendas at his expense. Many did both. They even warned the kawaga. To paraphrase an oft-heard interaction between a fox and the kawaga:

Thank you for coming, kawaga, and teaching us the ways of the West. Please don't think that I have lost my faith in Islam because I want to learn your ways, kawaga, for that is not true. Everything is the fate of God. It was He who sent you to revive us from our backwardness. Sadly, kawaga, there are those who will resist you or beguile you with appearances of friendship. Unfortunately, they are not as enlightened as I. Take care, kawaga, and don't be fooled by appearances. I will help you find the way.

What was their purpose in warning the kawaga? Why, to gain his confidence and turn him against their enemies. One had to get along. Did the kawaga listen? What choice did he have? He needed natives to do his dirty work, and friendly faces were preferable to those shooting at him. Like the lion, he had contempt for those whom he had conquered, and he rejoiced in the sure knowledge that Arabs would cut and run in the face of danger and sell out their countrymen for a pittance. It was the kawaga's view of the Arab psyche (Patai, 2002). Perhaps it was arrogance. Rare is the conqueror who doesn't suffer from a superiority complex. Or maybe there was a touch of naiveté or manifest destiny. Probably all of the above.

Besides, who could blame the kawaga for being beguiled by the Arabs? They were the living embodiment of *The Arabian Nights*, as charming and hospitable as they were mysterious and treacherous. A few kawaga became so enamored of the Arabs that they converted to Islam.

Some flavor of this struggle between the ways of tradition and the ways of the kawaga is to be found in the movies of the era, a few of which you can still catch on the Arabic movie channels. Alcohol mixed with loose women in low-cut evening gowns dancing with men in Western suits topped by a fez, while belly dancers swayed in the background, and lonely wives wept themselves to sleep in their grand palaces while husbands, returning from a hard night out, chased would-be lovers down marble staircases with shotguns and canes. Such movies, invariably produced in Egypt, had nothing to do with reality, but they became immensely popular throughout the region, with the exception of Saudi Arabia, Yemen, and other areas where they were outlawed as the work of the devil.

Political Behavior

Identity, Loyalty, and Collective Solidarity

Family and faith remained the primary Arab identities during the colonial era. It was ever thus. Daily life centered on the former, and spiritual matters centered on the latter. Both seemed ill suited to leading an

Arab uprising against the kawaga. Family identities fragmented society, while Islam had looked inward and had lost much of its zeal. Arabism, for its part, remained a vague concept far removed from modern concepts of nationalism. There was also little emotional attachment to kings and aristocrats who treated the masses as chattel. In Iraq, peasants in debt to the landlord, and that was most of them, were little better than indentured serfs. Some could not even leave the land without the landlord's permission. As for class consciousness, how was one to incite the proletariat against the capitalist class when there was no proletariat? A proletariat required factories to grind the workers into rebellion, but there were few factories to speak of in the Arab world.

How then was the small Arab elite to seize power for itself when the majority of the population, whatever their hostility to the kawaga, were either sleepers or bystanders? Talk wasn't going to sway the kawaga. Only a mass uprising would do.

If the Arab elite wanted to seize power for themselves, they had to inflame the masses against their colonial masters. So they did. It was a small Arab elite of intellectuals, merchants, religious leaders, and colonial employees who laid the groundwork for a vibrant Arab nationalism that would liberate the Arab world from the scourge of colonialism.

The details were sketchy, but they promised something for everyone. Islam would be rid of the secular heresy, Arab officials would seize control of the bureaucracy and military, factories would blossom, and merchants would prosper.

It would be wrong to suggest that anti-colonialism was a coherent mass movement. It wasn't. Rather, each segment of the Arab elites did its own thing in its own way with little coordination. In Egypt, the most advanced of the Arab states at the time, the Muslim Brotherhood emerged as a fundamentalist response to the challenge of Western immorality. It was joined by Young Egypt, a Nazi party inspired by the rise of fascism in Europe. Communists and socialists organized unions among rail and factory workers, but their numbers were few. Military officers formed secret societies in the name of Arab nationalism, while business leaders and aristocrats rallied behind the Wafd, a charismatic independence movement. Students in the high schools and colleges established by the colonial powers screamed slogans of all varieties (Berque, 1972).

For all of their differences, they all came together in demonstrations against the British and French, usually led by students in the hope that the masses would join in. There was no organization, merely a volcanic outpouring of emotion. The very specter of a mass uprising forced the British to grant the Egyptians formal independence. I say formal, because the British continued to rule under the guise of a puppet king. The French were less easily swayed and ruled with an iron hand in Algeria until their losses became so stark that France, itself, was threatened with revolution.

The spontaneous nature of the independence movement didn't force people to choose between Arab nationalism and their faith. Both could be served at the same time. Many of the members of the free-officer movement who seized power in Egypt following WWII, were members of both the Muslim Brotherhood and the Arab nationalist movement. An identity crisis? Perhaps among intellectuals torn between East and West, but not for most people. The immediate goal was getting rid of the kawaga. Identities and everything else would get sorted out with independence.

Life, however, did become confusing for those seeking to emulate Western lifestyles. Such lifestyles were foreign and unnatural, and they often violated many of the individual's ingrained views of how he should behave. Not only did a psyche attempting to live dual lives create identity crises and internal turmoil within individuals, but it placed them at odds with those around them, a most painful situation in the tight-knit societies of the Arab world. This was the stuff of early Arabic novels which doubted that people could ever be both Eastern and Western. Others doubted that Arabs could ever become truly Western, while still others wondered whether Arabs could remain Eastern having tasted the ways of the West.

Expressions of Spiritualism

Devotion to Islam, always reflected in Arab behavior, seemed to become more pronounced during the colonial era. More than being a testimony to God in a Muslim universe, prayer now became a sign of resistance to the crusader kawaga. How could the kawaga fail to see the slight bruise on Muslim foreheads caused by their bow of submission to God? The message was clear. Muslims would always submit to God, but never to their occupiers. This didn't mean that Islam was able to present a united front to the kawaga. Quite the contrary. The clerical establishment continued to debate the finer points of doctrine while popular religion, including Sufis, faith healers, and various mystics, captured the popular imagination. Calls for modernizing Islam, while profound, generally fell on deaf ears. Membership in the Muslim Brotherhood, by contrast, soared.

The Muslim Brotherhood and the Origin of Modern Islamic Mass Movements

Mass movements thrive on several key ingredients. First and foremost, they thrive on a large body of people who are suffering the pain of despair, humiliation, hopelessness, and helplessness. Second, the presence of a charismatic leader or guide, a Mahdi if you like, is most helpful. Whatever you call him, people who are hurting often search for a savior to lead them from their misery. If they could have solved their own problems, they wouldn't be hurting. Third, the hero should be a larger-than-life figure with unequivocal signs of charisma, the gift of grace. The Arabic word is baraka, or God's blessing. Human powers won't do. Things work better if God or some mystical force is involved. Fourth, the hero's program has to fit the emotional needs of the dispossessed. Finally, the movement, if it is to last, has to evolve into a viable organization that can transcend the passing of the hero-Mahdi. Barring this, the movement will simply collapse with the hero's death or fall from grace. There is nothing like a loser to spoil a good movement.

It was only toward the end of the colonial era, however, that conditions became ripe for the emergence of an Islamic mass movement capable of sweeping the Arab world. That movement was the Muslim Brotherhood, a youth organization founded in 1928 by Hasan al-Banna to provide religious instruction to the illiterate, to make Islam relevant to the problems of daily life, and to return people to the spiritual concepts of "Jesus, Moses, Abraham, Noah, and other prophets whose wisdom was incorporated into the Koran" (Husaini, 1956, 46).

The evolution of the Muslim Brotherhood is of particular importance to our study of the Arab psyche and American frustrations, because it provides a direct link between the Islamic movements of the Islamic era and the Islamic movements of today, of which the Muslim

Brotherhood remains the largest. Specifically, it adapted the organizational and indoctrination techniques of the radical extremist groups, discussed in the preceding chapter, to the modern era. As we shall see in the next chapter, the jihadists, who splintered from the Muslim Brotherhood, took them one step farther. One way or the other, you can't understand the politics of the region without understanding the origins of the Muslim Brotherhood.

Al-Banna would later describe his organization as a "Salafite movement (one of the four schools of orthodox Islamic teaching), an orthodox way, a Sufi (mystical) reality, a political body, an athletic group, a scientific and cultural society, an economic company, and a social idea" (Cited in Husaini, 1956, 15). In sum, there was something for everyone.

Al-Banna, a schoolteacher, was very much a popular preacher in the Sufi mode. Like popular preachers before him, he offered his followers pride in their religion, a clear path to paradise, and the confidence that they could achieve paradise by resisting the kawaga. While the religious elite regaled the masses with the finer points of doctrine, Al-Banna spoke to their hearts. In the words of one of his followers,

> People are arguing back and forth, theologians theorizing, would-be philosophers philosophizing, and cultured people are delving in all fields; but Hasan al-Banna does not believe any of it, no matter how the ulema [religious scholars] and the specialists plunge themselves into it. He cites for you a verse from the Koran and the matter is settled and decided.... People wear themselves out searching hither and yon, while al-Banna with his Koran has no need for these (Cited in Husaini, 1956, 31).

Al-Banna began his mission by holding discussion sessions in nearby mosques. Eventually, he and his disciples would open their own mosques. Al-Banna, himself, visited village after village speaking of pride, honor, hope, dignity, salvation, oneness with God, and the mutual caring of a brotherhood and family. He even spoke of nationalism and social justice, for all were one in Islam. It was one to one and heart to heart, and the urban poor and rural peasants listened intently. So did a growing number of educated Muslims. Branches and newsletters followed, paving the way for the spread of the Muslim Brotherhood throughout the Arab world.

The masses were looking for a Mahdi to guide them, and al-Banna fulfilled that role by combining Sufi mysticism with a practical program of social and political action that guaranteed dignity on earth with an eternity in paradise.

Did al-Banna have the gift of grace? Husaini describes al-Banna's charisma:

His mastery over his followers was a complete, total mastery approaching wizardry. For each person he had a special story, a special manner and a special logic.... The mastery of al-Banna over these different groups, the way he attracted constant supporters in Egypt and abroad, and the rapid growth of his movement in steadfastness and stability are manifestations of his intelligence and resourcefulness (Husaini, 1956, 33).

But the Muslim Brotherhood was about more than talk. Emulation is deeply rooted in the Islamic world, and members of the Muslim Brotherhood were to serve as models for others. Al-Banna also built houses for the wretched, opened schools for the illiterate, and established health and welfare programs for the poor. Preaching and welfare, in turn, led to political activism. Morality, according to the Muslim Brotherhood, did not lie in passive acceptance of immoral leaders who emulated the godless ways of the kawaga. He even wrote to presidents and kings, imploring them to change their ways. When they refused, the Muslim Brotherhood turned against them. The model of today's political Islam had been born.

Beyond his charisma, al-Banna was a master of organizational skills. "Members were divided into grades; first and second class and supporting and active members. They could not advance to a higher grade until they had passed certain examinations.... Active members were divided into spiritual units: nuclei (nawah), cells (khaliyah), families (usrah), and phalanxes (katibah)" (Husaini, 1956, 90). The above, in turn, were combined into branches, many of which contained military, or "rover," units. Various councils guided the affairs of the larger units, but lacked the authority to challenge the power of al-Banna. When al-Banna was assassinated in 1949, the ruling advisory council selected a new supreme guide, and al-Banna and his charisma became the guiding spirit of the organization and its mystical link to God. By killing a leader, the assassin had created a saint. Perhaps there was a message here for the U.S.

Searching for a Strong Support Base in a Shifting World

The Arab world was never a place for loners, and in eras past it had been the family and tribe that cared for most of the individual's needs. Guilds and religious brotherhoods had supplemented the family during the era of Islam, but seldom challenged its dominance.

Colonialism would not challenge the dominance of the family, but the allure of the kawaga often strained relations between younger and older generations. Beyond the allure of westernization, there was the need to deal with an increasing array of individuals from diverse economic classes, education levels, tribes, sects, and ethnic groups that the colonial enterprise had thrown together, most of whom were presumed to be hostile. They had to cooperate to resist the kawaga, but cooperation was difficult because of mutual distrust.

Arab nationalism was the easiest level of cooperation because it required nothing more than participating in raucous demonstrations and shouting antigovernment slogans. A few people were killed, but it was largely noise and posturing. Protests had a tremendous feel-good effect for the protesters, but it did nothing to address their most cherished needs other than to salve their pride, release frustrations, and offer mystical hopes of a brighter future.

At the more practical level, wasta trading became an art form among those families that had something to trade. Almost everyone close to the kawaga or his puppets had some influence that could be traded for a parallel favor or bribe. These exchanges often took place in the vast lobbies of elegant hotels where people of influence circulated, chatting casually with friends and acquaintances, but always conducting business or probing for information. Among the poor in the cities, spontaneous self-help groups sprung up to keep the wolf from the door.

Other options abounded for those who needed support beyond the family. Religious groups such as the Muslim Brotherhood deepened their roots in society by providing welfare services to the poor. They also provided a sense of belonging for lonely students and others cut off from their families by work or migration. Combining care, spiritualism, and belonging was a powerful formula for capturing the loyalty and devotion of members. Primary loyalty remained with the family and its kinship extensions, but attachments to the Muslim Brotherhood were strong and had to be reckoned with.

Tensions between family and religious loyalties were muted, for the Muslim Brotherhood stressed family values. It needed the support of families as well as individuals to weave its influence networks.

Expressions of Satisfaction and Discontent

Political expression took on a whole new dimension during the colonial era as experiments with parliamentary procedures flourished in the more westernized mandates. Nationalist demonstrations soared, but focused on independence rather than meeting the practical needs of the people. Elected officials were largely members of the economic elite and had little interest in equity.

Practical concerns continued to be addressed by petitioning tribal and religious leaders who had the influence (wasta) to get things done. The dramatic pace of change during the colonial era had hampered their influence, however, and people were forced to place greater reliance on an emerging class of powerbrokers, or zaim, to protect their interests.

This applied to both families and individuals because in classic Arab style, families formed the base of the zaim's empire. Strong families fared extremely well and dealt with the zaim directly. Individuals lacking a strong family counted for little. Unless, that was, they had connections with the kawaga, were skilled fighters, or wrote articles for an exploding number of newspapers, few of which had a high regard for the facts.

Powerful local leaders were nothing new in the Arab world, but the word "zaim" took on a whole new meaning during the colonial era as tribal chiefs and generals became massive landowners, members of parliament, large entrepreneurs, and, in some cases, drug lords. Their families ran everything. As an Iraqi friend explained with pride, one of his brothers was in real estate, while a second was a judge, the third a member of parliament, the fourth a general, the fifth a professor, and the sixth a distinguished man of religion. The father, while residing in Baghdad, was also the chief of a large tribe. I can't give the name, because it wouldn't be polite.

While being the client of a zaim or one of his lieutenants offered security and opportunity, it also had its risks. One voted as instructed and served in the zaim's militia should his conflicts with rival zaims or the kawaga erupt in violence. After all, the ability to field a well-armed militia at the snap of a finger was a key element of a zaim's power. How else could he acquire the money and government positions necessary to take care of his people?

Social Behavior: Getting Along by Going Along

Getting along during the eras of tribalism and Islam was a simple matter of conforming to the rules of the core groups while sucking up to their leaders, and doing your best to control everyone that you could lest they create problems for all concerned.

Things were far less simple during the era of colonialism. Conformity continued to be the easiest way for most people to get along, but that, too, had become complex. To whose rules was one to conform? The kawaga's? The tyrant's? The nationalist agitator's? The zaim's? The expectations of relatives and neighbors? The rigid piety enforced by fundamentalist organizations such as the Muslim Brotherhood? It was difficult to serve more than one master at once, especially when each was pulling in a different direction. Choices had to be made, painful choices, the outcomes of which were not always easy to predict.

One way or another, the peering eyes became more peering. Every building had a doorman, usually an illiterate peasant, sitting in the entrance and taking careful note of the comings and goings of its residents. They locked the doors in the evening and slept on a nearby mat to service late arrivals. Benign they were not. Some were ardent fundamentalists, while others were in the pay of the security services or a powerful politician. Some may have been in the pay of all. Then, as now, information was a very salable commodity.

The choices outlined above were particularly difficult for urbanites and especially for Arabs drawn into the service of the kawaga. The rural populations remained "sleepy," and even a vast majority of urban dwellers continued to be bystanders. When revolutions came, it was usually at the hands of the military or a westernized elite with strong ties to the military.

Being political bystanders or even sleepy villagers didn't mean that colonial Arabs weren't tempted by the delights of westernization portrayed in the movies and emulated by glitzy lifestyles of the rich and famous. But how were the people of the era to have it all while still pretending to conform to all the forces that demand their allegiance? Obviously, it was a job for the fox.

Defeating the Kawaga: The Ways of the Fox

While the timeworn strategies of conformity, following a strong leader, and shoring up one's base of support offered the surest way to survival during the colonial era, they didn't allow beni colonial to soar.

Given the passivity and cautious nature of the prevailing Arab psyche and the rigors of daily survival, it is doubtful that beni colonial was pre-occupied with thoughts of soaring. People did, however, have to cope with the instincts and appetites that came naturally to their species, all of which were now sharpened by the example of the kawaga and the movies of the era.

For the most part, people of the colonial era played it safe when the eyes peered and adventured when they didn't. The growing complexity of colonial society made things tricky, but the fox was the most adaptive of creatures.

The kawaga was the fox's favorite target because the kawaga con-trolled just about everything, including money, jobs, politics, weapons, commercial permits, visas, educational opportunities, and even land. The trouble was that the fox could never get more than crumbs until it got rid of the kawaga. Then, and only then, could it feast on everything that society had to offer.

Thus, the fox, tricky fellow that he was, set about exploiting the kawaga while simultaneously destroying him. Actually, it was a three-level game. The fox also had to position itself to take over once the kawaga left. At the very least, he couldn't be too closely tied to the kawaga when he bailed out.

The fox, of course, had an advantage because the kawaga was new to the game, and the fox had been honing his skills for centuries and passing them on from generation to generation in song and story. Each was learning the ways of the other, but the fox seemed a bit quicker than kawaga. He had to be. The lion was stronger.

It is not that the kawaga hadn't been warned. *The Arabian Nights* were a big hit in the West, and the kawaga feasted on these marvelous stories of sex, subversion, and intrigue. So, why didn't the kawaga listen? Because kawagas never listen. They roar like a lion and are pleased when the fox runs. Arrogance? Perhaps.

Despite the best efforts of the fox, the kawaga never left the Arab world. The struggle between the lion and the fox during the colonial era was merely the first chapter in an enduring saga that will endure as long as the kawaga ventures into the Arab world and its Muslim environs. The fox learned the painful lessons of the colonial era. The kawaga didn't, so each generation of kawagas has been fated to repeat the mistakes of its predecessors as if it were reading The Arabian Nights for the first time.

How did the fox go about dealing with the colonial kawaga? I highlight the key points below so you can look for them today.

The fox knew that the kawaga was armed, dangerous, and fond of fox hunting. So the fox studied the kawaga with great care, looking for ways to exploit his immense power without getting burned or worse.

This meant learning how to play the kawaga's game. First came learning the kawaga's language. What choice did the fox have? The kawaga, with the rarest of exceptions, didn't speak Arabic. The fox didn't mind. The kawaga's inability to speak Arabic made the kawaga dependent on the fox for dealing with the natives. It also forced the kawaga to accept the fox's translations of local publications and interpretations of what was happening in the native community. Did the kawaga know when the fox was mocking him? The kawaga had his suspicions when others smirked at the fox's jokes, but he couldn't be sure. Probably not. The natives were always smiling, and the fox's servility was disarming. They knew their place and that was good. Servility was humiliating, but what choice did the fox have? One had to get along. Besides, the fox knew that it was a game. His game.

Having learned the ways of the kawaga, the next challenge for the fox was to get close enough to the kawaga to exploit him without incurring his wrath, the envy of other foxes, accusations of apostasy by religious fanatics, or equally dangerous accusations of treason by a surging nationalist elite intent on destroying the kawaga. The trick was being close to the kawaga, but not too close.

The best opportunities for young foxes were in the security forces and the bureaucracy. The pay was low, but even a little authority went a long way among the poor of the rural areas and the slums. One could look the other way for friends and family and put in a bad word for traditional enemies. All became symbols of status and increased the fox's opportunities for wasta (influence peddling) and baksheesh (small bribes). Nothing got done without baksheesh or wasta, for the colonials couldn't be bothered with the riffraff of society.

Even the kawaga's servants lived better than the poor of the slums and rural areas. Food was ample, discarded clothes helped the family, and the kawaga tended to talk freely in front of them. The kawaga was also more generous with servants than their Arab masters, who paid them little and often beat them. Egyptian maids from the rural areas often worked free for wealthy patrons until they could be married off (Amin, 2000).

By the end of the colonial era, it was the natives in military and bureaucracy who formed the core of the newly independent governments. Not only had the fox positioned itself for the present, but he was staking his claim on the future.

Positioning was important, but the real key to exploiting the kawaga was gaining his trust and confidence. It probably wasn't that hard, for the kawaga was always searching for good Arabs to do his dirty work. What was a good Arab? It was obvious. He spoke the colonial language, dressed Western, was duly subservient, and provided good information on potential troublemakers, usually the enemies of the fox. Requests for advice and the delegation of authority followed suit, providing the fox with new vistas for wasta and bribes, as well as placing relatives in lucrative positions and destroying one's enemies, including the kawaga.

The more the fox captured the kawaga, the more the elite foxes formed a barrier or filter between the colonial powers and the masses they ruled. While the colonial powers pillaged the resources of their colonies, the foxes sucked the blood of the masses. Who got blamed? Why, the colonial powers of course. When nationalism soared, it was the foxes who filled their ranks.

The ability of the fox to capture the kawaga during the colonial era was small stuff compared to his ability to capture the American kawaga in Iraq and Afghanistan, but it was a start.

And so the game endured. The fox and just about everyone else played by the colonial rules when forced, but otherwise took pride in evading them. Venality followed suit, as duping the kawaga with lies and theft became badges of honor. Small victories against the kawaga to be sure, but they added up with time and were much admired by friends and family. Arab folk heroes always defied authority.

Keeping up appearances also took on an added dimension during the colonial era, as foxes working for the kawaga longed to impress others with their status and potential influence. Such things were important for trading wasta and arranging marriage contacts. Family status remained vital, but so were wealth and influence. As always, the emphasis on appearances made it impossible to admit error or display a weakness of any sort. There was little place for losers in the world of the fox.

In a curious irony, opposition groups such as the Arab nationalists and the Muslim Brotherhood had to go out of their way to appear excessively brave in their hostility to the kawaga. Not too brave, mind you, for that could bring reprisals and made supporters nervous, especially those pretending to be friendly to the kawaga.

Even the cleverest fox was beni Adam and suffered from all of his inherent defects. When a fox became too greedy, too power hungry, too spiteful, or too anxious to gain respect by boasting of his nefarious deeds, other foxes were waiting.

The fox also tended to live for the moment. When the world turned and the kawaga left, the fox was left at the mercy of the dispossessed. They knew who he was, where to find him, and what to do to him and his relatives. As the world closed in on the old fox's space, those who survived took their money and fled. Many became refugees in neighboring countries. The cleverest of the old foxes fled to England, France, and the United States, where they plotted their return by selling the kawaga tips on how to destroy the newly independent regimes. In the meantime, new foxes were waiting in the wings.

RED-FLAG ISSUES: EXTREMISM, VIOLENCE, GOVERNANCE, DEMOCRACY, AND DEVELOPMENT

Extremism Versus Moderation

The roots of extremism, as we have seen in the preceding chapters, had already been embedded in the Arab psyche before the advent of colonialism.

Everything in the colonial enterprise intensified extremism, not the least of which were assaults on Islam, oppression, the breakdown of social traditions, fear of the unknown, the humiliation of rule by the Christian kawaga, the frustration of rising expectations that defied fulfillment, and the despair of poverty. These and more were inflamed by the anger of religious and political leaders dispossessed by the colonial powers and longing for a return to power. Adding to the fray was the frustration of awakened Arabs who had tried to become modern, only to be scorned by the colonial masters as a subhuman species. Hopelessness, powerlessness, and self-doubt prevailed, and more than ever, Arabs longed for a savior. Would it be a new Saladin or a return of the Mahdi? Perhaps they would be one and the same.

Unwittingly, the colonial experience also divided Arab extremism into two warring camps: secular Arab nationalism and Islamic fundamentalism. The former was forward looking and the latter backward looking. The two currents cooperated to drive the kawaga out of the Arab world, but independence would soon pit one against the other.

Violence Versus Reconciliation

The causes of violence during the colonial era were much the same as the causes of extremism, one often fueling the other. The more colonialism endured, the more religious and nationalist agitators inflamed anti-kawaga passions. Organized violence was sparse and poorly coordinated, but the pot had started to boil.

Social violence such as honor killings and feuds remained part of life in the Arab world and its Muslim environs, as did brigandage and clashes between rival warlords and zaims, most of which overlapped with tribal and clan jealousies. Tribes and warlords still ruled the remote areas and were generally ignored by the colonial authorities as long as they didn't upset the colonial enterprise. If Arabs wanted to kill Arabs, so be it.

Much social violence during the era was the direct result of tensions inflamed by colonialism, not the least of which were the divide-and-rule policies of the colonial powers, the temptation to deviance provided by the kawaga and the elites that emulated them, the introduction of alternate moral cultures, the greater opportunities for deviance provided by migration to the cities, and the laxer social environment of the colonial era. Yet another key element in the violence of the colonial era was the breakup and redistribution of traditional tribal lands. Revenge for humiliation could be delayed, but not the loss of land. No wonder violence in the colonial settler states such as Algeria and Palestine surpassed all others.

Added to the above had to be the violence produced by an environment of changing rules and uncertainty. No one was ever sure of how long the kawaga would stay or who would replace him.

Recall also that much of the colonialism in the Arab world occurred between the two world wars, both of which saw the colonies drawn into the violent conflicts of Europe. Spies and sedition abounded, all of which added to violence that erupted between hostile groups betting on an uncertain future. The fox, as always, played each side against the other with little concern for interests other than his own.

The point is that violence in the Arab world from the colonial era forward had as much to do with global pressures as it did with predispositions of violence inherent in Arab society. If the Arab world has seemed to become increasingly violent with time, it is because of a merging of traditional problems and global pressures in a region increasingly caught in a vortex of change that started with the colonial era.

By the end of WWII, sporadic violence against colonial targets became wars of independence that the colonial powers, devastated by WWII, were too exhausted to quell. The era of European colonialism was drawing to a close, and the Arab world would soon be faced with two new kawaga, the Americans and the Soviets. Neither would formally occupy an Arab country. They merely transformed them into puppet allies in their Cold War struggle for colonial dominance.

Fragmentation Versus Solidarity
The appearances of Arab unity that emerged toward the end of the colonial era promised hope of an Arab revival that would see a people—united by language, history, culture, and faith—emerge as a major actor on the world stage.

This prospect scared the colonial powers, who feared that anti-colonial sentiments would push the Arabs into the Nazi camp. The intensity of anti-colonial demonstrations in the lead-up to WWII fueled such fears, as did fascist sympathies among many generals in the region who believed that Nazism was the wave of the future and their ticket to power.

Fearing for their own security, both Britain and France did their best to sew dissension in the Arab ranks, much of which focused on using Islam as a counterweight to Arab nationalism. Puppet kings were warned to keep nationalist emotions in check, lest they be overthrown by pro-Nazi generals. The colonial military presence also increased dramatically throughout the region, further stoking anti-colonial sentiments.

In reality, such fears were exaggerated, for displays of unity were largely emotional and lacked an organizational base. The true test of unity would come during the era of independence.

Tyranny Versus Democracy, Equality, and Equity

The mandate system established by the League of Nations at the end of WWI called upon the occupying powers to prepare the Arabs for independence. This was to include lessons in democracy, effective administration, and economic development.

The colonial powers were minimally concerned with either democracy or teaching the Arabs effective administration. Democracy was viewed as a threat to colonial rule, and bureaucratic positions of any significance were reserved for expatriates. And so it was that the Arabs attained independence with little experience in either democracy or effective administration. The economic situation remained equally dismal as most Arab countries continued to be economic dependencies of their former colonial masters.

This said, the colonial era did provide the Arabs with a model of democracy, of rule by laws and institutions, of human rights, and of effective administration that would provide the model by which all future Arab regimes would be judged.

Sadly, the colonial powers provided the Arabs with the rules of democracy and effective governance without teaching them how to apply them. In reality, it may not have been possible for the European powers to teach the Arabs how to achieve either democracy or effective governance in the short and traumatic era of colonial dominance in the Arab world, even if they had wanted to.

Democracy and effective governance in Europe had developed over the torturous course of European history and had gradually become ingrained in the European psyche. In England, it had taken about a thousand years. It was not merely a matter of following a set of procedures, but of wanting to follow them and knowing how to follow them. Beyond that, it was also the confidence that other people would follow the rules.

The colonial powers could teach the Arabs the formal procedures of democracy and governance, but could they instill the desire to follow these procedures in a people whose psyche had evolved in such a vastly different historical environment in twenty or thirty years?

Let me give you an example in the area of governance.

The British model of an ideal administrator was an individual who, having been selected on the basis of merit, was responsive to the policy directives of elected leaders, efficient and impartial in exercising his duties, creative in finding solutions to society's problems, courteous and helpful in dealing with the public, objective in offering advice, and sparing in the expenditure of public funds.

Obviously, not all British civil servants lived up to this model, but it was on their minds. None of this, as we have seen, was part of the Arab psyche's historical experience.

It was the same in the far more emotional areas of democracy, equality, and equity. Yet, the seeds of all had been planted during the colonial era and remain the core of Arab political rhetoric today. How long it will be before words give way to deeds remains to be seen.

Of all of the colonies, only India established a viable democracy. Unlike the Arabs, India had been subject to a century of British rule. More important, the Indian political elite had been educated in Britain and was intent on establishing democracy in India. This was not the case in the Arab world. The puppet kings put in place by the British had little interest in democracy.

Stagnation Versus Development

Colonialism changed the Arab world forever, but did it place the Arab world on the road to enlightenment? The answer to that question remains a matter of debate, but there can be no question that colonialism dragged the Arab world into the modern era and presented Arabs and Muslims with a view of the world totally different from what had prevailed during the long decline of the Ottoman Empire. Suddenly, Western secularism and Islamic theology were placed in a bitter struggle for the Arab soul. Which side won? The question has yet to be resolved forms a central theme in the chapters that follow.

CHAPTER 5

THE ERA OF INDEPENDENCE: THE RISE AND DECLINE OF ARAB NATIONALISM

The surge for independence in the Arab word began shortly after World War I, when Britain granted nominal independence to Egypt and Iraq. British troops continued to occupy strategic positions in both countries, and economic ties with Britain remained much as they had always been. In both cases, the British embassy remained the power behind the throne. Why the charade? The British simply found indirect rule to be cheaper and less bloody than direct rule. Not so the French, who ruled their colonies with an iron hand.

Whatever their style of colonial rule, World War II sounded the death knell of the British and French empires. The British saw the writing on the wall and threw in the towel rather than struggle through colonial wars that were doomed to failure. The French, less pragmatic than the British, clung desperately to their North African colonies for another decade, but to no avail. The more the French resisted the inevitable, the stronger and more radical the independence movements became. Perhaps this was a lesson for future kawagas.

THE ENVIRONMENT OF INDEPENDENCE: OPTIMISM AND TURMOIL

The surge of Arab independence unleashed a chain of events so profound that the Arab psyche would never be the same. In some ways, the Arab psyche is still attempting to recover from an era that many Arab intellectuals view as paradise lost. It was also the era that saw the U.S. and the Soviets emerge as dominant kawagas of the region. Both would find the Arab psyche a formidable adversary.

The Arab world that emerged from the era of colonialism was a mosaic of independent countries, none of which possessed the attributes of a state in the modern sense of the word. And what a curious patchwork it was.

Egypt, Iraq (Mesopotamia), and Syria were large countries whose roots stretched to antiquity. They had shaped the Islamic empires of yore. It was now they, ruled by populist dictators, who vowed to lead an Arab revival that would again see the Arabs rank among the most powerful and developed nations in the world. Modernization, industrialization, and militarization were to be the key to the future. Arab nationalism was to be the rallying cry of the masses, and socialism was to provide the path to industrialization and equity. Democracy would come once economic development had been achieved. In the meantime, Christians and Muslims were to be as one as they looked to the future rather than the past.

Most other Arab countries were tiny enclaves, such as Jordan and the Gulf sheikhdoms, that were created by the whim of the colonial powers and ruled by puppet kings. Saudi Arabia and Yemen were antiquated tribal kingdoms that faced the future by clinging to the past.

The British evacuation of Palestine in 1948, unleashed the first Arab-Israeli war and resulted in the rebirth of Israel. Egypt and Jordan assumed control of the areas of Palestine that remained under Arab control until Israel occupied them in 1967. For the Jews and many Christians, the rebirth of Israel after some two thousand years of exile was the fulfillment of biblical prophecy. For Arabs, Christian as well as Muslim, the creation of a Jewish state in Palestine was a devious Western conspiracy to plant a new kawaga in their midst. The rest, as they say, is history.

For all of their diversity, the Arab states were unified by language, religion, pride in their Arab heritage, and the dream that independence would, indeed, lead to an Arab revival. The artificial borders that the colonialists established would be washed away in a spontaneous rush for unity. Wealth and power would follow.

This said, the tribal kings had little interest in a rush to modernization that would spell their doom. Who could blame them? There was little place in the modern world for tribal kings locked in a time warp of the Middle Ages.

Egypt, Syria, Iraq, and Algeria referred to themselves as the "progressive" Arab vanguard and scorned the tribal kings as being reactionary lapdogs of the kawaga. In reality, it was tough sledding for both the progressive revolutionaries and the conservative forces, as the tribal kings referred to themselves.

The Progressive Forces and the Dream of Modernity

The goal of the modernizers (revolutionaries) was no less than the total transformation of the Arab world into a unified industrial-military power on par with the countries of the West. Only then, in their view, could the Arabs regain their former glory and be free from the scourge of occupation.

Their leader was Abdul Nasser, the junior officer who had orchestrated the overthrow of Farouk in 1952. Farouk had sealed his doom by sending Egypt's ill-equipped and poorly led army to liberate Palestine from Jewish control in the 1948 Arab-Israeli War. According to the Hasan Youssef Pasha, the head of the royal diwan (cabinet), Farouk assumed that the Jews couldn't fight and that, in a day or two, he would add Palestine to his kingdom (Youssef, Interviews, 1983). The Jews humiliated the Egyptian forces, and Nasser and his Free Officers overthrew Farouk a few years later. Farouk quipped as he sailed for Italy on his private yacht, "There will soon be only five kings left in the world. The king of England and the four in a deck of cards."

Nasser put Farouk on his yacht rather than dragging his body through the streets as the Iraqis would do to their prime minister a few years later. The prevailing international environment dictated his leniency. Colonialism was alive and well, and Nasser didn't want the murder of Farouk to provide the British with a pretext for reinvading Egypt.

The British were kept at bay as long as they thought that they could control Nasser, but that illusion passed with Nasser's seizure of the Suez Canal in 1956. A joint British, French, and Israeli plot to seize the Suez Canal and overthrow Nasser followed. Alas, the conspirators forgot to check with the Americans who, fearing a Soviet takeover of the region, forced a withdrawal of Israeli forces from the canal zone. Nasser, at least in the eyes of the Arabs, had scored a miraculous victory over the combined forces of the British, French, and Israelis. It was a political victory rather than a military victory, but so be it. A victory is a victory, and it was the first Arab victory since the era of Islam.

Was Nasser the new Saladin? How could there be any doubt? Within a few years of seizing power, Nasser had evicted the British from their Egyptian military bases, liquidated foreign control of the Egyptian economy, distributed land to the peasants, shattered American control of Middle East by purchasing weapons from the Communist Bloc, nationalized the Suez Canal, thwarted a joint Anglo-French-Israeli attempt to seize the Suez Canal, and began construction of Aswan dam, a massive undertaking that would tame the Nile's legendary floods and provide electrical power for Egypt's industrial revolution. This was heady stuff, miraculous even, for an Arab psyche trampled by centuries of decay. If Arabs were looking for a superhero, they had surely found him. In mystical circles, rumors soared that Nasser was the new Mahdi.

Unlike Ataturk, the Turkish general who had launched a devastating attack on Islam a few decades earlier, Nasser chose to bend Islam to his modernization program. Islam could not be divorced from the Arab psyche. Both would have to be modernized.

The modernizing goals of Nasser and other progressive leaders of the era were as admirable as they were elusive. Colonialism had divided the Arabs into twenty-plus states, each with a narrow elite intent on clinging to power, whatever the costs. Their populations remained largely rural, illiterate, wedded to the past, and fragmented into a multitude of religious sects and kinship networks. As Abdul Nasser would lament, the British had their revolutions one at a time. First came the industrial revolution, then the social revolution, and finally the political revolution. The Arabs were fated to have all of their revolutions at once.

Nor were the former colonial powers interested in seeing the Arabs unified. They no longer ruled the Arab world, but they remained dependent on its oil resources and covetous of its strategic location. The plot thickened with the ever-deepening Cold War between the Communist Bloc and the U.S. that had emerged from the ashes of WWII. The nationalistic slogans of Nasser and the modernizers smacked of socialism and hostility toward the West. To the American strategists of the time, a unified Arab nation allied with the Soviet Union could well tip the balance in global politics toward the latter. Concern became panic with the Soviet's launch of Sputnik, the world's first satellite, in 1957. Fearful of having lost its technological edge in its struggle against the Soviets, the U.S. could not afford to lose the Middle East.

Despite environmental adversities, the Arabs had cause for optimism. United, they could have everything the modern world had to offer, including wealth, military power, and industrialization. Divided, they had nothing. Surely, Nasser believed, the Arab masses would seize the moment by putting their shoulder to the wheel of industrialization and overthrowing their decaying tribal monarchies.

Enlightened leaders, for their part, would allocate the resources of the state, however meager, in a wise and egalitarian manner. Revolutions in education and healthcare would fuel an industrial revolution that would provide jobs and prosperity for all. Economic democracy would, with time and education, lead to political democracy. Force would be necessary to crush reactionary opponents of the revolution, but only as a last resort. When everything was in place, powerful Arab armies would crush what remained of the tribal kingdoms and restore Arab pride by pushing the Israelis into the sea.

Such was the dream of Nasser and the other revolutionary leaders of the era. It was all summed up in their slogan "Unity, socialism, freedom." The order of the words varied from country to country, but the basic concept was the same.

Dream on, sweet prince. How was there to be a political revolution in the Arab world when the existing political institutions were controlled by landowners, aristocrats, and other elements linked to the past? How could there be unity when the existing political parties caused dissension by inflaming ethnic, religious, and class differences? How was there to be mass education when there were few teachers? How was there to be an industrial revolution when there were few factories, little technology, few resources, and a workforce that consisted of peasants with little appreciation of time or discipline? How was the state to allocate the meager resources that existed in a wise and judicious manner when what passed for a bureaucracy were the corrupt sons of the aristocracy? How was there to be a powerful army when the generals were aristocrats, and the only weapons available were hand-me-downs from the colonial powers? And the cruelest question of all was, how could the masses be harnessed to the wheel of modernization when the prevailing Arab psyche was overwhelmed with passivity, petty jealousies, and distrust of the government?

One could not help but feel Nasser's pain when he lamented upon seizing power,

> Every leader we came to wanted to assassinate his rival. Every idea we found aimed at the destruction of another. If we were to carry out all that we heard, then there would not be one leader left alive. Not one idea would remain intact. We would cease to have a mission save to remain among the smashed bodies and the broken debris lamenting our misfortune and reproaching our ill-fate.... If I were asked then what I required most my instant answer would be, "To hear but one Egyptian uttering one word of justice about another, to see but one Egyptian not devoting his time to criticize willfully the ideas of another, to feel that there was but one Egyptian ready to open his heart for forgiveness, indulgence and loving his brother Egyptian (Nasser, 1955).

The only solution was to rebuild everything from scratch, including Arab society and the Arab psyche. Nothing was to be gained by changing the bottles if they were to be filled with the same old wine.

The revolutionary modernizers were also men in a hurry. Who knew how long they had before their opponents, including the West and Israel, launched a countercoup? Time was of the essence, and neither Nasser nor his Syrian, Iraqi, or Algerian counterparts had any experience in running a country. Mistakes would be made, but such was the nature of the beast. They would be sorted out with time.

One fact was clear. There could be no revolution without the active participation of the Arab masses. The sleepers had to be awakened and the bystanders activated. Everyone and everything had to be mobilized to the cause of modernization.

Faced with a hostile environment and the reality that the masses were still locked in the past, Nasser and the other modernizers seized upon the communist model of forced modernity. If Russia and China could transform themselves into world powers within a few decades, so could the Arabs. Both the Soviets and China, moreover, were anxious to help the Arabs modernize as part of their Cold War strategy. While America clung to the tribal kings, the Soviets proclaimed themselves the champions of development and progress throughout the world.

Huge factories built and equipped by the Soviets mushroomed overnight, while the peasants were forced to join government-controlled cooperatives. Everything was managed from Cairo and the other progressive capitals.

Nasser and the modernizers weren't communists. Rather, they were Arab nationalists who were willing to follow the communist model to achieve their dream of a united and powerful Arab state. Far from being ideologues, they were pragmatic populists who viewed themselves as an historic vanguard charged with shaking the Arabs from their deep slumber, whether they liked it or not (Ba'ath Party, 1964–1965). With time and education, the Arab psyche would see the light and get its priorities straight.

Nasser and other modernizers had little choice but to do the best with what they had. Massive bureaucracies were built to provide employment for ever-larger waves of high school and college graduates taught by teachers with minimal training. The new Arab bureaucratic class, accordingly, lacked the skills to administer a modern state, not to mention the mammoth task of building factories, managing production, and fixing prices on everything from rents to rice. But at least it was a start. Glitches were expected, but things, the modernizers assured their subjects, would improve with experience and on-the-job training. Anyway, there was no choice in the matter, because the private sector had been abolished in the name of ending exploitation of the masses.

Oppression and economic frustrations were papered over with smoke and mirrors as government propagandists painted ever more dazzling pictures of the Arab future based on socialism and unity. Glitches too glaring to be papered over were blamed on America, the "little kings" as Nasser referred to the rulers of Jordan and Saudi Arabia, and Israel. Never mind, Nasser consoled the Arab masses, all would be well when Israel had been defeated and the little kings were no more.

Oppression, however packaged, was nothing new to the Arab psyche, but the authoritarian modernizers added a level of intrusiveness unknown in previous eras. They weren't totalitarians in the communist sense, but they were zealous, erratic, and poorly disciplined. In the meantime, rare was the Arab who didn't fear that a slip of the tongue or act of vengeance would see them disappear into one of the region's bulging prisons.

Expressions of religiosity were particularly tricky in the progressive states. Prayer and attendance at the mosque were expected, and the slight bruise on the forehead continued to serve as a sign of sincerity in bowing to God. It was also common among members of the modernizing elite who were anxious to demonstrate their Islamic credentials. Their intent was not to destroy Islam, but to mold it to the goals of modernity. Government propagandists emphasized that the socialist policies of Nasser were not Marxist socialism, but Islamic socialism based upon the Koranic emphasis on equality and its rejection of economic exploitation.

The rub came when the Muslim Brotherhood and other fundamentalist groups saw the hand of the devil in the policies of the modernizers. Particularly offensive were the mingling of the sexes and the glorification of Western values. Unlike the colonial era, in which Islamic fundamentalists and modernizers had joined forces to defeat the colonialists, Nasser's charge for modernity placed the two visions of the Arab future on a collision course.

It was the fundamentalists who struck first, with the Muslim Brotherhood's failed attempt to assassinate Nasser in 1954. Nasser's response was swift and brutal. Stories of the era, later published by the Muslim Brotherhood, recount the plight of a young man who, being given a notebook to record telephone numbers as a gift, didn't have his own number to record. Rather than lose face by admitting that he didn't have a phone, he entered the number of a friend in his notebook. To his bad luck, the friend whose number he had borrowed happened to be a member of the Muslim Brotherhood. With cudgels raining on his head, he too confessed to membership in the Muslim Brotherhood and disappeared into a prison reserved for enemies of the revolution.

Another story recounted the ill luck of a young pharmacist who had signed up for flying lessons, unaware that an unknown person in his class was a member of the Muslim Brotherhood. The secret police assumed that he, too, was a member of the Muslim Brotherhood, and he disappeared into one of Egypt's nefarious prisons without a trace. So, too, did any member of the Muslim Brotherhood, real or imagined, whom Nasser's security forces could place their hands on. The Muslim Brotherhood, seemingly defeated, went into remission. Secularism had defeated Islamic fundamentalism. Or had it?

Things Fall Apart and the Decline of Arab Nationalism

For a while, it appeared that the dream might become a reality. Factories mushroomed, and education and healthcare reached the masses. It wasn't great, but it was. Massive armies marched in lockstep, their mighty Soviet weapons striking fear throughout the region. Egypt and Syria were unified briefly in 1958 with Iraq, Yemen, and others promising to follow suit. I recall living in Egypt during the early 1960s and being terribly impressed by the whole thing. A new era was at hand.

Then, the nationalist dream started to unravel. Rural peasants rushed to the cities in search of work, only to find themselves living in squalid slums, many without basic utilities. The government bureaucracies, mired in confusion and corruption, became an obstacle to modernization rather than its patron saint. So bad were the facilities of the average bureaucrat that some officials had to share desks. Much the same was true of the massive single-party organizations designed to link the masses to the regime. Rather, both served as a wall separating well-meaning leaders from the masses they had pledged to serve. Nasser even spoke openly of forming an alliance with the masses against the rapacious officials who filled the administrative and political bureaucracies that he had created to serve as the foundation of his development program.

It was the same on the regional front. The union between Egypt and Syria lasted but three years, and Iraq never did join. The worse things became, the more the reformers relied on force and ever more dazzling portrayals of a future that would never be.

The smoke and mirrors of the nationalist dream were brutally shattered by Israel's crushing of the Arab armies in the June War of 1967. Actually, the grizzly defeat took only about four days. The Israelis occupied the Sinai Peninsula, what remained of Palestine, and Syria's Golan Heights. Once again, a tiny Jewish state had humiliated the Arabs.

Surveying the wreckage of the 1967 war, Nasser launched a scathing critique of his regime at an emergency meeting of his Revolutionary Command Council. Nasser said that

What is important is that the leaders do not criticize and carp at each other because it is we, the high-ranking officials in the system, who have caused it to crack. Each one of us is destroying what another one is doing.... Moreover, sensitivity among us has reached the point where we are afraid to criticize each other at meetings. I believe that the only solution is for us to create a real "challenge" in the true sense of the word, to hasten to correct the mistakes that have been committed (Farid, 1994, 87–88).

The performance of the socialist-nationalist regimes in Syria and Iraq was equally dismal, as was the bitterness of their self-criticism. The Iraqis were particularly candid:

For years Iraq had witnessed savage strife among the national [modernizing] forces. The blood of all these forces was spilled in every part of the country without any positive results achieved for national aims or the public interest (Iraqi Ba'ath Party, 1974, 30).

The Arab Environment as a Rudderless Ship

The decade that followed the Six Day War saw the Arab world mired in confusion as Nasser died and was replaced by Anwar Sadat, his vice president.

The one bright spot, from the Arab perspective, was Egypt's defeat of Israel in the Arab-Israeli War of 1973, the October War. It wasn't really a victory because the Israelis, flush with a massive infusion of U.S. aid, ended up on top. But in the wonderland world of the Middle East, it was a stunning Arab victory that continues to be celebrated throughout the Arab world. Israel may have come out on the top in the end, but the damage had been done. Egypt had liberated the Suez Canal and forced a full-scale Israeli retreat into the Sinai Peninsula. The Arabs had demonstrated their capacity to fight, and the myth of Israeli invincibility had been shattered. Saudi Arabia, and other oil-producing countries, while not engaging in battle, shook the global economy by slashing oil exports to the West. At long last, the Arabs had used their oil weapon. Curiously, it would be the last time that they would use it.

The Israelis, too, acknowledged that the October War was a devastating defeat. Without American aid, the future of the Jewish state could well have been in danger. Israeli intelligence had monitored the Egyptian buildup, but they just didn't believe it. The reason for their defeat also remains a hot topic of debate in Israel today.

In retrospect, the Israelis didn't have cause to worry. Sadat, the hero of Suez, forged his own cult of the personality and began referring to Egyptians as his children. His goal was personal survival, and that meant destroying his former colleagues on the Revolutionary Command Council, most of whom leaned to the left. But how was he to destroy leftist adversaries deeply entrenched in the military, the ruling party, and the labor unions? Easy.

Sadat, clever fox that he was, gave the Muslim Brotherhood and its extremist spinoffs free rein to destroy the leftists, and so they did. The jihadist extremists assassinated Sadat, but not before he had thrown Egyptian politics into turmoil by becoming an American puppet and making peace with Israel. The lead player in the Arab world had jumped ship. If Arab nationalism hadn't died in the June War, it died with Sadat.

The situation wasn't better in the other progressive countries of the Arab world. All careened from coup to coup and ended up as military dictatorships, spouting nationalistic slogans and quarreling with each other while they took bribes from the Saudis.

Saudi Arabia and the Conservative Forces

The woes of tribal kings were the mirror image of those facing the progressive forces. Their popular support, if any, was based on tribal loyalties buttressed by ignorance and passivity. Saudi pilots, inflamed by Nasser's speeches, defected to Egypt with their planes and into the waiting embrace of Nasser. Even a few members of the royal family defected to Egypt and were duly tabbed the "red princes." Students, equipped with newly invented transistor radios, thrilled to Nasser's rhetoric on remote sand dunes. It was a small step, but the revolution in modern communications had made its mark.

The Saudis, the leader of the conservative block, attempted to block the appeal of Arab nationalism by preaching Islamic unity, but it was a hard sell. Left to its own devices, it is doubtful that either its soaring oil wealth or control of the holy cities could have saved the Saudi monarchy. If the Saudis fell, it would be but a matter of time before the remaining conservative countries followed suit. All were wracked by the rebellion and sedition spawned by Egypt and other revolutionary states.

The United States managed to keep Saudi Arabia and the other tribal-religious monarchies afloat during the first two decades of independence, but only at the price of propping up the most repressive and backward tribal monarchies of the era. It was Saudi Arabia, moreover, that was propagating the virulent anti-American versions of Islam that are haunting the United States today. It all seemed to make sense at the time, but the seeds of America's present frustrations had been planted in the most fertile of soil.

It wasn't only the political environment of the Arab world that had changed with the advent of Saudi wealth, but its economic and social environments as well. It was the *Arabian Nights* all over again, as palaces bloomed in the desert and former revolutionaries from the progressive states rushed to lucrative positions in the Gulf. It was more smoke and mirrors, as medieval tribal monarchies disguised their soul in a glitzy veneer of superhighways and dazzling skyscrapers.

But that wasn't all that the oil kings spent their money on. Cradle-to-grave welfare schemes became the order of the day as the tribal kings attempted to buy the love of the masses. Legitimacy, however, required more than welfare. It required faith, piety, and good works, a particularly hard sell for a bunch of pampered epicureans whose only claim to glory was the luck of having been sired by an unusually talented individual. Or was it God's will? In an effort to gain the appearance of piety, the Saudis built elegant mosques throughout the Islamic world and funded extremist Islamic doctrines in Pakistan, Afghanistan, and just about everywhere else in the region. It was faith, but it was also the self-preservation of tribal kings using Islam to stifle a rebirth of a virulent Arab nationalism that had vowed their destruction. The quest for Arab unity was giving way to the quest for Islamic unity.

One way or another, the explosion of oil wealth propelled Saudi Arabia into the forefront of Arab and Islamic affairs. The conservative forces couldn't defeat the progressives by force, and so they simply bought them.

It was more, however, than just a shift of regional power. The internal balance of the Arab countries was also destabilized by the sudden wealth of the millions of poor Arabs who had flocked to the oil states in the hope of transforming their lives. Even peasant farmers and manual workers returned to Egypt and other progressive states with undreamed-of wealth, and the bureaucrats, lawyers, and teachers even more so. They had become the nouveau riche of their societies, their wealth far surpassing that of the bureaucrats and military officers who had previously dominated the Arab middle class.

Oil wealth also transformed the entire social and political structure of the oil kingdoms. People who once worked their fingers to the bone for the sake of survival now became accustomed to handouts from the government and gave up work for consumerism. Whether intentionally or not, the tribal kings used their newfound oil wealth to strip their subjects of their work ethic, spirit of freedom, and many of the other tribal values discussed earlier. Merchants, clergy, intellectuals, bureaucrats, and military officers all succumbed to the lure of free money and bowed to the will of the palace. Pride and honor reigned in family affairs, but not in dealings with the royal family. The oil Arabs enjoyed the bounty of Allah from on high, while legions of foreign workers performed the tasks that were either beyond the skill of the oil Arabs or below their dignity.

FORGING AN ARAB NATIONALIST PSYCHE

Both Nasser and the other progressive Arab leaders understood that the Arab psyche of fear, self-doubt, passivism, and mutual hostility (inherited from the colonial era and before) would provide a poor foundation for their dream of an Arab revival based on modernity, industrialization, and military power. They, the vanguard, could lead and cajole, but it was the Arab masses that would have to bring the dream to life. A true Arab revival would require a new Arab nationalist psyche that united the rulers and the ruled in a common quest for power, prosperity, and pride.

What would this new Arab psyche look like? Nasser wasn't terribly clear on the topic, but a reading of his collective speeches called for the pride and courage of a Bedouin warrior, the moral discipline of the Prophet Mohammed, the zeal of the Islamic invaders, and the discipline and respect for the law of the British. All were part of the Arab experience. All that remained was to put them together (Nasser, *Collected Speeches, 1954-1965*).

Nasser's efforts to remake the Arab psyche relied heavily on three basic assets. First, as commander in chief of the security forces he had a monopoly of coercive force. He could crush his opponents and force the masses to carry out his orders. His Soviet allies were experts on the subject and had done wonders in developing his secret service.

Second, Nasser controlled the Egyptian economy. Having nationalized most businesses of any size, he was able to guarantee all Egyptians a job, healthcare, and a free education. Surely they would be grateful and support his program.

Finally, Nasser's charisma soared. The Arab hero had arrived to lead them to the Promised Land. The long-awaited Mahdi or not, his victories conveyed unequivocal signs of God's blessing. His victories became their victories, and he was their father and guide. It was their obligation to follow and obey, as Arabs had always followed and obeyed their patriarchs. Such is the nature of charisma, at least as long as it lasts.

These were powerful weapons, but each had a fatal flaw. Military power, alone, could not force people to buy into his vision of an Arab revival. If past experience were any guide, Arabs knew how to deal with tyrants. They responded with appearances of conformity while they subverted the regime by playing the fox. Nasser knew the drill and also had doubts about the loyalty of his own security forces.

It was the same in the economic sphere. Nasser controlled the economy, but it was a bankrupt economy shattered by erratic efforts to impose socialism on a largely rural population. Massive Soviet-style factories were built in an effort to transform Egypt into an industrial power, but they consumed more wealth than they produced. Jobs were provided for the masses, but the pay was pathetically low. It was the same in the bureaucracy. Things were to be sorted out with time, but that time never arrived.

Hero worship also had its weaknesses. Nasser was a product of his culture and understood the power of heroes and holy men to sway the masses. He also knew that the power of heroes and holy men required an endless series of victories and miracles. One slip, and their aura would fade, and the masses would desert the ship in search of a new savior. The circus had to continue, and so it did, all the way to Arab's disastrous defeat in the 1967 Arab-Israeli War.

As a result of these weaknesses, Nasser was forced to place ever greater reliance on the Soviet Union for military and economic aid. In the process, a new kawaga roamed the streets of Cairo, a rough and insensitive kawaga who had neither the humanity nor generosity of the British. Had Egypt become a Soviet satellite? No, but it seemed that way to many Egyptians officers who bristled at the arrogance of their Soviet advisors.

FLAWED INDEPENDENCE AND THE EMERGING ARAB PSYCHE

The pace and depth of change during the Nasser years were too profound not to leave their stamp on the Arab psyche. Yet, the Nasser era was too chaotic and disorganized to remake a deeply rooted psyche that had evolved over the centuries. This would be the work of decades, if not centuries, and Nasser had but fifteen years before his dreams turned to dust in the calamity of the 1967 Arab-Israeli War.

Just how devastating was the 1967 defeat to the Arab psyche? In the words of El Sayeed Yassin, the director of Egypt's major think tank and author of the *Arab Personality*, "Fifteen years of forced industrialization and massed armies had produced nothing but humiliation, defeat, and the devastation of Arab confidence in themselves. There was nothing left, only a psychological void" (Yassin, 1993, 17–21).

It were almost as if the era of independence had produced two psyches: a psyche of pride, hope, and optimism and a psyche of humiliation, fear, and despair. The Arab psyche could never return to what it was before the Nasser era, but neither was it clear that it could go forward. The Sadat years that followed merely added to the confusion by destroying the myth of Arab unity and inflaming the seeds of a resurgent Islam. This dilemma was reflected in all dimensions of the Arab psyche, surveyed below.

Trading New Identities for Old?

The cataclysmic events of the era of independence forced Arabs to question who they were and how they fit into the world around them as never before in their long and checkered history. Family and faith remained the bedrock of the identity of independence, with not too much overlap between them. As always, the family and its extensions guided the earthly realm, while faith took care of the hereafter.

Even here, there were problems. Urban migrations had divided families and forced the need for supplementary attachments. It was the same with Islam. It wasn't enough to be a Muslim. One had to choose between being a nominal Muslim or a fundamentalist Muslim, not to mention the various shades in between.

For Muslims who found a supplemental family in the Muslim Brotherhood or the more extremist groups, the tension between family and faith became lethal. Membership in the Muslim Brotherhood was not only dangerous to the individual, but to his family and all others associated with him. Faith had suddenly put the family in jeopardy.

Those who identified with Nasser as a demigod found themselves torn between hero worship and Nasser's attack on deeply entrenched social values such as the equality of women. How could it be otherwise when family honor depended on female virtue? It was the same throughout the progressive Arab countries. Imagine the ruckus when Qadaffi, the Libyan dictator, ordered the creation of female military brigades in what remained a largely tribal society.

These were but the most extreme identity crises produced by the era of independence, but there were others as well. More than ever, people had to choose whether they were forward looking or backward looking. Arab identities also began to clash with local identities in the years following the collapse of the union between Syria and Egypt. Without going into details, suffice it to say that both the Egyptians and the Syrians thought that they were more intelligent and cultured than the other. The Iraqis knew that they were smarter and more cultured than either (Heikal, 1962; Kerr, 1965; Palmer, 1966).

Political identities also had to be dealt with and often melded with religious and ethnic identities. Many urban Shia in Iraq, for example, were token Muslims but became ardent communists. Or was it the other way around? They didn't forget their Shia identity, but they used communism to resist the dominance of the Sunni rulers. The moral of this story is that outward political labels aren't always what they seem.

A particularly interesting identity crisis was illustrated by a Libyan friend who confessed to feeling inferior because the Italians had taught the Libyans that they were toads. He also confessed to feelings of superiority because of Libya's sudden oil wealth. "It's hard," he lamented, "to be a rich toad. Sometimes I am one, and sometimes I am the other."

This is not an incidental anecdote, but continues to be played out on a daily basis between the Saudis and their Egyptian workforce. The Saudis treat Egyptian workers as if they were hired trash, while the Egyptians mock their hosts as unlettered clods. It's the same throughout the oil countries, but less stark than Saudi Arabia. The same class distinctions appeared in Egypt, as millions of poor workers returned home from the oil states to form a new class of nouveau riche, with all of the odious connotations of the term (Amin, 2000).

This point was brought home with a vengeance when one of my Saudi students rose to a high position and employed an Arab classmate, who was also my student. The Saudi held a great feast in my honor during a visit to Saudi Arabia and was effusive in insisting that the non-Saudi attend, but it was all for show. When the guests arrived, there were no non-Saudis among them. The non-Saudis hadn't really been invited. The Saudi and the non-Saudi Arab had been great friends in college, but it was a marriage of convenience in Saudi Arabia. The Saudi was the patron and the non Saudi the supplicant. Wealth, among other things, had sharpened class identities within the Arab world.

Adding complexity to the picture was the dramatic shift in identity patterns that followed the Arab defeat in the 1967 Arab-Israeli War and Sadat's peace treaty with Israel. Where were identities with Nasser and Arab nationalism to go? Both had lost their feel-good effect and become downright painful.

Perhaps worse was the psychological void that El Sayeed Yassin described. How were people to get along when they weren't sure of who they were or how they fit into the environment around them? The most common shift was from Arab nationalist identities to an intensification of Islamic identities. Something had to fill the void, and other secular identities such as communism and democracy had been crushed.

Local identities also sharpened, making hopes of Arab unity ever more remote. The dream continues, but it remains little more than a dream.

Arab Motivations during the Era of Independence

The Arabs of the era of independence wanted what they had always wanted: security, food, shelter, wealth, honor, dignity, love, sex, belonging, and the whole nine yards. The fiery rhetoric of Nasser and the other modernizing leaders promised it all, with the exception of sex. Never mind, the Arabic movies, mostly made in Egypt, promised that as well. It was all pretty tame by today's standards, but it was hot stuff for the era.

The colonial era had also exposed Arabs to a number of new learned wants, not the least of which was the rule of law and institutions rather than the whim of tyrants. These also were promised by Nasser and the other progressive leaders of the region, as were jobs for everyone, free education, and cradle-to-grave welfare services. Not only did they promise a socialist paradise, but they taught the masses that these services were their right and could not be denied. Mass expectations soared as scholars of the era spoke of a revolution of rising expectations.

People of the time spoke of a social contract between the revolutionary leaders and the masses. Demands for political democracy were traded by the masses for economic democracy, expressed in the form of jobs, education, and welfare. Eventually, the two would merge and become as one, but not before the enemies of the Arab revolution, foreign and domestic, had been defeated. The more the socialist regimes faltered, the more grandiose their promises became. Expectations kept pace, as did popular frustrations.

The social contract, like everything else, was shattered by the cataclysmic Arab defeat in the 1967 Arab-Israeli War. Talk about a social contract continued, but it was soon exposed as the empty slogan that it was. Leaders in the progressive countries enriched themselves as they ruled by force and became ever more distant from their impoverished subjects.

This was not the case in Saudi Arabia and the oil sheikhdoms, as cradle-to-grave welfare programs provided Saudis with the finest services that money could buy. Students returned home with doctorates to become chairmen and directors as soon as they stepped off the plane. Need a house? No problem. Simply get a loan from the government that would never be repaid. The royal family skimmed off the cream, but there was enough for all.

Complaints mounted whenever oil royalties faltered, but not to the extent of alarming the security forces. An emerging middle class, mostly educated in the West, kept mumbling about a need for more freedom and democracy, but the social contract held. Besides, the stifling environment of the Kingdom, as the Arabs refer to Saudi Arabia, could always be eased by a trip to Paris or London.

It was the same in the other oil sheikhdoms. One of my Kuwaiti students complained that the poor Arabs mocked him by saying that he spent his weekends in Switzerland. This, he protested, was a blatant lie. Beirut, maybe, but not Switzerland. Funny, no one from the oil monarchies complained about too much work. That was because few people in the oil states did much work. They supervised poor Arabs, but did no manual labor. They were above it.

Guilt and Conscience

In return for his promised paradise, Nasser begged the Arab masses to embrace the revolution with their souls as well as their voices. The revolution, he preached, was not his victory but their victory. The revolution could only succeed, he warned, if people embraced the Arab nationalist psyche, outlined above, as a sacred obligation, a conscience so to speak. Sinners were to feel the pain of guilt and repent. For those who repented, according to Nasser's collected speeches, the forgiveness of the stern but compassionate father awaited.

Did the Arabs embrace the Arab nationalist psyche, body and soul? This question will be addressed in the discussion of Arab behavior that follows. For the moment, suffice it to say that it was difficult to create a new conscience within a few chaotic years, especially when the politicians were preaching one message, the popular clergy a second, and the family elders a third. Guilt and conscience worked better for a Muslim Brotherhood already rooted in the Arab psyche than it did for the revolutionary leaders.

The Emotions Fired by Independence

The tumultuous events of the era of flawed independence triggered an avalanche of conflicting emotions, the likes of which the Arab world had never seen. Or maybe it was the torrent of conflicting emotions that made the era of independence so tumultuous? Whatever the case, the key word was "conflicting."

Let's start with the thrill of victory and the agony of defeat. For a vast number of Arabs, Nasser's early victories unleashed an outpouring of euphoria that washed away the humiliation of conquest and heralded a new dawn of power, pride, and prosperity. Keep in mind that Nasser was more than an Egyptian hero. He was an Arab hero.

Only the sense of euphoria that reigned as Nasser moved from victory to victory could explain the agony that gripped the Arab world with its defeat in the Arab-Israeli War of 1967. A people desperate for hope and dignity had built Nasser into the superhero they so ardently craved, and he had failed them.

Nasser may have played upon the Mahdi complex that was so strong in the Arab psyche. It is also probable that the outpouring of mass euphoria that accompanied his victories beguiled Nasser into believing that the adulation of the Arab masses would translate into self-sacrifice and dedication to the Arab cause.

Sadly, superheroes are supposed to do everything themselves or, as in the case of the Prophet Mohammed, with the will of God. The Prophet Mohammed possessed the spirit of God. Nasser did not, although those who identified with him wanted to believe that he did.

The thrill of victory and the agony of defeat were the most visible emotions of the era of independence. Lurking just beneath the surface was a latticework of equally contradictory emotions. Nasser's charisma inspired the emotions of hope, pride, power, superiority, satisfaction, optimism, and self-confidence. Even the strength of these emotions, however, could not shake the deeply entrenched feelings of fear, insecurity, suspicion, inferiority, frustration, alienation, and resignation inherited from the past.

Fear and insecurity remained core problems. Fear and suspicion of the government ran deep in the Arab psyche. They were not to be washed away by words, especially when police were everywhere and arrested people on the slightest whim. What choice did Nasser have? The revolution had to protect itself from its enemies, and Nasser even encouraged the masses to uncover them. It was the same in all of the Arab countries, progressive and conservative. Scary stuff, indeed.

Thoughts of change also made people nervous. A few intellectuals may have welcomed Nasser's attacks on society's backward-looking traditions. Not so the masses that were wedded to their traditions. Traditions were the core of their psyche and were presumed to be the will of God. Particularly sensitive were Nasser's calls for female equality and his attacks on tribal customs that the less educated equated with Islam. The Muslim Brotherhood and popular mystics even hinted that Nasser was leading the Arabs toward godless communism.

Added to the fray were jealously, envy, and the fear of being left out of welfare programs promised by the revolutionaries. The new class of bureaucrats and soldiers did quite well because they had contacts (wasta), and the revolutionaries needed their support. This was not true of the poor of the slums or the peasants in the countryside. I was living in Cairo in the early 1960s and recall watching the poor buy a piece of pita bread and a ladle of beans (foul medamas) for a penny or two from a passing vendor. It wasn't much, I thought to myself, but at least they were eating. "Not, so," corrected an Egyptian friend. "Those aren't the poor."

Despite Egypt's problems, faith in Nasser remained strong, as those who saw him as a savior focused their frustrations on those who surrounded him. This was not the case in the other progressive Arab countries. Their leaders, lacking either charisma or financial resources, had no choice but to rule by force alone. Coups were so common in Iraq and Syria during the 1950s and 1960s that it was hard to keep track of them all. Iraqi coups had sectarian overtones and were exceptionally violent. Fear of vengeance soared with each change of regime.

Distortions in the Reasoning Process

The drill never changes, and so there is little need to cover past ground other than to note that emotions, generally speaking, are the enemy of reason. This was particularly the case during the Nasser years that sent emotions soaring and placed a premium on action rather than long-term planning.

I'm still fond of the image of a small person lodged in the control panel of the brain. It isn't terribly scientific, but putting yourself in the role of an average Arab ego should help you keep pace with the torrent of events assaulting the Arab psyche during the heady days of the

Nasser era. It may also help you to understand the depth of despair that followed its collapse.

The mental confusion of the era, however, was not merely a matter of emotions. The Western media had propelled Nasser into the role of superhero by blaming him for all of the West's woes in the Middle East. Better yet, the Israelis vilified him as the reincarnation of the devil. What more could he ask for? The Soviet media, by contrast, played their role in hero building by idealizing Nasser as the inspiration of oppressed people everywhere. No wonder *Time Magazine* crowned him Man of the Year. If the kawaga thought that Nasser was a superhero, who were Arabs to argue? The kawaga knew everything.

Also bear in mind that superheroes fit well with the mystical reality of an Arab psyche awaiting the return of the Mahdi. This was the stuff of faith rather than science, and the Arab view of the world was faith-based.

Arabs throughout the region identified with Nasser because it made their spirits soar. Much like people identify with the hero in a movie, they vicariously became at one with Nasser, a larger-than-life hero. Identification with Nasser provided a tremendous psychological high for people whose lives were drab, at best. For some, it may have been an addiction that they couldn't live without. They rationalized his faults, and blamed others for his failures. Conspiracy theories, blaming the West and the tribal kings for his problems were believed because people wanted to think that Nasser was, indeed, the historic Arab hero that their imaginations had portrayed him to be.

The collapse of the combined Arab armies in the 1967 Arab-Israeli War was followed by Nasser's passing a few years later. The Arab psyche yearned in vain for a new superhero. Qadaffi and Saddam Hussein tried to fill the void of defeat and Nasser's passing, but the masses weren't buying. The need for a hero/savior didn't disappear. It merely became stronger.

Language as the Soul of the Arabs

The Arab language also changed during the era of independence as the new modernizers, mostly from the lower-middle class, infused the language with the colloquialisms of their local dialect and neglected the grammatical rigors of the classical language that the scholars of the past had so carefully guarded. This made it easier for Nasser and others to churn the emotions of the masses, but it also reflected a loss of rigor and discipline. Foreign words were simply added to the language without becoming Arabized. Some of the common expressions were a combination of both, the most common being "merci-awi," the French-Arabic equivalent of "thanks a lot."

For Galal Amin, a leading Arab economist, this change in speech reflected a change in the Arab psyche. He views it as a form of class conflict, as newer social classes that rose to the fore during the era of independence thumbed their noses at the symbols of an oppressive past (Amin, 2000, 90). Who knows? Perhaps it was a form of linguistic democracy.

Arab Nationalist Roadmap and Independence Poker

In one way or another, then, the psychological roadmap that the Arabs used to interpret their world had grown infinitely complex. Once again, the Arab psyche kept much of what it had while adding new wrinkles to cope with the challenges of a new and rapidly changing environment.

It was much the same with the game of independence poker. The opportunities for gain were greater, but the stakes were higher. The number of players had also increased dramatically, and one could never be sure what powerful patron an adversary held as an ace in the hold. Everyday, or so it seemed, brought a new shuffle of the cards. Those who had supported the last coup suddenly found themselves in dank prison cells, if they survived at all. Family and clients all ran for shelter. But for those who won, the rewards of power and wealth were enormous, at least for a while. Most people chose not to play, not that they didn't make small bets on the side.

FLAWED INDEPENDENCE AND ARAB BEHAVIOR

Efforts of the Arab psyche to adjust to the tumultuous environment of the era of independence followed the timeworn strategies of earlier eras. New twists were added to cope with the pressures of modernization, but the core strategies remained the same.

The special emphasis in this section is on the millions of poorly trained people forced to run the vast bureaucratic, military, political, and industrial establishments that had mushroomed overnight in Egypt and the other progressive states. Even if the flawed policies of Nasser and the other modernizing leaders had been perfect, the behavior of the Arab bureaucracies would have prevented their successful implementation. I stress this point, because nothing has changed. If anything, things have become worse. It was the era of independence that set the tone for the political malaise that led to the Arab revolutions of today (Palmer, Leila, Yassin, 1988).

The discussion also places special emphasis on the reluctance of the Arab masses to buy into the revolutionary programs of the era. Nasser and others proclaimed that they had acted in the name of the people, but the people were not involved.

Political Behavior

Distinctions are made between political, social, and economic behavior, but as always, the lines between politics, society, and economics were blurred. How could it be otherwise when politicians made all of the key economic decisions and dictated the version of Islam to be preached in the mosques?

Collective Behavior: Nationalism Versus Spiritualism

This is not to suggest that the Arabs were not enthralled with visions of an Arab renaissance. They were, but none more so than students and junior officers in the mushrooming armies of the region. Nasser's nationalist rhetoric filled the streets with surging crowds demanding Arab unity and the liberation of Palestine, the most bitter of Arab humiliations. The Arab nation was awakening, and Arabs everywhere were filled with hope, pride, and dreams of what could be. All that remained was to channel this phenomenal surge of emotional energy into the task of nation building. Surely those who screamed so vociferously for the defeat of Israel would put aside their petty jealousies and sacrifice heart and soul for the good of the Arab nation.

Alas, the Arab psyche saw little connection between shouting nationalistic slogans and the need to make personal sacrifices for the good of the nation, the Arab nation. It was as if they were living in two different worlds—one a world of dreams and the other the real world of daily survival. Dreams were fine, but one had to get along.

Perhaps the nationalist dream would have fared better if the newly independent Arabs didn't have to spend hours, if not days, waiting in line to bribe a petty bureaucrat to sign some meaningless form. Unless, of course, they had connections. In that case they would be ushered into a side room, the form signed, the requisite identity picture over-looked, and the token of appreciation paid. Efforts to stamp out corruption resulted in more forms and signatures until the Arabs soon faced death by bureaucratic strangulation. The threat increased with time and shows no signs of easing.

Did requiring more forms and signatures make bureaucrats honest? Not at all. It merely required more wasta and increased the cost of bribing a government official.

Nasser and other modernizing Arab leaders well understood that Islam was too deeply entrenched in the Arab psyche to be tamed, so they attempted to make it subservient to the regime. Formal religion was encouraged and popular mysticism tolerated as long as it focused on internal salvation.

Political expressions of Islam, by contrast, were crushed without mercy. The attempted assassination of Nasser by the Muslim Brotherhood in 1954 led to a witch hunt of any and all associated with the organization. The Muslim Brotherhood's challenge to the Syrian regime resulted in the slaughter of from ten thousand to thirty thousand Muslim Brothers. Radical Islam was driven underground, and people avoided any form of religious expression that the security police might deem suspicious.

The forced religious moderation of the Nasser era exploded in a wave of religious extremism in the decade following the Arab defeat in the 1967 Arab-Israeli War. It was this period that gave rise to a vision of jihadist radicalism so violent that it was reminiscent of the Assassins of old. The Muslim Brotherhood seemed tame by comparison.

The situation in Saudi Arabia was the opposite. The Saudi monarchy welcomed the surge in Islamic emotions while arresting anyone suspected of Arab nationalist tendencies. The battle between the progressive and conservative poles of the Arab world had become a battle between secularism and Islam.

The Arab psyche, for its part, became ever more adept at playing the game of appearances. Its life depended upon it. In all probability,

THE ARAB PSYCHE AND AMERICAN FRUSTRATIONS

outpourings of nationalism were exaggerated in the progressive countries, much as mass displays of religiosity were exaggerated in Saudi Arabia and other conservative countries.

Establishing a Support Base in a Shifting World

Shouting nationalistic slogans kept the security police at bay, but it did little to secure a job, housing, or anything else in the tumultuous environment of the revolutionary era. Everything required connections (wasta) with a powerful individual. Families were still the core units in society, but the most powerful families were now those with connections to the ruling party, military, and bureaucracy. They controlled access to everything, and little could be done without their support.

Members of the old regime also retained considerable influence. The revolutionary elites had little practical experience in running an economy and soon relied on the old business elite to run the firms they had so hastily nationalized. The revolutionary leaders, most drawn from the lower-middle class, also had an inferiority complex of sorts and, despite their socialist rhetoric, continued to hold aristocrats in awe. I recall renting an apartment overlooking the Nile from Nasser's niece, a charming lady who went to great pains to inform me that she possessed Turkish blood, a sure sign of aristocratic origins.

Little by little, the new political elite began to form marriage alliances with the old business and aristocratic elite. It began slowly and eventually became a rush. After all, each had what the other needed. Nasser and other revolutionaries had power, the old aristocracy had prestige, and the capitalist entrepreneurs had vital skills and foreign contacts. They also had foreign bank accounts.

People with influence strengthened their powerbase by building networks of supplicants to do their bidding. The larger and more influential a patron's client network, the more influential the patron. Patron-client networks had emerged during earlier eras, but they became the fabric of politics during the era of independence.

Of course, it was essential that the patron took care of his clients. Those who didn't would soon see their support base wither. Taking care of clients was an expensive proposition that could only be fed by favoritism, nepotism, and corruption.

I recall the story of a good Arab friend who, having acquired a global reputation as a scholar, was asked to head a new Arab university. His rules were clear. He would accept the position on the condition that American procedures would apply and that there would be no external political influence. It wasn't to be. The family that sponsored the university had just lost control of the surrounding community to an opposing clan, and with it, their ability to find jobs for their clients. Their solution was to create a university to glorify the family name and provide positions for their clients. An American-style university it wasn't, and my friend was rewarded with a heart attack.

For supplicants, the task was to consolidate their position by currying the favor of superiors, be they bureau chiefs, local leaders of the ruling party, commanding officers, shop foremen, or local officials. Their superiors not only expected such deference, they demanded it, a situation caustically illustrated by the following editorial from an Egyptian newspaper of the era:

> No sooner is an official promoted to the post of manager than he ceases to accomplish any constructive work. His primary concern is to receive the compliments indiscriminately leveled at him from every quarter and to smile with condescending magnanimity at the servile flattery lavished at him by his former colleagues.
>
> Such a state of affairs has naturally developed out of a corrupt system of bureaucracy fostered and consolidated over the years, as a result of a deeply rooted fear in the hearts of juniors toward their superiors. Managers have actually capitalized on this fear in order to force more submission and humility on already humble juniors and to extort from them every possible kind of service and every conceivable kind of flattery.
>
> With such material and moral accouterments adorning the post of manager, it is only natural that officials should be vying with one another to attain this post though all the means available, not excluding hypocrisy, bribery, backbiting, double-dealing and deception (The Egyptian Gazette, March 24, 1982).

In Saudi Arabia and the other monarchies, it was links to the king or senior princes that counted. If not the king and senior princes, then lesser princes and princesses would do. This was not an insurmountable task, for the royal family in Saudi Arabia is reputed to have between ten thousand and thirty thousand members. If ties to the royal family proved difficult, the next step was somebody close to the royal family or someone close to someone close to the royal family. Maybe, perhaps, the chief of a powerful tribe, religious leader, big merchant, or large landowner. If not them, a lesser figure would do. A close friend of mine in one of the monarchies spoke freely of the matter, lamenting that his ties were with the crown prince rather than the king. All would have been well if the crown prince had become king, but he didn't.

It didn't matter whether it was Saudi Arabia or Egypt. The principle was the same, as everyone struggled to consolidate his position by becoming the client of a powerful patron. It was the same for families, clans, and even tribes, all of whom curried the support of a powerful patron.

Expressions of Loyalty

Expression of loyalty came in many forms. Loyalty to the family, clan, and tribe were assumed but not flaunted for fear they would reflect disloyalty to the regime. Expression of religious loyalties depended on the circumstances but were subdued in the progressive countries to avoid the attention of the security police. Loyalty to patrons had much to do with their ability to take care of their clients. The more powerful the patron, the more loyal his clients. One had to get by, and association with a fallen patron was dangerous. The tricky problem was bailing out in time.

Two common expressions of loyalty to the regime were shouting and the syrupy submissiveness of the opportunist. I recall listening to a Syrian talk show a few years ago, when a Syrian worker called in and kept screaming at the top of his voice how much he loved Syria's president for life. The caller was allowed to drag on for several minutes because the host of the show, while embarrassed, was reluctant to terminate praise for Syria's president for life.

Shouters, however, had their purpose. It was they who flooded the ubiquitous demonstrations of support for the anointed leader. Sincere or not, they gave the impression of mass support and made others think twice about resisting the regime.

The opportunists were far more lethal. They joined the ruling party and its various affiliates for the sole purpose of personal gain. The best discussion of the topic that I have encountered was a pamphlet titled, *The Revolution and the Problem of Opportunism*, published by the revolutionary party in Syria during the 1960s (Syrian Ba'ath, no date). Opportunists, according to the pamphlet, are flawed individuals totally lacking in morality who will support any leader, group, or cause that promotes their personal interests, regardless of the good of the revolution. Beyond seizing opportunities, they plot to create opportunities by pushing leaders to the fore, only to betray them in a blink of the eye if it suits their interest. Much like the hypocrites of the Islamic era, the modern opportunists have no cause, ideology, or morals other than selfish gain, be it material wealth or fame. This, of itself, makes their public statements hollow and meaningless.

Opportunism is also a group affair in the Arab world, as prominent people gather supporters around them to bolster their influence. The zaims discussed in the preceding chapter were leaders of opportunist groups, the members of which were concerned with their own gain and survival. So are the patron-client networks that permeate Arab governments.

The author of the pamphlet makes it clear that opportunists come from all classes and professions, including the military, the bureaucracy, the economic institutions, the peasant cooperatives, the official political parties, the clergy, and even the intellectual elite that, like the poets of old, spend the time glorifying leaders and praising their miraculous feats.

Sadly, the author laments, the mass revolutions ignited by Nasser and other modernizing leaders were riddled with opportunists who had perverted revolutionary ideals into a cruel farce. It could not be otherwise, he cautions, because the instability produced by revolutions are the feeding ground for opportunists and lesser foxes.

Far worse, according to the author, the activities of the opportunists precluded the Arab revolutions from establishing efficient institutions capable of achieving the rule of law, stability, economic growth, and popular democracy. Thus, the Nasser revolution gave way to a most opportunist Sadat, and Sadat to the even more opportunistic thirty-year reign of Mubarak.

The only way an Arab revolution could survive, the author concluded, was to destroy all opportunists, individuals as well as groups. I wonder who he thought would be left.

Such complex thoughts were expressed by Neguib Mahfouz, Egypt's Nobel laureate, in a simple phrase: "The revolution is conceived by dreamers, carried out by the brave, and manipulated by the opportunists (*Egyptian Gazette*, February 23, 2011).

An Obsession for Control

Because loyalty was so iffy, patrons and other power figures became obsessed with controlling the actions of those below them in life's impermeable web of dominant-submissive relationships. The principle was not new, but it reached such intensity in the era of independence that all of the political, bureaucratic, military, and state-run industries created to serve the revolution were immobilized by micromanagement, the excessive centralization of authority, a refusal to share information with peers and subordinates, fear mongering, and the obstruction of the successes of talented juniors. There were other subtleties, but these will do for our purposes.

The logic of centralizing authority was obvious. The chances of sedition were reduced and the harvest of bribes increased. Also increased was the ability to trade favors (wasta) with others. Why should these opportunities be wasted on underlings whose job, at least in the view of most supervisors, was to serve them? During a more recent era, I headed a research center in a major Arab university but couldn't order a ten-cent cover for an electric outlet without permission of the dean. It was all downhill from there.

Seeing that the top person decided everything, everyone who was anyone demanded to see the top person. No one else could get anything done. This caused bottlenecks, especially because superiors displayed their power by coming in late and leaving early. What good was being a superior if you had to show up on time?

It was pretty much the same everywhere. The Saudis were still developing their bureaucracy and relied heavily on Egyptians and Palestinians to staff the technical positions while the Saudis supervised from on high. Tribal authoritarianism blended perfectly with the bureaucratic authoritarianism (Al Gosaibi, 1998).

Just to be on the safe side, the wielders of power, whether political leaders or bureaucrats, found it to their advantage to provide subordinates with as little information as possible. The less subordinates knew, the less able they were to conspire against the leader. More often than not, superiors gave conflicting misinformation to different subordinates just to keep them off guard.

Control also meant instilling fear among subordinates. It was almost impossible to fire anybody, but they could be passed over for promotion or transferred to a remote province. Not only did such transfers terrify other workers into conformity, it made room for friends and supporters of the superior and his superior. Both had relatives and supporters to care for, and all were more than anxious to trade favors (wasta) with each other.

More confusing was the bureaucratic and academic practice of not giving subordinates the tools they needed to succeed unless it served the interests of the superior. Again, why give credit to a subordinate when he might use it to climb over your head? It just wasn't logical. It was far better that subordinates fail than the security of the supervisor be jeopardized. The superior's boss might complain, but a lack of production could always be blamed on incompetent employees. Besides, everyone was playing the same game. Everyone, that was, except the modernizing leaders who became ever more frantic as they saw their dream dissolve into a morass of bureaucratic confusion and public indifference.

Now, look at things from the perspective of the average bureaucrat, barely able to survive on his government salary. The penalties for committing a serious mistake or upstaging a superior could be devastating, but there were few penalties for foot dragging or avoiding responsibility. Government employees, and that was most people, soon learned that the key to getting along was to do as little as possible, avoid responsibility, follow regulations to the letter, and demand their supervisor's signature for even the most routine of matters. This left them open to charges of being lazy, but clever bureaucrats created the impression of great activity by walking around with a bundle of papers in hand while they searched for the missing supervisor, who was seldom to be found. That was, of course, unless they were on break, sick, grieving, or otherwise indisposed. The Egyptian press suggested that the average bureaucrat actually worked about two hours a day, and that was on good days. As a highly placed friend lamented, "How can we expect them to work when we pay them so little?"

This didn't mean that subordinates wouldn't conspire against superiors when the time was ripe. They would and they did, which only served to perpetuate the cycle of control and subordination. In the meantime, they would seek the security of powerful patrons who could counter the power of their superiors. Perhaps it would be a powerful political or military figure, or even a tribal (zaim) or influential religious leader. For that matter, subordinates might seek patrons from among the powerful rivals of their superiors.

The above description applied to the average government employee, a category often referred to as survivors. Survivors did so little to rock the boat that they were generally acceptable to any cabal that seized power. After all, someone had to run the government when all of the prized positions went to the high rollers who had risked all to pull a coup. Those who succeeded became rich, famous, and powerful, at least until the next coup. Those who failed, and that was most of them, simply perished as enemies of the people.

Place yourself in the position of government employees in Syria and Iraq during this period, countries in which coup d'états were so frequent that you needed a program to keep score. No one knew who would be in charge following the next coup, but they did know that supporters of the old regime would find themselves in hot water, perhaps literally. While a few people were high rollers willing to stake all on a roll of the dice, most were not.

Perhaps the distinction between survivors and high rollers is overdone. When an Egyptian intellectual complained about survivors to Egypt's President Mubarak, the president simply replied, "We are all survivors." Survive he did, for thirty years before being forced from office by mass protests.

Every Arab country suffered from the same disease, but none more so than Saudi Arabia and the other oil states that allocated positions in the bureaucracy as a means of buying support among a restive population. Government jobs were considered a right, and no one was really expected to work (Al Gosaibi, 1998).

Passive resistance extended to the rural areas as well. Peasants welcomed land reform, but they resisted efforts to be organized into cooperatives controlled by the government and administered by the ruling party according to the bureaucratic principles outlined above. While the government demanded ever more production to provide cheap food for the urban areas, the peasants saw little incentive to work harder when the leaders of the cooperatives skimmed off the fruit of their labor.

As one frustrated Iraqi official complained, "They will only work hard if we beat them." Another Iraqi official told of efforts to increase production by providing the peasants with improved seeds. The peasants ate the seeds, and so the administrators poisoned the seeds. Some of these stories were told in a long-lost Iraqi venture into self-criticism. Others were told to me by an Iraqi friend at the Iraqi Agricultural College who, peering out the window at the vast acreage below, lamented that all of the college's experimental test sites had become saline as the result of flawed irrigation practices ordered by politicians in a frantic effort to increase production.

Egyptian assessments of their efforts to mobilize the peasants lamented that nothing they tried was able to change the mindset of the peasants who continued to view government officials with "fear and deep suspicion" (Al-Manoufi, 1979, 79).

The moral of the story is simple. Frantic decisions made by desperate leaders and implemented by a fear-based bureaucracy could not succeed in forcing peasants to support a revolution that, for all of its slogans, offered them nothing but grief.

Expressions of Satisfaction and Discontent

How were individuals in the progressive states to express satisfaction and discontent when the ruling party orchestrated both elections and demonstrations?

People couldn't protest against the ruling tyrant, but they could mock them with jokes so lethal that Nasser even established a separate organization just to keep track of them (Hamouda, 1990). My favorite joke began with Nasser's son, a boy of philosophic nature, asking his father questions.

"Who are you, father?" asked the boy.

"I am the father of the country," replied Nasser.

"And who is mother?" continued the boy.

"She is the people," replied Nasser.

"And who am I?" pressed the boy.

"You, my son," replied Nasser, "are the hope of the future."

Later that evening, the boy awoke hungry and, going to the refrigerator for a snack, found it empty. Adding to his dismay was the sound of his parents making love in the adjoining room.

"My God," thought the boy. "The father of the country is screwing the people while the hope of the future starves to death."

I don't recall many Saudi jokes. But then, the Bedouin didn't have that much imagination. Remember that all of the prophets of old came from settled populations.

The Saudis didn't bother with faux elections, but retained the tribal custom of allowing people to petition the king or other senior princes for special favors, a topic to be discussed in later chapters. People didn't have rights, but the king was generous to his children.

The passive resistance discussed above was also a common form of mass protest throughout the Arab world. Tyrants could force people to bow their heads, but they couldn't force them to work. Even shouting slogans praising the tyrant became a form of mockery.

Plots and coups were also common during the early years of independence, but most were the work of the military. There were few mass uprisings in the region.

Social Behavior

Politics aside, much behavior during the era of independence fell into two categories: getting along by going along, and attempting to beat the system.

Conforming to the Pressures of Culture and Tradition

Most people simply kept out of politics and did what they always had done, as long as it didn't upset the forces that be. This was particularly the case with women, who despite Nasser's efforts to bring them into the revolutionary mainstream, remained isolated from the political realm.

Galal Amin, for example, tells a fascinating story of not being able to recall seeing his mother outside of the kitchen:

Nothing but a cramped little place with very poor ventilation, no comfortable place to sit or work and no glimpse of beauty...where she spent most of her time...dripping with sweat as she prepared food for one son after the other as they arrived home from school at various hours of the day without making the slightest effort to exchange a few words with her beyond a critical comment on this or that dish (Amin, 2000, 79).

What makes this story so interesting is that Amin was the son of a university professor who represented the cream of Egypt's intellectual middle class at the time. Imagine, then, the pressures for social conformity of the vast majority of Arab women. As Amin continues,

They were raised to regard men as their source of economic security, but a very unreliable source at that. A woman therefore had to develop skills to retain her man, for if she did not she would be exposed to an unenviable fate. It is no exaggeration to compare the relationship between a husband and wife in Egypt at the time with a political relationship governed by the arts of war and diplomacy, of cunning and craft, rather than love and friendship.

Like most Egyptian women of her generation, my mother learned from childhood the crucial lesson that a wife must clip her husband's wings if he was not to fly away and that the most effective way of achieving that was to bear him as many children as possible (Amin, 2000, 81).

I mention this story here because it illustrates the profound task that Nasser and other modernizers faced in awakening popular support for their modernizing revolutions. How were their revolutions to succeed with 50 percent of the population effectively taken out of the workforce at the same time they were fueling a population explosion?

The situation was far worse in the more conservative countries in which women were secluded. I recall accompanying a Libyan colleague as he carted the ladies of the extended family from one appointment or another almost every hour of the day. I had to wait in the car while he made the arrangements, and it was during his long absences that I suddenly realized that the seclusion of women did more than remove half of the population from their country's development process. While one half of the population was sidelined, the other half was preoccupied making sure that they stayed that way.

Men, too, were attempting to get along by conforming to the pressures of the day. The difference between the situation of men and women was the tremendous pressure placed on men to join the ruling party and its government-controlled labor unions and agricultural cooperatives. At the very least, men were expected to attend political rallies and shout praise for their leader. Both the carrot and stick were at work. Those who participated in official organizations received jobs and other benefits. Others had a harder time of it, and refusal to do so was noted by the secret police.

Social Deviance: The Fox against Society

The opportunists who hovered in the corridors of power have already been discussed. They were the princes of foxes. For society at large, however, the principle was the same. Playing the fox was the only way for ordinary people to get their share of the cake and a bit more. How could it be otherwise in a world ruled by opportunists?

The wiles the fox that had been honed to deal with tyrants and the kawaga were easily adapted to the era of independence. New ploys also emerged to deal with the greater risks and opportunities that the surge to modernization provided. All remain very much part of governance in the Arab world today.

Appearances of wealth and power continued to be an essential component of the fox's strategy. How was an aspiring powerbroker to attract clients without the symbols of power? After all, who was going to follow a weak leader in a political system dominated by powerful individuals rather than institutions?

The same principle applied to those in power. The slightest sign of weakness was an invitation for desertion. So the fox studied its leaders with the skill of a chess master, noting each nuance of power and decline. It was a game played between the rulers and the ruled, as leaders attempted to convince their subjects that rebellion would be useless and the fox probed for signs of weakness.

Just as appearances were vital to the fox, so was his ability to change roles at a moment's notice. The fox had studied the lion with great care, and government officials never refrained from wearing the cloak of the lion when it offered the opportunity for extorting a bigger bribe or shielding themselves from the demands of the public. "I'm so sorry sire, but we are honor bound to uphold the law, and I have no choice in the matter. Come back tomorrow." Few people had any idea of what the law said, and it didn't make much difference if they did. The legal systems of the region were a mishmash of contradictory laws originating in the Ottoman and even Islamic eras. If one law didn't get you, another one would. It was simply easier to pay a bribe or use wasta (influence) than fight the system.

A variation on this theme was the tendency of lower officials to play the fox by using the same impenetrable morass of laws and regulations to avoid work and responsibility. Orders of superiors couldn't be disobeyed, but neither could superiors order their subordinates to break the law, at least not without a favor in return. So it was that laws became a shield against the public and superiors alike. Superiors might scream and shout, but not much more. The fox cowered, and all was well (Palmer, Leila, and Yassin, 1988).

As always, the fox had to hover close to his prey if he were to strike at a moment's notice. Even here, however, life was not easy. The fox had to decide what his aspirations were. Was he content to live off the fat of the land, or did he want to go for the gold and have it all?

For the high rollers, the trick was to enter the security services or official party and gradually position oneself to overthrow the government. This was best accomplished by entering the service of a patron on the rise, ever ready to bail out if necessary. This was the path followed by many of the region's dictators, including Hafiz al-Asad and Saddam Hussein, America's sometimes puppet and eventual adversary.

The less adventurous foxes chose the Mr. Clean technocrat strategy. The trick was to be close enough to the ruling elite to have influence, without being destroyed by its fall. Technocrats, in the curious world of Arab politics, blended a reputation for honesty with high technical skills generally acquired by a foreign education. They were also skilled opportunists.

Did the people cheat, bribe, steal from the government, ignore the law, and evade taxes and military service? Naturally. They had no other option if they were to survive oppressive and corrupt regimes that stuffed the government with their own relatives and supporters, all of whom had carte blanche to rip off the masses and just about everyone else. The progressive states pretended to be governed by institutions and laws, but it was still their rulers who became presidents for life unless they were overthrown by a coup d'état.

Wasn't it immoral for people to rip off the government? How could it be when their governments were immoral, and the focus of their moral obligations remained the family? They simply had their priorities straight. Both the fox and the person who cared for his family were honored members of society.

Arabs could be courteous to a fault among friends, families, guests, superiors, and potential supporters, but they were also adept at getting to the head of the line. How else were they to get home on infrequent buses stuffed to the brim, while the poor clung perilously to the bumpers or roofs? It was the same in endless lines needed to get a form signed or to buy subsidized goods at the government co-ops that were always short on supplies.

This said, one of my passions was riding the public buses in Cairo. Once I had connived my way to the front of the line, a kind hand would appear to draw me inside one of these human pressure cookers. As for my bags of groceries, they would disappear from view, only to reappear when it was time to descend. It didn't work that way in the first-class coaches of the commuter trains, only among the poor.

Trust during the era of independence was limited to a narrow circle and, even then, with extreme caution. The problem was that traditional circles of trust were too narrow to deal with the complexities of modernization. New networks of trust had to be built in order to maneuver through the exploding array of military, bureaucratic, economic, and political institutions. Marriage and tribal alliances helped, but sooner or later you had to trust someone from outside traditional circles. Invariably, those trusted individuals were friends of long standing who had stood the test of time. For example, the power structure in Syria during the thirty-year rule of Hafiz al-Asad was tightly controlled by family, sect, and long-time friendships that President Asad had made with members of other sects during his years as a military cadet (Seale, 1988).

Kinship and enduring friendships eased suspicions, but even they were fragile. Asad, for example, recovered from a serious illness only to find that his brother was on the verge of seizing power. Armed conflict threatened when, in a fascinating mix of tradition and modernity, Asad stood down his brother, saying, "I am your elder brother to whom you owe obedience" (Seale, 1988, 430).

It wasn't just political alliances that were fragile. I recall a good Palestinian friend who, upon returning home with his doctorate, was anxious to publish an article on his dissertation research. Deeply engrossed in his work, he was annoyed when a lifelong friend shouted from the garden.

"Come on," the friend shouted. "The trees are ripe with figs. Let's eat them."

"I'm busy," shouted the scholar to his friend. "You eat the figs."

A friendship was lost.

The rush toward socialism during the era of independence filled government offices with poorly trained officials who found it difficult to ignore the tempting opportunities for corruption and revenge that overwhelmed them at every turn. Invariably, this opened the gates to wholesale accusations, rumors, slander, and innuendo, only some of which were justified. The responses of the accused, guilty or not, were both predictable and forceful: blame others, scapegoat, stonewall, deny, and flare up in anger at the slightest confrontation.

Flare ups among men were easily quelled by neighbors and colleagues, but not so accusations against women who now entered the universities and workforce in large numbers as part of socialist modernization programs. Most were helpless victims of male bravado, but innuendo shattered reputations, and family tensions flared. It wasn't merely a matter of honor, but also of eligibility for marriage. An unmarried woman was a burden on the family and suffered the pain of living as a spinster in a society that demanded marriage.

The conservative states, still largely tribal, solved the problem by heavy veiling and the strict segmentation of education systems. They also prevented women from being alone with a man who was not a close relative. Women driving? Perish the thought. They couldn't even

THE ARAB PSYCHE AND AMERICAN FRUSTRATIONS

be in a car with a strange man other than their driver, let alone being left to their own devices. An unguarded woman was an invitation to sin and the unleashing of rumors that could shatter the fragile calm of the kingdoms with tribal feuds. Islam was the justification, but tribalism was the cause. But who was watching the driver?

Economic Behavior: Productivity and Welfare

For all of their differences, both the progressive republics and the tribal monarchies became welfare states during the era of independence. The progressive republics turned to socialism in the quaint hope that people would selflessly give according to their abilities and take according to their needs. The oil monarchies attempted to buy love with their newfound oil wealth. All had also become police states.

What this meant, in practice, was that few people in the Arab world had much incentive to work very hard. The Saudis and other oil monarchies encouraged their subjects to enjoy the good life and to enrich themselves while foreigners did all of the work. The socialists provided everyone with a job, but they were too poor to pay a living wage. Either way, there was no incentive for Arabs to work.

The fact that all of the Arab countries were police states added to the decline of the Bedouin work ethic by making innovation dangerous and unproductive. Neither the ruling elite nor the royal families wanted competition from independent people who might challenge their authority. That is, of course, unless they got a good share of the profit.

Besides, how were people to innovate and get ahead in a work culture that pulled people down rather than encouraged cooperation? A few succeeded, but most just got along by doing as little as possible. All but the fox, that is. He did very well for himself and didn't care about anyone else outside of the family.

Time and Space

The enduring concepts of time and space also reshaped behavior in the era of independence and modernization. Everything was accelerated: urbanization, education, industrialization, arrests, wars, and coup d'états. Who could predict what would happen next? Opportunities came with blinding speed and disappeared just as quickly. While people in the West planned for decades, those in the Arab world planned for the moment, gathering what they could and then struggling to keep it from the rapacious eyes of the state. Those with wealth smuggled their money abroad, but they were the elite. Those with lesser means invested in apartments and land, both being more stable than bank accounts subject to the whims of socialist dictators desperately in need of money. Rent controls were imposed, but only made things worse. Natives would go homeless while landlords rented to foreigners on a short-term lease. If worse came to worse, the building stayed empty until a suitable tenant could be found.

Space, too, had taken on a new dimension. An exploding population and the search for opportunities had pushed people to the cities, but where were they to live? Private investors, as we have seen, had little interest in renting to the poor. Those who did so demanded huge bribes paid in advance. Governments rushed to build housing for the masses, but the lines were long and the bureaucratic forms impenetrable. It was the land speculators and supporters of the ruling party who reaped the harvest. The same pattern emerged in the new desert cities built to ease the pressure on Cairo and keep urban sprawl from overrunning ever-larger swatches of Nile farmland. They, too, went to people with money and wasta. And so the poor continued their relentless trek to the hideous slums of Cairo.

RED-FLAG ISSUES IN THE ERA OF INDEPENDENCE

The era of flawed independence offered hope that the Arab world would come to grips with the red-flag issues so vital to the dream of an Arab revival. All were incorporated in the revolutionary slogan, "freedom, unity, and socialism." How well did they do?

Extremism Versus Moderation

Religious extremism was muted during the early years of independence, when Arab nationalism soared and dreams of an Arab revival swept all before them. Perhaps extremism would have remained muted if Nasser and other modernizing leaders of the era had succeeded in achieving their dream of social, economic, and political development.

Sadly, they failed on all counts, and their flawed efforts unleashed a vortex of disjointed change that fueled every known cause of religious extremism, including fear, crumbling social institutions, oppression, frustrated expectations, instability, attacks on traditional values, and a pervasive foreign presence in the form of Soviet and American advisors.

All simmered under the iron hand of the modernizers, only to explode into the most virulent form of jihadist extremism following the devastating defeat of the Arab forces in the Six Day War of 1967. Saudi money fueled the explosion while the U.S. and Israel applauded from the sidelines. The threat of Arab nationalism to American, Saudi, and Israeli interest had vanished. The roots of an imperceptible U.S., Saudi, Egyptian, and Israeli alliance were taking shape. Keep it in mind as you read future chapters.

Violence Versus Reconciliation

The early years of Arab independence were a pageant of violence, including continuous scrimmages with Israel, a brutal war of independence in Algeria, civil wars in Yemen, Lebanon, and the Sudan, and an endless chain of coups in Syria and Iraq. Announcements of plots and conspiracies became the mainstay of the government-controlled media, and repression and torture followed. Feuds, revenge, crime, sectarian strife, and honor killings continued unabated.

The religious extremism unleashed by the 1967 Arab-Israeli War increased the carnage, as jihadist groups maimed and murdered in a frantic effort to purify Islam by force. Iran and the Sudan became Islamic republics, and Egypt was pushed to the brink of civil war. The details will be provided in the next chapter, "Islamic Resurgence and the Arab Psyche."

Religious violence was to be expected, for the same factors that fueled extremism also fueled the violence that was becoming endemic to the region. The absence of anything approaching democracy made the peaceful resolution of conflict impossible. Violence and submission were the only options left.

Fragmentation Versus Unification

The West had always viewed Arab unity as a threat to its influence in the region, and it played a major role in keeping the Arabs divided. The master stroke of America's divide-and-rule policy was pushing Egypt, the dominant power in the Arab world, to make peace with Israel. In so doing, it assured that an Arab world divided against itself would cease to threaten the survival of the Jewish state. The Arabs squabbled among themselves, and the dream of an Arab revival grew ever more distant.

By contrast, the Americans encouraged Islamic solidarity as a counterweight to the spread of communism in the region. The activities of the Muslim Brotherhood, and even the jihadists, were embraced in America's fight against the Soviet menace.

American interests were served during the early years of the era, but radical Islam soon turned on the U.S., and half of the squabbling Arab states ruled by American puppets turned into swamps that bred anti-American terror. The picture in Israel was no brighter. Rather than confronting poorly motivated secular armies with little zest for war, Israelis found themselves confronting intensely motivated religious forces that courted death in the name of God. Again, more of this is in the following chapter.

Tyranny Versus Democracy
All of the countries in the Arab world during the era of independence evolved into brutal dictatorships with the exception of Lebanon which evolved into civil war. Dictators soon lost touch with the masses, and the moribund bureaucracies, discussed throughout the chapter, proved totally incapable of meeting the material or spiritual needs of the populations. As a result, all of the pressures that led to extremism and violence intensified.

The U.S. assisted its puppet kings and presidents for life in keeping the lid on with brutal force, but only at the price of forcing political opposition into the radical Islamic camp.

Keeping the lid on also meant stifling the emergence of democracy and human rights in the Arab world. Secular parties, other than the official party, were empty shells created to give the impression of democracy. In reality, all groups and associations not controlled by the ruling party were crushed. As a result, radical Islamic currents became the only effective opposition groups to which people could turn. Islam was too much a part of the Arab psyche to be crushed.

It all seemed so logical at the time, and American lawmakers nodded in agreement as Hosni Mubarak explained to the U.S. Congress that

> *The country was under pressure for years and years, and when you open the gate for freedom, you will find many terrible things taking place.... We have to give a gradual dose so people can swallow it and understand (New York Times, October 12, 1993, A3).*

That may be true, but there were no gradual doses of freedom in the Arab world for people to swallow. Keeping the lid on doesn't lead to democracy. It leads to extremism and violence.

However, all was not in vain. The idea of democracy and popular rule, however vague, did become rooted in the Arab psyche. Even the Saudis would get around to holding local elections some thirty years down the road, but only on an erratic basis.

Inequality and Equity

In contrast to democracy, progress in the area of equality was not a farce. The progressive states did launch massive literacy programs and initiated vigorous programs to bring women into the labor force. Industrialization required no less, and gender equality was actively pursued in the government-controlled media of the progressive states.

One of the most moving films that I have ever seen was an Egyptian portrayal of a mother holding her daughter while the girl's brother beat her. The girl's sin was kissing an air force officer. It was shocking to me, but I'm not sure that it was shocking to less-enlightened Egyptians. Nevertheless, this and similar films ignited a sexual revolution in the progressive states. The tribal kings would have none of it.

This didn't mean that women were equal to men in the progressive states, but they did flock to educational institutions and defended their new rights with vigor. Even the Saudis eventually got around to mass education programs. Much to the Saudi's dismay, educated women are now a major force in the tribal kingdom's social revolution.

The socialist ideology of the progressives also championed economic equity, and most people were spared from the starvation of eras past. The progressive states, however, were too poor to support more than a rudimentary welfare system. They also lacked bureaucracies capable of distributing their meager resources in an efficient manner.

Most people may have survived, but those with connections got most of what there was to get.

Saudi Arabia and the other oil monarchies were flush with money, at least some of which trickled down to the masses as a reward for their quiescence. The Saudi budget remained a family affair, so nobody knew how much money the kingdom had or how much remained in the hands of the senior princes. Transparent, it wasn't.

Stagnation Versus Growth

For all of their failures, the modernizing leaders of the era of independence dragged the Arab world into the modern era. Progress was made, but it was slow and shallow. As Sadiq Azm lamented in his *Self Criticism after the Defeat*, the Arabs had experienced a political revolution, but not a social revolution (Azm, 1979). People still clung to their faith and families for support, and the fox ruled.

The oil states didn't develop economically. They merely became consummate consumers, the likes of which the world had never seen. They spent, but they didn't produce.

In reality, both the progressive states and the tribal monarchies had adopted flawed economic systems. The progressive states placed their hopes on socialist economic systems that wasted resources while destroying initiative and individual effort. The oil monarchies simply lived off of their oil revenues. Foreigners drilled the oil, refined the oil, and marketed the oil. The Saudis and others spent their fabulous wealth on foreign goods, arms included, and hired foreigners to manage their affairs. As a result, the oil Arabs were not in control of their own economic system.

CHAPTER 6

ISLAMIC RESURGENCE AND THE ARAB PSYCHE

W ho was to fill the psychological void left by the Arab defeat in the Six Day War? The answer was as simple as it was seductive. "God is the solution." It was broadcast from minarets, scribbled on walls, whispered on crowed busses, and screamed on banned cassette tapes that passed from hand to hand. Almost overnight, Islamic fundamentalism had become the dominant ideology of the Arab world. It was everywhere, and it was relentless.

Sadat's unleashing of the fundamentalist currents in the early 1970s had been nourished by the U.S. as a counterforce to the spread of Arab nationalism and communism in the region. It was a stunned America, accordingly, that struggled to come to grips with the Ayatollah Khomeini's overthrow of the Shah of Iran in 1979. How was it possible for a bunch of bearded mullahs to overthrow America's major ally in the Muslim world, not to mention an ally who claimed to have the fifth most powerful army in the world? It would be but the first of America's frustrations in the three decades that followed. The era of Islamic resurgence that began with Khomeini's overthrow of the shah in 1979 would reach its crescendo with bin-Laden's 2001 attacks on the United States.

Unlike Americans, the Arab psyche was not bewildered by the shah's fall. There was but one explanation. It had been the will of God. If the

Mahdi hadn't arrived to answer their prayers, the signs of his coming were irrefutable. The role of Muslims was to prepare the way. For the doubters, there was the flawed American attempt to rescue its hostages from Tehran. No sooner were the U.S. helicopters air born than a mystical force blew sand into their engines, and they came tumbling down like the walls of Jericho. The age of miracles hadn't passed, at least not for the much battered Arab psyche.

Not all Arabs and Muslims saw the fall of the shah as the will of God, but the view was prevalent. The Arab psyche, as we have seen, was mystical and inclined to search for otherworldly solutions for its woes. This was certainly the case after the failure of the Arab world's brief experiment with secular nationalism and its devastating defeat in the 1967 Arab-Israeli War.

American experts had long noted the decay of the shah's regime, but none had predicted its collapse in the face of a mass uprising fueled by aging clerics. When reality set in, the same experts predicted that the populist revolution would be short lived. The mullahs, in their view, could revolt, but they couldn't rule.

Again, the experts were mistaken. The Ayatollah Khomeini launched an Islamic revolution that, he vowed, would sweep the West from the lands of Islam. Sunni or Shia, it made no difference. Iran, with its arms and oil wealth, would help all who wanted to join the cause.

Things had changed, but it would take a long time for American policymakers to adjust to the new realities of the Arab world and its Muslim surroundings. Perhaps that is because they focused on the realities on the ground rather than on the realities in the mind.

THE ISLAMIC MOVEMENT

This chapter focuses on the new realities that the Islamic resurgence created in the Arab world and its Muslim environs. It is impossible to limit the discussion to Arabs alone, for the Islamic resurgence transcended national and ethnic borders. It also transcended the sectarian conflicts that had long divided Sunni and Shia. All remained part of the picture, but all were muted by the surge of religious emotion sweeping the Islamic world. Nationalism had failed. Now it was Islam's turn.

The term "Islamic movement" evolved in the Arab media as a convenient way to refer to the total mass of individuals who sought a stronger role for religious morality in the social and political life of their countries. Arab scholars preferred the term "political Islam," but it came down to the same thing. Whatever you called it, a growing number of Muslims were intent on achieving a more Islamic state by political means. Collectively, their numbers were staggering.

American commentators merely referred to the Islamic movement as "Muslim fundamentalism," a term that reflected the similarities between Protestant and Muslim revivalism. Both advocated a stronger role for religious morality in social and political life. The Islamic movement, however, was this and much more. While many members of the Islamic movement would be content with greater morality in government, others demanded nothing less than an Islamic government that ruled on the basis of Islamic law.

The Arab press solved the matter by using "fundamentalist" interchangeably with "Islamic movement" and "political Islam." People had a vague idea of what they were talking about, but that was about it.

It was all very ambiguous and caused American policymakers a great deal of frustration. How were they to cope with the Islamic resurgence sweeping the Arab world without a clear idea of the menace they were facing?

The Arab psyche was less concerned. Ambiguity was its forte, and it was far more adept at reading between the lines than Western analysts.

A brief guide to the Islamic movement follows, but be warned. The lines between the different components of the Islamic movement are blurred and shifting. Other words, such as "Islamists," keep being added to the debate, but only serve to make things even more confusing. The discussion moves from the most extreme elements of the Islamic movement to the most benign.

Radical Islamic Extremists: The Salafis and the Jihadists

Literally translated, "salafi" means followers of the ancestors or founding fathers. The Salafis view themselves as followers of the Prophet Mohammed, the founding father of Islam. As the goal of the Prophet Mohammed was to establish a moral society in the corrupt environs of early Arabia, the Salafis are intent on establishing a moral society in the corrupt environs of the modern era. Their logic is simple. Pure societies produce pure minds.

The Salafis stress the proposition that man was born in sin and cannot, of his own will, win the battle against the devil. Society's role is to enable people to achieve paradise by eliminating temptation and forcing them to comply with God's will as outlined in the Islamic scriptures. The Salafis' model of a moral society is that of the Prophet Mohammed's rule in seventh-century Arabia.

A living model of Salafi rule in the modern era is that of Taliban rule in Afghanistan following the withdrawal of Soviet troops around 1980, the beginning of the era of Islamic resurgence. "Taliban" is the Arabic word for students. The Taliban who seized power in Afghanistan were students in a seminary of the Deobandi doctrine of Islam that shares much in common with the Wahabi doctrine of Saudi Arabia. It was these well-organized zealots who provided an element of stability in broad areas of Afghanistan torn by civil war. Girls' schools were closed, full veiling was required, music was banned, and all vestiges of Western influence was obliterated. Even soccer games were frowned upon. It was Taliban-controlled Afghanistan that sheltered bin-Laden as he plotted his 2001 attacks on the United States.

The most deadly of the Salafis are the jihadists who believe that modern Arab societies are beyond reform and must be purified by force. Bin-Laden's al-Qaeda organization exemplifies the jihadist passion for purification by violence. In his view, all threats to the creation of a pure society had to be destroyed. This included secular governments in the Arab world. It also included Western countries that spewed secularism, greed, and lust into the Muslim world.

Not all Salafis were wedded to violence. Some Salafis, for example, built pure communities in the desert, far removed from the immorality of modern life. The Wahabi doctrine of Saudi Arabia is a Salafis doctrine, albeit one softened by efforts to maintain social purity in an environment of phenomenal wealth. Movies and the mixing of sexes are banned in Saudi Arabia, but Europe and Beirut beckon.

Radical Moderates

Next in line came groups such as the Muslim Brotherhood and Hizbullah. The Muslim Brotherhood was a Sunni organization headquartered in

Egypt, while Hizbullah, the "Party of God," operated in Lebanon and other Arab countries with large Shia populations. Both vowed to create a modern Islamic state by political and social means, including violence if need be. I refer to them as radical moderates because they were willing to pursue their radical goal of an Islamic state by moderate means if possible. The details remained sketchy, but both blended the benefits of modern science with Islamic morality. Both were also well organized, possessed a military capacity, and provided a vast array of social services to the poor. Were they democratic? The Muslim Brotherhood's answer was suitably ambivalent.

> This depends on your definition of democracy. If democracy means that people decide who leads them, the Ikwan [Muslim Brotherhood] accept it. If it means that people can change the laws of Allah and follow what they wish to follow, then it is not acceptable.... Ikwan accept personal freedom within the limits of Islam. However, if by personal freedom you mean that Muslim women can wear shorts or Muslim men can do Haram [forbidden] stuff, then the Ikwan do not approve of that (Muslim Brotherhood, Homepage).

Both the Muslim Brotherhood and Hizbullah operated within the context of Islamic law and did not excommunicate Muslims by declaring them to be nonbelievers. That was God's call and not their own. Both, however, called for enforcement of Islamic morality and dedicated themselves to fighting the external enemies of Islam, the most visible and emotionally sensitive of which was Israel.

Arabic satellite channels such as Al Jazeera and Al Arabia use the word "Islamists" to refer to all radical Islamic groups intent on replacing the established order with an Islamic state, by fair means or foul. Islamists, as they use the term, include the ultraradical Salafis as well as radical moderates such as the Muslim Brotherhood, Hizbullah, and Hamas, the Palestinian offshoot of the Muslim Brotherhood.

Islamic Democratic Parties

After the radical-moderates come a variety of Muslim political parties that denounced extremism and vowed to provide a normal economic and social life within an Islamic framework. The details of their program remained sketchy, but they claimed to be no different than the Christian

Democratic Party in Europe. Their opponents accused them of being a seductive front for the Muslim Brotherhood and similar groups. The argument was moot, because none were allowed to exist for more than a few months before the tyrants of their respective countries crushed them. These parties are now coming to the fore in the Arab world and are clearly part of the Islamic movement.

Establishment Islam

The tyrants of the era attempted to dull the zeal of the Islamic movement by having government-appointed religious leaders sing their praises and testify to their piety. The religious establishment generally consisted of a grand mufti (chief religious judge), minister of wafqs (religious endowments), and the rectors of Islamic universities, such as al-Azhar in Egypt, the oldest of the Muslim institutions of higher learning. "Establishment Islam," as the government-owned religious elite were referred to in the vernacular, also included the clergy that controlled the elegant mosques built by Muslim tyrants as a symbol of their piety.

The message of establishment Islam, then as now, was one of passivity and submission to the will of their leaders, regardless of how oppressive and tyrannical they might be. God, so their message went, had put their leaders in power for a purpose, and it was he who would judge them when their time came. In the meantime, Muslims were not to rebel.

Was establishment Islam part of the Islamic movement? That depends on what country you are in and whom you ask. Radical currents, while muted, have always been present within establishment Islam. Many among the ranks of the lower clergy used the intricacies of the Arab language to conform to the letter of the law while subverting it with intonations and the use of words with flexible meanings. Remember, intonations can be more meaningful than words in the Arabic language, and the Arab psyche was most adept at reading between the lines. You may want to think of these radical currents as a fifth column lurking within the ranks of the secular-controlled religious establishment. They were part of the Islamic movement during the era of Islamic resurgence and exploded into a dynamic force during the era of rage and chaos.

The role of establishment Islam in Saudi Arabia and other kingdoms, by contrast, was to keep their countries from evolving into a more liberal and tolerant vision of Islam. Creeping secularism was a constant threat in the oil-rich kingdoms, all of whom were beholden to the U.S., the great Satan. Rather than subverting the monarchies, the role of establishment Islam in Saudi Arabia and the other kingdoms was to hold the feet of tribal kings to the fire of faith. They were part of the Islamic movement.

Sufis

The Sufis, in sharp contrast to the Salafis, focus on achieving a true Islamic society by building pure minds. Heaven, in their view, comes from oneness with God and not from forced conformity to politically imposed restrictions. To the contrary, the human environment is irrelevant to those who have found unity with God, a euphoric state that can only be acquired through faith and following the path outlined by a rightly guided leader or guru who possesses the gift of baraka (grace).

The search for purity and oneness with God had led the Sufis along strange paths, including mysticism, reliance on questionable sayings of the Prophet Mohammed, and the worship of holy men and their tombs. There is not one Sufi way, but hundreds.

Were Sufis part of the Islamic movement? Yes and no. Yes in the sense that Sufis are devout Muslims who aspire toward a pure Islamic state based on oneness with God. Indeed, there could be no purer Islamic state than one in which all people had achieved oneness with God.

They were not part of the Islamic movement in terms of political activism designed to transform the countries of the Arab world into Islamic caliphates, patterned on the Prophet Mohammed's rule in early Arabia. Some were even hostile to such efforts.

All of the visions of Islam surveyed above are evolving. Both the Salafis and the Sufis are now establishing political parties to market their wares. Sheikh Yousef Qaradawi, the dean of Islamic philosophers and television preachers, called for making Salafis Sufis, and Sufis Salafis. As o explains,

The Sufi takes from the discipline of Salafis in not following fabricated Hadith, polytheist rites, and tomb-side rites, and we want the Salafis

to take from the Sufi tenderness, spirituality, and piousness. From this mixture we get the required Muslim (Qaradawi, 2010).

THE ENVIRONMENT OF ISLAMIC RESURGENCE

The struggle to the death between the jihadists and the ruling tyrants gained momentum throughout the era of Islamic resurgence. By 1993, Egypt's minister of the interior, the country's top cop, was forced to declare, "We are at war, people will have to die on both sides" (*New York Times*, November 28, 1993, A3). Algeria, Lebanon, the Sudan, and Iraq were already at war with radical Islamic currents in one guise or another. Egypt, often referred to as the mother of the Arabs, was the dominant power and pacesetter in the Arab world. If Egypt fell to the jihadists, it would be but a matter of time before the remainder of the Arab world followed suit. Scary stuff, indeed, for the vast majority of people just trying to get on with their lives.

The struggle to the death between the tyrants and the jihadists touched every dimension of political, economic, and social life in the Arab world. Politics became a deadly game, as security services had a license to kill and targeted jihadists and advocates of democracy with equal zeal. Both had become sworn enemies of the tyrants. Fear immobilized bureaucracies, and the quality of services, always dismal, declined further.

The jihadists, for their part, had seized control of urban slums and rural villages in Egypt, Algeria, the Sudan, and Lebanon. All became launching sites for terror.

The economic picture was equally bleak, as fear and political instability stifled economic growth and sent national debts soaring. The tyrants in Egypt, Algeria, and other poor states sank so far into the red that they could only keep afloat with massive loans from the U.S. and the EU. The U.S. complied, but only on the condition that its pet tyrants rationalize their economies by laying off excess government employees, the majority of the workforce, and cutting subsidies on food and other necessities. It made sense to Western economists attempting to force the Arabs into a global free market, but not to the millions of poor Arabs who faced unemployment and a loss of the state subsidies upon which their survival depended.

It was the same in the social sphere, as displays of Islamic piety became acceptable. They were mandatory in the Arab kingdoms. The eyes of neighbors continued to peer. So did the eyes of the jihadists and the security forces.

The regional and international environments were equally lethal, as the Sudan slipped under Islamic control midway during the era of Islamic resurgence. The Sudan became a center for funneling arms and money from Iran and Saudi Arabia to jihadist groups throughout the Arab world. Bin-Laden was a key player in this process.

The U.S. was slow to react to the surge of Islamic emotions and soon suffered a series of terrorist attacks against American targets. In 1983, seventeen American lives were lost when a truck loaded with explosives leveled the U.S. embassy in Beirut. A marine barracks followed suit a few months later, with the loss of 214 American military personnel. Both were assumed to be the work of Iranian-sponsored terrorist groups, and the U.S. withdrew its troops from a war-torn Lebanon.

In 1993, Jihadist attacks forced U.S. military troops to withdraw from Somalia, another country consumed by civil war. The same year witnessed the first jihadist attack on the World Trade Center in New York. Casualties were light, but the warning was not heeded. In 1995, the battle shifted to Saudi Arabia when jihadists attacked a Saudi National Guard barracks in Riyadh. Five Americans were killed and scores wounded. A few months later, the target was the Khobar Towers, a U.S. Marine facility in the Saudi city of Dhahran. Two hundred and forty-one Americans were killed. The bombing of U.S. embassies in Tanzania and Kenya followed in 1998. Both were attributed to a global jihadist network.

The chain of U.S. defeats outlined above altered the struggle between the jihadists and the U.S. in two key ways. First, jihadist strategists became confident that they could force the U.S. to retreat from the Muslim world by the use of sustained violence. Anti-U.S. violence increased accordingly. Second, the jihadists had made it known to one and all that they could strike anywhere in the world, the U.S. included. The Arab psyche took note.

The Muslim Brotherhood bided its time while it waited for the tyrants, the jihadists, and the U.S. to destroy each other. The tyrants and the jihadists would be history, and the U.S. would be driven from the region. Then, and only then, in their view, would the path be clear for the Muslim Brotherhood to establish a moderate Islamic state strengthened by the technology of the modern world. In the meantime, the Muslim Brotherhood and Hizbullah strengthened their bases of popular support by providing for the needs of the poor. In the process, they also established a reputation for efficiency and honesty, something that the tyrants had never been able to do.

FORGING AN ARABO-ISLAMIC PSYCHE

So there you have the environment in which the Arab psyche sought its fortune during the era of resurgent Islam. On one side stood the corrupt and oppressive dictators who ruled by force with the support of the United States. On the other was a much fragmented but increasingly vibrant Islamic movement. Who would win? The Islamic movement had the momentum, but it was too close to call. Situations had to be assessed and strategies plotted, not once but continuously.

The Arabo-Islamic Identity
Many Arab writers use the term "Arabo-Islamic psyche" to stress the distinction between Muslim Arabs and Christian Arabs. It is also used to stress the distinction between Arab Muslims and non-Arab Muslims. The three identities form overlapping circles, yet each remains separate and distinct from the others.

This distinction came to the fore during the era of Islamic resurgence when the close cooperation between Christians and Muslims in forging an Arab nationalist movement dissolved into bitter conflict as Christians recoiled at the prospect of being forced to live under Islamic rule.

Hostile relations between the Arabs and Iran, by contrast, softened as many Arab Muslims began to seek greater Muslim cooperation within the region. Although he was an Iranian Shia, the inspirational impact of the Ayatollah Khomeini on Arab Muslims was profound. Shia Arabs were the most deeply moved by Khomeini's rise to glory, but even Sunni Muslims were moved by his baraka.

Some Arab scholars even suggested that Islam had become the new beacon of Arabism, much as it had been during the era of Islamic expansion. Arabs, so the argument went, were the soul of Islam and indivisible from Islam. Islamic victories were Arab victories, whether they were achieved by Arabs or by Iranians such as the Ayatollah Khomeini. Arabs remained the chosen people of God because He had selected an Arab to be his final messenger. It would be Islam, accordingly, that provided the ultimate path to a true Arab revival. In this view, there could be no Arab revival without Islam and no Islamic revival without the Arabs (Shahrour, 1994).

This said, all three psyches continued to be fragmented by kinship identities, sectarian identities, and increasingly, by narrow country identities. One might question, for example, whether Iran's Islamic revolution was really an Islamic revolution or whether it was a Shia revolution, or for that matter, an expression of Iranian nationalism? Iran's Islamic revolution seemed to incorporate all three identities.

Particularly confusing for Arab Muslims was the need to choose their preferred interpretation of how best to serve God. Reduced to simplest terms, a jihadist identity inclined people toward violence, while those who identified with the Muslim Brotherhood inclined toward the patient pursuit of an Islamic state. Muslims who identified with establishment religion were passive, while Sufis were ethereal. These were major differences when it came to the politics of the era. They still are.

The Motivations of the Islamic Resurgence

People wanted pretty much what they always wanted during the era of Islamic resurgence, and more. Most people continued to want the higher quality of material life that had been promised by Nasser and the other progressive leaders. They also wanted the advantages of modernity in a reasonably moral environment that respected Arab and Muslim traditions. This didn't mean jihadism, but it did mean an end to oppression, cults of personality, corruption, and incompetence.

Saudi Arabia became a model for the millions of poor Arabs who flocked to the oil kingdoms to make their fortune. The Saudis had it all: faith, luxury, and power. In the minds of many poor Arabs, the wealth of the Saudis had been God's reward for living an Islamic life. Perhaps He would do the same for their countries if they followed the path of true

Islam (Habib, 1989). Or as a secular Muslim Arab friend said at the time, "We have tried everything else to ease our despair. Why not try Islam?"

Why not, indeed. The Arabo-Islamic psyche had never made the sharp divide between religion and state so common in the West. If Islam could provide a better way of life in a moral environment, so much the better.

This attitude was prevalent throughout the region and posed a daunting challenge to the Ayatollah Khomeini in his efforts to transform Iran into a living model of Islamic rule. Faith had conquered the shah and kept the Americans at bay, but could a vision of Islam that looked to the past meet the needs and wants of Muslims in the modern era?

Much like Nasser, the Ayatollah Khomeini was a profoundly charismatic individual. Khomeini, however, was that and more. Nasser had accomplished miraculous feats and was followed as a hero. Speculation that he was the reincarnation of the long-awaited Mahdi was rampant, but that was largely wishful thinking. Not so with the Ayatollah Khomeini, a gifted Islamic scholar who was considered by his followers to be the earthly agent of the Hidden Imam. There were some people who believed that he was the Hidden Imam. The ayatollah denied such assertions, but made it clear that he had been sent by the Hidden Imam to prepare the way for the Mahdi's return by cleansing sin and corruption from the earth. In Shia practice, it was the obligation of the followers of an ayatollah to emulate his behavior, and Khomeini's followers were legion.

Conscience and Superego

At least among Shia, this suggests that the Ayatollah Khomeini had become a conscience or superego for those who identified with him. He was more than a hero. He was a divinely inspired source of emulation. His example promised heaven, and deviation from his example promised hell. If he had not become the superego of those who identified with him, what explains the sacrifice of the Basiji (irregular volunteer fighters) in Iran's decade-long war with Iraq? The Basiji could

> be identified by his tattered leftover uniform and mismatched boots (often picked up on the battlefield), the bright red or yellow headband stretched across his brow declaring God's or Khomeini's greatness, and the large, imitation brass key, the key to paradise, that hung

around his neck. The Basijis gained fame as human minesweepers.... Boys as young as twelve, shaped by the fanaticism of the revolution, walked across minefields to clear the way for the advancing...army (Mackey, 1996, 323).

There is no doubt that Khomeini's mystical hold over his followers could mobilize them to fight to the death for the sake of Islam. The tricky question was, could the moral conscience inflamed in Iranians and Arab Shia by the Ayatollah Khomeini motivate them to put aside their appetites and petty squabbles for the sake of transforming Iran and the Arab world into an Islamic paradise? Or conversely, would they ignore their conscience and go about their affairs, much as they always had, while waiting for their hero-cum-Mahdi to banish sin and want from the world with a wave of the hand?

I recall reading a bitter statement by Ayatollah Khomeini chastising Iranians for grumbling about disruptions in utility services caused by the revolution and his war in Iraq. The exact words elude me, but the basic messages was, "If you put material concerns above serving God, why did you vote for me? The Islamic revolution is about God, not about personal comfort."

The above discussion focuses on Iranians and Shia Arabs because they were the most ardent supporters of Khomeini and his Islamic revolution. The pattern, however, follows earlier discussions of the Arab psyche in which conscience was an important motivator in seeking salvation, but gave way to a family-based conscience in dealings with the government and other people.

The Sunni rejected notions of a Hidden Imam and were less inclined than the Shia to accept Khomeini as a conscience or moral guide. Few Sunni, however, doubted that Khomeini possessed mystical powers. This didn't mean that they had lost faith in a Sunni savior on par with the Ayatollah Khomeini.

The Emotions of the Islamic Resurgence

The dominant emotional triggers that tormented the Arab psyche during the era of Islamic resurgence were anxiety and fear. It couldn't be otherwise, as Arabs of the era struggled with the prospect of an Islamic revolution sweeping all before it, as it had in Iran. Even scarier was the prospect of a battle to the death between the jihadist fanatics and the deeply entrenched dictators supported by the United States. Neither side was willing to give quarter to the poor souls caught in the crossfire of their deadly struggle. Neither seemed to care. It was time to place bets, but prediction was impossible for all concerned, including the tyrants and the United States.

Questions about which current of the Islamic movement would dominate also loomed. The more flexible doctrine of the Muslim Brotherhood could be negotiated, but not the fanaticism of jihadists intent on the violent cleansing of societies irreparably scarred by the modernity of the era of independence. Such worries were less frequent in Saudi Arabia, where Wahabi doctrines shared much in common with the world view of the jihadists.

Underscoring anxieties over the future course of the Arab world was the ever-present fear of chaos. Civil war raged in Lebanon, Algeria, and the Sudan, and it loomed in Egypt and elsewhere. Even the jihadists, in the eyes of many, were preferable to total lawlessness. It was this emotion that fueled the dominance of the Taliban jihadists in Afghanistan.

Fear of peering eyes and wagging tongues also took on a new intensity, for it could be they that led the jihadists and the security agencies to their next victims. Both assumed the worst and acted accordingly.

For the legions of government employees, the mundane fears of betrayal by colleagues and associates continued to haunt, while youth feared unemployment and a life destitute of marriage. Such fears were particularly bitter among young girls who faced the specter of spinsterhood. The Lebanese civil war, of itself, had virtually eliminated more than a generation of eligible husbands, a situation that currently exists in Iraq.

Intense feelings of frustration and despair joined fear and anxiety in the litany of emotions that shaped the era. Both soared as welfare programs initiated by the modernizers were neglected by the heirs of Nasser, who were minimally concerned about social and economic equality. Rather, inspired by American faith in free-market capitalism, they gutted subsidies and welfare programs and allowed the masses to go into an economic free fall. American economists acknowledged that there would be a period of adjustment, but they oozed confidence that things would work out for the best as money wasted on welfare subsidies gave way to productive investment.

It was a great theory, but the people who rode the stinking buses of Cairo and other human conglomerations, didn't seem to understand. Or maybe they did. Little of the wealth generated by privatization and other World Bank reforms pushed by the U.S. found its way into productive investments. Rather, it lined the pockets of the ruling elite and swelled their foreign bank accounts. If you have any doubt in the matter, check the billions of dollars that the dictators had amassed in foreign bank accounts before being swept away by the revolutions of rage in 2011.

The masses were angry, but it was anger muted by the emotions of resignation and hopelessness. Everything, or so it seemed, was beyond their control. The parallel emotions of hate and revenge simmered beneath the smiling faces.

Invariably, the emotions of despair and helplessness gave way to a longing for a new superhero graced with the mystical powers to right all wrongs. As in the case of Nasser, it was this longing that transformed the Ayatollah Khomeini into the superhero of the Islamic movement. God was the solution, and an Islamic state governed by Islamic principles would be both equitable and just, much as it was during the golden days of the Prophet Mohammed.

It was this vision that gave the dispossessed hope and filled them with a vicarious thrill of victory as Khomeini soared from victory to victory. A new Sunni hero also beaconed. His pictures adorned the mosques of Saudi Arabia and the Gulf. His name was Osama bin-Laden, the Arab mastermind of the Soviet defeat in Afghanistan.

The prevailing emotions among those who identified with the Ayatollah Khomeini and bin-Laden were righteousness, pride, and a feeling of superiority. It was as if they had answered the call of God and achieved salvation. Many appeared to feel a sense of euphoria that had been reserved for the Sufis. They may not have achieved a Sufi oneness with God, but there was a new confidence that God had not forgotten Arabs and Muslims who sought his grace. Potent stuff, indeed.

Distortions in the Reasoning Process

Was it possible for the Arab psyche to make rational decisions in the emotional pressure cooker described above? Clearly, the cards were stacked against it. Information poured in from all sides, much of it confusing and highly politicized. Even keeping track of what was going on was difficult, let alone separating myth from reality.

Then, add the faith-versus-science debate to the reasoning process. Faith won the day, as few people could evaluate the events swirling around them without reference to God. How could they when faith was so deeply imbedded in the Arab psyche? (Zakriya, 1998).

Defense mechanisms were also in full swing, not the least of which was identification. Khomeini had become the new superhero, and his word was tantamount to law for those who gained a sense of power and redemption by identifying with him as the agent of God. This practice was particularly intense among the Shia, but Sunni, too, recognized him as the new man of destiny. They rejoiced in his victories over the United States at the same time that they feared the spread of the Shia doctrine.

Regression, as a psychological term, refers to individuals who, troubled by the strain of the present, revert to behaviors associated with earlier and happier times, usually in their childhood. In the case of the Arab psyche, the concept of regression seems to fit the longing of more extreme Muslims for the peace and serenity of the days of the Prophet. This also involved a great deal of fantasizing, but so be it. The era of Islamic resurgence was shaped by extremist dream merchants, who played upon the despair and frustrations of the masses and by giving hope to desperate souls without hope. "God is the solution," said it all.

Naysayers did not deter those who dreamed of a return to paradise past. Doubters became enemies of Islam, and they were attacked without mercy. This would seem to have violated Islamic law, but violence against secular Muslims was rationalized by decreeing that they had forfeited their claim to Islamic compassion by serving the devil. Death was their justice. As for the innocents, their sacrifice had assured them a place in heaven.

The rationalization process, according to Jabri, a leading student of the Arab psyche, was strengthened by the tendency of the Arab psyche to see the parts rather than the whole. For those intent on a return to the past, the realities of the present were simply stuffed into a separate mental compartment and didn't influence the reasoning process. Their total attention was focused on the establishment of an Islamic state. The details would be sorted out with time.

Finally, add the list of common Arab psychological traits to the discussion. Authoritarianism, hero worship, the longing for a strong leader, and mysticism were all rooted in the tribal era and persisted over the course of the centuries. They had helped propel Nasser into a superhero, and they now did the same for the Ayatollah Khomeini and bin-Laden.

Arabic as the Language of the Islamic Revival

Jabri's assertion that pronunciation in the Arabic language tends to take on a meaning of its own has already been noted. What you see and what you hear are often two different things.

In dealing with the era of the Islamic resurgence, Jabri takes his argument one step farther. The emotional power of pronunciation in the Arabic language, he suggests, enabled Salafi preachers to use their verbal skills to convince people that their extremist version of God's word was the correct version, even though it contradicted the literal meaning of the Koran.

Once a Muslim orator had used the power of pronunciation to convince believers that he had the true interpretation of God's will, according to Jabri, the psychological mechanisms discussed above kicked in, and the orator became an authority figure to be followed and emulated. Guilt didn't enter the picture because the supplicant was following the true word of God (Jabri, 2007).

This, however, was only part of the linguistic picture during the era of Islamic resurgence. The use of terms such as "Islamist" in the secular press, for example, was often an attempt to scare people away from the Muslim Brotherhood by tarring them with the brush of jihadist violence. All Islamists, regardless of their stripe, if one relied on popular magazines such as *Rose al-Youssef,* were intent on returning Muslims to the age of darkness.

Roadmaps and Poker in the Era of Islamic Resurgence

As a general rule, the mental roadmaps that emerged during the era of Islamic resurgence encouraged the Arab masses to cling to whatever elements of stability existed in their lives. There wasn't one roadmap, but several, depending upon whether you were the rulers or the ruled. There was also a separate roadmap for those who basked in the oil wealth of the Gulf and another for the dispossessed of Cairo and Algiers. The principle was the same. Cling to what you have while clutching opportunities to escape from the looming storm.

For many, perhaps most, the roadmap pointed to support for a more religious state governed by Islamic principles of equality and justice. There appeared to be few alternatives, other than migration to the slums of Europe in hopes of building a new life in an environment of stability. For some it meant both.

Even then, it wasn't a clear roadmap. The Islamic movement, while pointing toward a more religious state, was a hodgepodge of conflicting and ever-shifting ideas on how best to attain an Islamic state or what that state should look like. The prevailing roadmaps of the era also urged prayer for the appearance of a divinely guided leader.

Clear roadmap or not, the Arab psyche in the era of Islamic resurgence had to place its bets. The stakes had never been higher or more dangerous. For the dispossessed, the present was intolerable, but the thought of chaos and retribution was terrifying. For the rulers and their supporters, the fear of sedition and rebellion became ever more frightening as images of the Ayatollah Khomeini and bin-Laden haunted their dreams. If the U.S. couldn't save the Shah of Iran, its favorite puppet, how could it save the Saudis?

HOW ARABS TENDED TO COPE WITH THE ERA OF ISLAMIC RESURGENCE

How, then, did the Arab psyche's struggle to navigate its tumultuous environment translate into the way the people of the era actually behaved? The pot was boiling, but the security forces and the jihadists had become ever more dangerous. As a result, what the Arab psyche yearned to do wasn't always what it did.

The lines between political, social, and economic behavior continued to be blurred during the era of Islamic resurgence. Everything was political in one way or another, not the least of which was religion. There was also a tremendous amount of variation in the way people behaved during the era, but the behavior patterns discussed below were sufficiently prevalent to have a major impact on Arab politics and American frustrations.

Political Behavior

Political behavior during the era of Islamic resurgence ran the gamut from expressions of nationalism to expressions of mass discontent. All were colored by the religious emotions that surged throughout the era.

Nationalism Versus Religiosity

Displays of Arab nationalism didn't disappear during the era of Islamic resurgence, but they were eclipsed by the surge of religious emotion that became a rush with the Ayatollah Khomeini's overthrow of the Shah of Iran. Shia friends in Lebanon, youth at the time, still recall their frenzied excitement at the Ayatollah's stunning success. The excitement was not theirs alone. Arabs and Muslims everywhere took heart at the miraculous defeat of America's foremost puppet in the region. Their excitement was more than the feel-good effect of a temporary victory over Western domination of the region. It was a sign of revival, of a shift of forces, of hope and empowerment. It was the knowledge that the Arabs and Islam could defeat the West. And finally, it was a stunning rejection of the myth of Arab and Muslim inferiority propagated by the West and Israel (Yassin, 1993).

Local nationalisms remained weak during the era and offered little resistance to the Islamic tide. Indeed, Saudi Arabia and the Gulf states were still struggling to create a sense of local nationalism (Melikian, 1981). This wasn't difficult to understand. How could countries ruled by a tribe attract the loyalty of other tribes when the ruling tribe controlled everything? They could buy their docility, but docility wasn't loyalty. Sectarian differences between the ruling tribe and other tribes didn't help matters.

Displays of Religiosity and Spiritualism

The resurgence that began in the 1970s became a groundswell, as Islamic dress proliferated and Islamic groups of all persuasions entered the political fray. Islamic student groups seized control of the universities, and Islamic candidates swept to victory in professional and labor organizations long dominated by the ruling party. It was also during this period that Islamic financial institutions established themselves as an alternative to Western banking practices. Faith was more than talk. It was also putting your money where your mouth was.

But it was more than that. Leaders throughout the Arab world sensed the dangerous shift in the public mood and put on an Islamic face to avoid its backlash. Egypt and Algeria toyed with rigged elections, but many were cancelled to avoid the wrath of the Muslim Brotherhood and other Islamic groups. The Saudi king, always anxious to display his religious credentials, increased his support for the extremist Wahabi doctrine throughout the Islamic world. Just to be on the safe side, he changed his title from "His Majesty," to "His Majesty, the Protector of the Two Holy Shrines" (Mecca and Medina). Interestingly, he didn't add Jerusalem, the third of Islam's holiest shrines, to the list.

Arab leaders struggled to contain the Islamic tide, but to no avail. No segment of society was immune to the surge of religious emotion sweeping the Islamic world. Some observers equated it to a massive locomotive threatening to sweep all before it as it careened through the deserts and valleys of the Arab world and the regions beyond (James Bill, personal communication).

Was this hyperbole? No, not at all. The Islamic movement didn't sweep all before it, but there wasn't much left behind. The main problem, as in most mass movements, was the difficulty in giving focus to an emotional surge that was unified only by a simple if seductive slogan. "God is the solution." Seductive, indeed, but nagging questions remained. How best to serve God, and which of the diverse currents of the Islamic movement was to be in charge?

Other problems also divided Islamic emotions, not the least of which were sectarian conflicts and the uncertain relationship between Islamic groups and the powerful warlords (zaim) who dominated local politics throughout much of the Arab world. Local warlords, including tribal leaders, cooperated with the Islamic extremists when it suited their purposes and attempted to crush them when it didn't.

It was much the same at the regional level. Iran's Islamic revolution fueled extremist activities throughout the Middle East, but Arab and Sunni hostility toward Iran, the powerbase of Shia Islam, made cooperation difficult. Iranian money was welcome among Sunni Arabs, the vast majority of Arab Muslims, but the seductive mysticism of Shia theology was not.

My own research, as well as election results and public-opinion surveys, suggest that the intensity of support for an Islamic presence in politics followed the standard bell-shaped curve sketched in Figure 6-1. These figures are from the more westernized countries such as Egypt, Algeria, and Lebanon. Reliable data from Saudi Arabia, Yemen, and other totally closed societies was not available.

The least supportive of an Islamic state were the secular Muslims who preferred a separation of religion and politics. This didn't mean that they weren't religious, but merely that they viewed religion as a personal matter.

Secular Muslims probably constituted around 20 percent of the population in the more westernized areas of the Arab world and were largely limited to the better educated and middle sectors of society. While giving Islam its due, they weren't anxious to have religious constraints on their Western lifestyles.

Next came the Islamic Democrats who, like the Christian Democratic Party of Europe, acknowledged that religion was part of society and could not be ignored in the democratic process. Islam would have a political voice, but only within a democratic framework in which multiple views were represented. The Islamic Democrats probably represented about 30 percent of the population in the more westernized Arab countries. Again, their numbers predominated among the more westernized segments of the population.

The Islamic Democrats, in turn, gave way to what Americans refer to as the moral majority. The moral majority wanted a strong and pervasive role for Islam in politics, but stopped short of wanting to live in an Islamic theocracy. The moral majority would probably constitute about 30 percent of the populations in the more westernized Arab countries, with heavy representation among the middle and lower classes.

The moral majority, a symbolic term, blended with advocates of enlightened theological rule. The moral majority would almost certainly have voted for the Muslim Brotherhood and Hizbullah in their respective areas, even if it meant the superiority of Islamic law over civil law.

Their numbers fall to the 15 percent range, with heavy representation in the rural and poorer classes.

Finally came the supporters of a hard-line Islamic theocracy based upon the strict enforcement of the Koran and Sunna. They would have voted for the most radical Islamic parties available and supported the establishment of an Islamic state by nondemocratic means, including violence. This didn't mean that all who yearned for a return to the idyllic model of the Prophet's rule were violent, but it did mean that democracy was not high on their priority list. Their numbers probably ranked in the 5 percent range, with heavy representation in the rural and poorer classes.

The actual jihadists were few in number. The CIA estimated that fanatical Muslims constituted no more than about 4 or 5 percent of the world's Muslims. Potential fighters were put at about 120,000 or less than 1 percent of the Muslim population (Gunaratna, 2002, 95). The trouble with these figures was that they didn't include the millions of Arabs of all stripes who passively supported the jihadists in the hopes of toppling the tyrants who had locked them in a state of despair.

The line separating the different visions of Islam's role in politics were blurred and shifted according to the circumstances. The jihadists, for example, had a Robin Hood aura during the early years of the era, but the intensity of their violence against Muslims soon led to a tangible lack of support. Nevertheless, each of the five categories of Arab Muslims preferring a greater role of religion in politics had its own center of gravity.

The figures presented in Table 6.1 continue to be ballpark and suggest that it is doubtful that Islam will ever be able to rule with a single voice. This said, the figures also suggest that parties expressing the Islamic moral majority are likely to control about 30 percent of the seats in parliament if fair elections are held in the Arab world. In the case of Turkey, this was enough to place a moderate Islamic regime in power over a period of several years.

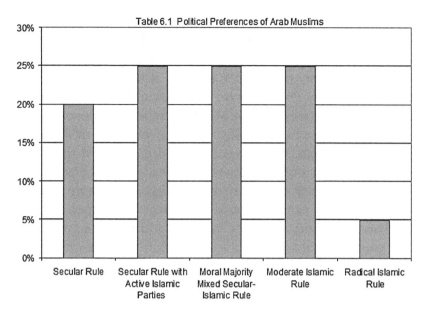

Note: Percentages are based on a variety of research projects, election results, and expert opinion. Most are in general agreement. Election results in elections conducted during the current eras of rage also support these figures.

Searching for a Strong Base of Group Support

As might be expected, the traumatic shift from the chaotic world of the modernizers to the violent world of the jihadists sent people scurrying for an island of stability wherever they could find it.

The family remained the core of the individual's support base, but the need for a patron beyond the family had become ever more urgent. In the rural areas, this meant clinging to tribal attachments or the patronage network of the local zaim. Landowners and generals also gathered the weak under their wings, as did local representatives of the ruling party. Often, they were one and the same.

For those cast from the rural areas into the uncertain world of the city, it was the Muslim Brotherhood and Hizbullah that ministered to their material and spiritual needs (Keilani, 1990; Hamzeh, 2004). The state bureaucracies, as discussed in the last chapter, were too corrupt, self-serving, and incompetent to provide the poor with even a rudimentary level of service.

The jihadists, for their part, were too harassed by the security services to establish sustained welfare networks. They had their own ramshackle mosques in abandoned buildings, but they had become prime targets of the security police. One entered at his own risk.

Both the Muslim Brotherhood and Hizbullah placed special focus on the youth, especially college and high school students, who were the most daring, impressionable, and vocal element of Arab society. In Egypt, for example, it was the Muslim Brotherhood that provided poor students with books, clothes, healthcare, and the tutoring they required to pass their exams. Hizbullah played the same role among Shia in Lebanon and other countries with large Shia populations. Unlike more affluent students, the poor had few clothes, were generally hungry, and couldn't afford to buy the teacher's notes. The rich could, and they passed their exams without undue effort. The word "brotherhood" was not a misnomer, but a conscious effort to stress the family relationship that existed between the Muslim Brotherhood and its members.

The jihadist groups, while often led by fanatical students and intellectuals, recruited most of their foot soldiers from the ghastly slums of the region's exploding cities. Picture, if you will, the youth raised in the shanty towns of Algeria, in which one hundred thousand people were squeezed into some twelve thousand apartments with little in the way of water, sewage treatment, or electricity. Delinquency born of shattered parental authority and promiscuity was the norm. Gangs and crime flourished (Boukra, 2002, 109). According to Algerian police psychologists, many made easy prey for jihadist recruiters who understood their pain.

The jihadists, for their part, were more than a brotherhood. They were a mafia-type family under the strict control of a supreme guide who claimed to be divinely inspired. Beyond that, they offered their recruits a new identity as soldiers of God. Their status soared among the slum dwellers, and many adopted the names of famous heroes and movie stars (Awad, 2003).

The jihadists gave them more than a new identity. They also gave them guns, a license to kill, and a reservation in paradise. The thrill of power and plunder followed, not to mention the venting of pent-up emotions of hate, anger, humiliation, and revenge. It was this package that fueled the wanton and indiscriminate violence of many jihadist groups.

Some of the jihadist groups to emerge in Algeria and elsewhere were little more than street gangs masquerading as angels of God. Others were integrated into mainline jihadist organizations or were dispatched to Afghanistan for advanced training in bin-Laden's al-Qaeda organization. Those who survived often returned to their native countries to start their own jihadist cells (Palmer and Palmer, 2008).

Expressing Loyalty: An Obsession for Control

Issues of loyalty and control were accentuated by the turmoil that assaulted the Arab world during the era of Islamic resurgence. The tribal kings and presidents for life claimed to be loved by their subjects, but their behavior told a different story. Pretenses aside, they worried about the influence of soaring religious emotions on the loyalty of their subjects. The more they worried, the more they became obsessed with controlling everyone and everything that was in their power to control.

The control process began with the leaders of the diverse countries and worked its way down through the lower reaches of society, including the jihadist groups. They may have claimed to be the holiest of the holy, but their perverted views of Islam found little support in either the Koran or the Sunna. No wonder they worried and became obsessed with control.

In the case of Syria, a country plagued by a history of military coups, the Presidential Security Forces consisted of at least four separate intelligence organizations, including Political Security, General Intelligence, Military Intelligence, and Air Force Intelligence (Batatu, 1999). These were followed in order of importance by the Republican Guard, an elite force some ten thousand strong. The Republican Guard was supported by the Presidential Special Forces and other elite military units, albeit with a competing command structure that precluded any one unit from dominating the others. These military units, in turn, were kept in check by the militias and the intelligence organizations of the ruling party (Perthes, 1997). Every unit was watching the others, and all were watching the Syrian population.

All of the key units were commanded by a relative of Hafiz al-Asad, Syria's president for life during the era of Islamic resurgence and beyond. If a reliable relative could not to be found, a trusted friend of the president would do.

As recounted in the preceding chapter, Syrian officials at every level rode herd over their subordinates, demanding their praise and subservience. They also demanded a lion's share of the bribes and benefited from other forms of corruption that gave the security forces a vested interest in keeping the regime in power.

The same pattern was followed in Iraq during the long reign of Saddam Hussein that ended with the U.S. occupation of 2003. When a Kurdish revolt threatened, he gassed them. When the Shia threatened revolt, he assassinated their religious leaders. Shia leaders who cooperated, by contrast, were allowed to establish recruiting centers throughout the country and had free access to the media. They became the dominant voices in the Shia community, and they collected the charitable contributions of the faithful. It was the same with Saddam's treatment of Iraq's tribes. Hostile tribes were starved. Those who supported the regime had utilities, televisions, access to jobs, and the accompanying opportunities for corruption.

The Iraqi security services were similar to those in Syria, with the exception that all of the guiding figures came from the area of Takrit, the center of Saddam Hussein's family influence. As in the Syrian case, the Iraqi bureaucracy and security services followed the pageant of dominance and submission described in the previous chapter. Loyalists at the senior levels received a Swiss watch embossed with Saddam's picture as a token of appreciation and a symbol of influence. Wealth followed, as did support for the regime, based on the certain knowledge that they faced a dire future if the regime fell, which of course, it did.

An Iraqi friend and proud bearer of a Saddam watch had managed to acquire several million dollars when he decided to bail out and move to the United States. Much to his dismay, the necessary bribes threatened to exhaust his fortune. He could stay in Iraq with his money and live in fear of the security services, or he could live abroad in relative poverty. Higher rollers had money in foreign banks, but he didn't. At least, not enough.

Security in Saudi Arabia was equally tight. I recall discussing a large grant with the Saudis during the era. The discussions went well at first, but broke down when it was hinted that they wanted to use an unnamed

U.S. university as a surveillance center for Saudi students in the region. Western-educated students were a source of danger to the kingdom and had to be watched with care, lest they be seduced by American freedoms and other immoral ways of the West.

Loyalty and Control among the Jihadists

The starting point of control in jihadist organizations began with the leadership of a supreme guide or imam whose authority was based upon divine inspiration. As vicars of God, their authority was absolute and beyond question.

The very term smacks of authority and exalted religious leadership. Ali ibn Talib, the patron saint of Shia Islam, is referred to as Imam Ali. More humble jihadist leaders made do with emir, or prince of the faithful. This was but one of several mystical Shia practices adopted by the Sunni jihadists to embellish their authority over their followers.

This was a tricky proposition, for most of the jihadist leaders to emerge during the era of Islamic resurgence came from secular backgrounds and had little formal religious training to support their claim of religious supremacy. This was true of most of the seventy-plus jihadist groups to emerge in Egypt, many of whom were students majoring in engineering or medicine (Mustafa, 1995). It was certainly true of bin-Laden, who was an engineer and economist by training. All had turned to jihadism in response to a growing conviction that modern society had become so rotten that it was beyond salvation.

All were inspired by the works of al-Sayed Qutb, a breakaway member of the Muslim Brotherhood who was killed by the security police for the attempted assassination of Nasser. Pure Islam, according to Qutb, could never be established in a corrupt society. The pure of heart had no choice but to destroy society and rebuild it from scratch based upon the model of the Prophet Mohammed's rule in Medina. It would be they, guided by the true spirit of Islam, who reestablished the rule of the Prophet Mohammed on earth. They, and only they, would enter paradise.

The weak religious credentials of the jihadist leaders forced them to rely on the strength of their personalities to dominate their followers. Indeed, it was precisely because of their lack of religious credentials that the jihadist leadership relied on authoritative titles, such as imam and emir to broaden the psychological distance between themselves and their followers.

Personality dominance was very common in an Arab world in which holy men had traditionally attracted a large following based upon the force of their personalities and mystical illusions of religious power. We have already seen this process at work in Hasan Al-Banna's founding of the Muslim Brotherhood in the 1920s.

The same process was common in the founding of Sufi orders. All were led by a supreme guide whose mystical knowledge alone could pave the way to oneness with God. Thus, the common expression "the way of the Sufi."

Another example of this phenomenon is that of Colonel Qadaffi, the tyrant of Libya for more than forty years before being swept away by the Arab Spring in 2011. Qadaffi developed his first revolutionary cell while in secondary school and so dominated his followers that he would shave the heads of those who disobeyed him (Fathaly and Palmer, 1980). In addition to preaching Arab nationalism, Qadaffi also fancied himself a religious luminary. This was so much the case that he shocked the Islamic world by decreeing that the Muslim calendar should begin with the Prophet Mohammed's birthday rather than the traditional date of the Prophet's flight to Medina. The blend of Islam and Arab nationalism didn't pose a contradiction for Qadaffi because they had become the twin pillars of a personality that blended force with megalomania. Nasser's 1969 emissary to Qadaffi's newly proclaimed People's Republic of Libya described the new Libyan leader and his followers to Nasser, saying, "they are shockingly innocent—scandalously pure" (Heikal, 1975, 65).

The story of Qadaffi is told here because many of the jihadist leaders were shockingly innocent and scandalously pure in their vision of Islam. They also shared Qadaffi's dominant personality, megalomania, and blatant disregard for the Islamic traditions that had evolved over the ages. Much the same pattern, it will be recalled, was common among religious mystics of early Islam, including the Assassins.

The ability of a jihadist leader to establish control over his followers by the force of his personality was the easy part of the dominance equation. His real test came with the need to convince his followers that he was divinely inspired and that obedience to his orders, including the murder of innocents and other Muslims, would assure them an eternity in paradise.

Given a jihadist doctrine that called for the destruction of a corrupt society by force, only the violent destruction of the enemies of God could testify to the baraka (gift of grace) of a jihadist leader. The more spectacular the violence, the greater his baraka and the stronger the loyalty of his followers.

With his spiritual supremacy established, the jihadist leader was able to unleash the full range of his supporters' motivations. The most important of these were the need for belonging and the emotions of righteousness, pride, and superiority, not to mention the joy of revenge and the pious unleashing of their anger, hate, and frustration on a world that despised them.

It was this lethal package of motivations, then, that enabled the jihadists to survive as hunted animals in the desolation of Afghanistan and the stinking slums of Cairo and Algiers with little hope of earthly gain.

The jihadists may have been an infinitesimal segment of the world's Muslim population, but it was the intensity of their beliefs and underlying emotions that allowed them to reshape a confused, fragmented, and despairing Muslim world.

All of this, again, hinged on the belief that their leader possessed the gift of grace and that his perverted version of the Koran was the will of God. They had to be convinced not once, but continuously, lest they begin to doubt his baraka and search for a new supreme guide whose star was on the rise.

Violence facilitated control in other ways as well. The group's violent acts strengthened its internal cohesion by turning the jihadist group into a pack of hunted animals that could survive only by clinging together. It was them against the world.

Acts of violence also became an initiation ritual for new members of jihadist groups. It was a test of courage in a group culture that required courage and obedience for its survival. In extreme cases, this test might even include the murder of relatives, the most intense of Arab loyalties. For those who failed the test of loyalty, a most uncertain future awaited.

Ironically, it was the violence of the security police and their barbaric prisons that offered the jihadists one of their prime sources of recruitment. It was there that innocents arrested on the vaguest of suspicions were beaten, starved, cut off from relatives, and thrown into the company of dedicated jihadists, who became their guides.

Jihadist violence, then, was far more than an avenue to paradise. It was also a means of recruitment and organizational control.

This didn't mean that control of jihadist organizations was a piece of cake. Individuals willing to join a jihadist organization that promised little more than probable death and an eternity in paradise were not your average Arabs. They were willing to commit mayhem at the command of a supreme guide whom they believed to possess the gift of grace, but patient they were not. To the contrary, jihadist cadres wanted action. It was the key to paradise and glory. Jihadist leaders, accordingly, had to do more than continually prove their gift of grace. They had to run to keep ahead of the demands of their troops for constant action. This often forced the hand of the jihadist leaders and pushed them into rash ventures that resulted in defeat, death, or imprisonment at the hands of the security police.

To their followers, such defeats suggested that the leader had lost God's blessing. How could it be otherwise? Those blessed by God didn't lose. Perhaps temporary setbacks could be explained away, but they made the faithful nervous. Even minor doubts in the rank and file could trigger power struggles and desertion.

Under the best of circumstances, supreme guides often faced death or imprisonment for life. Their fall produced a crisis of succession, for how could the gift of God's grace be transferred from one mortal to another without God's intervention?

As a practical matter, the passing of a supreme guide gave way to the selection of a new supreme guide from among his ranking lieutenants. The new supreme guide immediately proclaimed his selection to be the will of God and guarded his authority jealously. This was not always easy to do, especially for second- and third-generation leaders who had been chosen by questionable means over disgruntled pretenders. This, of itself, was a recipe for fragmentation, as the new supreme guide viewed his former competitors as threats and attempted to quell their influence. Two potential supreme guides couldn't survive within the same organization.

As a result of this atmosphere of doubt and suspicion, many of the control techniques outlined in the discussion of Arab bureaucracies found their way into the management of jihadist organizations. Supreme guides created an inner circle of their most trusted followers, often longtime friends or relatives. Even then, the supreme guides shared information and authority sparingly and often gave different information to different lieutenants in a concerted effort to keep them off balance. They, in turn, applied the same tactics to their followers, and so forth down the line. Much like other organizations, the jihadists soon found themselves riddled with cliques and patron-client networks that made control and concerted action difficult.

For all of their presumed search for a world without sin, the jihadist cadres were not free of the earthly appetites of lust, greed, jealously, and the craving for power. Perhaps they had the best of both worlds, knowing that their violent sacrifice in the name of God would wash away sins past and present.

Also keep in mind that the members of the jihadist groups were products of the Arab psyche that has been traced over the course of Arab history. Pride, honor, distrust, and the other features of the Arab psyche were very much part of the jihadist milieu.

The weaknesses inherent in the jihadist movement led to a precipitous decline in its popularity by the early 1990s. The problems were many. Jealously among jihadist imams (supreme guides) made coordination and cooperation difficult. This meant that human and material resources were wasted rather than being applied to the task of seizing power from the tyrants.

Heavy casualties resulting from poorly conceived attacks had also taken their toll. Mounting arrests and increasing casualties led to rapid turnover in the leadership structure of the jihadist groups and diluted the mystical authority of their leaders. Even original jihadists rotting in the putrid jails of the region began to doubt the wisdom of the jihadist doctrine. If the jihadist leaders doubted themselves, what choice did the jihadist cadres have? Everything hinged on their faith in the holy blessing of their supreme guide, and that faith had now been shaken.

Far worse, according to Al-Zaiyat, the shadowy Islamic lawyer who hovered on the fringes of the jihadist movement, the jihadists had lost touch with the Arab psyche. As the tide of battle turned, so did an Arab psyche reluctant to bet on losers. The Arab psyche yearned for stability, and according to Al-Zaiyat, violence had become an end in itself that served no useful purpose. An Arab psyche that abhorred chaos found the brutality of the tyrants preferable to the reign of terror unleashed by the jihadists. At the very least, the tyrants were predictable. Such sentiments mounted as jihadist violence stagnated already weak economies and deepened the despair for Arab populations (Al-Zaiyat, 2002).

This, in turn, left the jihadists open to vicious attacks by respected moral majority preachers such as Yousef Qaradawi, who scorned the jihadist imams as being "soft boned," the Arabic equivalent of being immature or "green behind the ears." Yet, Qaradawi seemed to have a begrudging respect for the jihadists and compared them to the Kharijites of early Islam who had allowed violence to destroy a pureness of heart (Qaradawi, 2001).

Even sympathizers with the jihadist cause found the Koran-based doctrines of the Muslim Brotherhood far more appealing than the questionable and uncompromising views of the jihadists. Why live through a reign of terror to achieve paradise when patience would bring the same result? The Arab psyche was very rational in assessing pain and pleasure when it suited its purposes.

Did that mean that jihadist violence was a mistake? The jihadist philosopher Abu Bakr Naji admits that errors were made during the era of Islamic resurgence and devoted an entire chapter in his *The Management of Savagery* to "The Problem of Excessive Zeal and the Problems That Accompany It, Such as Rushing Operations, Stupidity, or Heresy" (Naji, 2006, 71).

These errors, according to Naji, did not discredit violence as the primary method for achieving a pure Islamic state based on the jihadist interpretations of the Koran and the broader way of the Prophet. The problem was not violence or "savagery," Naji's preferred term, but the management of savagery. While the human errors of excessive zeal and stupidity slowed the jihadist movement, they also provided it with much needed experience in the management and application of violence. That experience having been gained, however painfully, set the stage for the emergence of a rightly guided jihadist leader who could again capture the faith of the masses and focus their emotions of righteousness, pride, superiority, revenge, anger, hate, and frustration on America, the true enemy of Islam.

While the jihadist movement was brought under control in Egypt, Algeria, and other core areas, an ever-deepening environment of oppression and decay continued to generate untold legions of dispossessed praying for the emergence of an Islamic state that would provide the faithful with justice on earth and salvation in the hereafter. Most inclined toward the Muslim Brotherhood, but a hard core of dispossessed clung to the jihadist vision of a primitive Islamic state.

All that was required to revive the jihadist dream, then, was a new hero who walked in the shadow of God, a hero so powerful and so blessed that an Arab psyche perpetually searching for a savior would crown him the Mahdi and rush to his side.

Lo and behold, a new hero did appear. His name was Osama bin-Laden, the leader of the jihadist resistance to the Soviet occupation of Afghanistan, and the genius who transformed his Afghan al-Qaeda organization into a jihadist network that spanned the globe.

Bin-Laden was a master psychologist and propagandist who understood the Arab psyche and who knew how to play upon its aspirations and frailties. The first step in his plan was curing the ills of the formative years of the jihadist experiment. Attacks on Muslims were curbed, and violence was focused on the U.S. and Israel, the two enemies of an Islamic revival upon which all jihadists could agree. Bin-Laden also understood that even small victories against the U.S. and Israel would bring joy to an Arab psyche burdened by the pain of humiliation and defeat. In their place would come the thrill of victory, and a surge of recruits and financial donations would follow.

As a military strategist, bin-Laden knew the folly of attacking security forces armed and trained by the Americans. Losses were too high and gains too low. So, bin-Laden guided the jihadists to regions torn by civil war in which they could gain maximum publicity by supporting whatever side was opposing American puppets. This pattern was established in Afghanistan where bin-Laden, backed by American support, assisted various Afghan forces in their struggle against the Soviets. In the process, he strengthened Taliban control in the region. From there, he added to the torment of civil wars in Sudan, Algeria, and Somalia while simultaneously sending Afghan Arab recruits back to their home countries to establish sleeper cells for future use.

Bin-Laden was also aware that the questionable legitimacy of jihadist theology had limited its appeal. To rectify the problem, bin-Laden formed an alliance with Hasan al-Turabi, the leading Islamic thinker of the era. Far from being "soft boned," Turabi possessed a master's degree from the University of London and a doctorate from the Sorbonne. He applauded Western advances in science and law as the future salvation of Muslims, but was appalled by Western hedonism and moral depravity (Palmer and Palmer, 2008). Once the U.S. and Israel had been driven from the region, according to Turabi's doctrine, Arabs and all Muslims would enjoy peace, piety, power, and prosperity. The Arab psyche applauded.

Bin-Laden's successes mounted, but he needed a master stroke that would place an indelible stamp on his leadership of the jihadist movement and incite the U.S. to declare war on Islam. That masterstroke would be unleashed on September 11, 2001.

The Muslim Brotherhood: Complexity and Control

The Muslim Brotherhood had survived the tumultuous years of Nasser's repression by moving toward a policy of patience and moderation that positioned it as the middle ground between the violent oppression of the tyrants and the wanton violence of the jihadists. It had also made the difficult transition from an organization dependent upon the personalized charisma of al-Banna to a complex organization with institutionalized procedures for replacing a fallen supreme guide and providing welfare and religious services to the poor. Both centered on a vast network of mosques that the Muslim Brotherhood controlled. Their mosques also served as a political forum at the same time that they served the Arab need for belonging by creating a network of family and youth organizations that integrated their followers into the Muslim Brotherhood family. Politics followed, but never to the point of threatening the reigning power. The Muslim Brotherhood had learned the lesson of Nasser's repression and Syria's virtual eradication of the Syrian branch of the Muslim Brotherhood. First, it would concentrate on expanding the base of devout Muslims in the Arab world, and then it would seize power with minimal violence.

Unlike the jihadists, the Muslim Brotherhood's promise of progress and morality within an Islamic framework tapped the heart of the

Muslim psyche's desire for faith, stability, and development. As a result, it had grown into the largest Sunni Muslim organization in the world.

This didn't mean that the Muslim Brotherhood didn't have problems controlling its members. The jihadists had split off from the Muslim Brotherhood in revulsion against its shift to a centrist policy of moderation. In the process, the Muslim Brotherhood lost some of its brightest minds and most zealous members. The Muslim Brotherhood also faced succession problems as younger cadres, many in their fifties and sixties, grew restive with the authoritarian rule of aging supreme guides in their eighties. The younger leaders, in addition to champing at the bit for authority, simply believed that the older elite was out of touch with the realities of the modern era.

The massive organization built by the Muslim Brotherhood left it vulnerable to the control techniques of Arab bureaucrats, including nepotism, favoritism, dissimulation, and micromanagement. Added to the bureaucratic problems of the Muslim Brotherhood was the strain of being a secret organization penetrated by the spies of the security service. Distrust was pervasive, and leaders at all levels were reluctant to share either information or authority. Invariably, patron-client networks proliferated, as ranking members of the Muslim Brotherhood gathered a powerbase of junior members who sought the influence of a powerful superior. Added to the mix were the earthly appetites of lust, greed, jealously, and the craving for power, the visibility of which led to charges that the Muslim Brotherhood had sold out to the tyrants in return for positions, bribes, and the ability to operate freely as long as they kept a low profile.

The Muslim Brotherhood, the jihadists charged, had become part of a corrupt system of rule. Patience was merely its excuse. I have provided a fictional picture of the tense struggle between the Muslim Brotherhood and the jihadists groups in a novel titled *Egypt and the Game of Terror*. It was easier to protect my sources that way.

Expressions of Satisfaction and Discontent

The surging religious emotions of the era were there for all to see. They couldn't be ignored. But what did they mean? The tyrants attempted to convince the U.S. that the surge of Islamic emotions was the work of a few troublemakers, but posed no risk to the regime. For most observers, they represented a ringing condemnation of rule by oppressive and corrupt tyrants unable or unwilling to meet the needs of the Arab population.

Even here, however, ambiguities remained. Were Arabs really intent on establishing Islamic rule of one form of another, or were they merely using the Islamic movement to protest the miserable conditions in which they lived? These questions raised the ghost of Iran's collapse in 1979. Almost every political current in Iran, the far left included, had supported the Ayatollah Khomeini's Islamic revolution in a collective effort to get rid of the Shah and his corrupt cohorts. Leftists assumed that they would soon dispatch with the aging mullahs, and Iran would be theirs. It didn't work out that way. It was the secular leftists who were dispatched, most to hideous prisons.

This posed a problem for American officials charged with gauging the strength of the Islamic movement in Egypt and other key Arab countries. They certainly didn't want a repeat of Iran. But how were they to gauge the intensity of the Islamic movement when elections, opinion polls, and all other indicators of popular opinion were a charade without meaning?

As always, they consulted with informed sources, much as they had done in Iran. Alas, their informed sources in Iran had been in the pay of the Shah. While condemning the shah as a brutal and corrupt tyrant, they assured American officials that his power was unshakable. American officials in Egypt, wary of the Iranian experience, were less trusting of their informed sources. Nevertheless, they played it safe by supporting the tyrants. No one, it seemed, wanted to be the bearer of bad news.

The tyrants remained, and the pent-up emotions of the Arab masses continued to simmer. The U.S. was minimally concerned as long as the surface waters remained calm.

Social Behavior

Adding to the weakness of the Islamic movement was the reality that its members, for all of their piety, were still beni Adam and subject to all the frailties of humankind. Like the rest of the human race, most went about their daily business of clinging to what they had and plotting to get a bit more. Their strategies were the same as those discussed in previous chapters, the only difference being the need to adapt to a more Islamic and increasingly chaotic environment.

Conforming to the Pressures of Religion and Tradition: To Veil or Not to Veil?

Most people during the era of Islamic resurgence continued to get along by going along with the social and political pressures of the day. This requires little added elaboration other than to note the growing emphasis on Islamic dress, especially among women. Indeed, Islamic dress suddenly became stylish among women and was often referred to as "Islamic chic," a sarcastic reference to the ability of Paris designers to make Islamic dress as seductive as it was pious.

Paris gowns were the preserve of the rich, but even they couldn't disguise the initial pain of being forced to conform to the demands of pious dress that accompanied puberty. The wife of the Turkish prime minister, for example, was told by her brother to wear a headscarf when she was fifteen and confessed to thoughts of committing suicide. It was only after she met successful ladies who dressed in an Islamic manner that she realized that a "Muslim lady could be modern, cultivated, and also covered at the same time" (Yalcin, 2008).

Does Islam require veiling? It is difficult to answer this question without distinguishing the three types of veils available to Muslim women. A simple headscarf covering a woman's hair is referred to as a *hijab*. The woman's face remains uncovered, often to stunning effect, but the general tenor of her dress reflects modesty. A full veil that covers all but a woman's eyes is called a *niqab*. In many cases, the eyes are also veiled in public, forcing a woman to view the world through a thin layer of black gauze. The total or head-to-toe veil is referred to as the *bourka*.

The Koran requires the covering of the head, a requirement met by a simple headscarf. For Saudi Arabia and other deeply conservative Muslim countries, the requirement for total veiling is provided by the sayings and deeds of the Prophet Mohammed, as reported by his followers and their followers for several generations. The spirit of Islam, in the Saudi view, requires full veiling of women. Even here, there is some dispute on the issue. Does full veiling require covering both eyes in public, or will covering one eye, as a Saudi cleric suggests, suffice? Revealing two eyes, in his view, is an invitation to the use of seductive makeup, where revealing one eye lessens that problem (BBC, October 3, 2008).

The total veil, eyes included, also raised safety issues. Could they see well enough to drive without endangering themselves and others? This wasn't much of a problem in Saudi Arabia where women weren't allowed to drive, but it became an issue in Egypt and other modernizing countries.

Suggesting that veiling was merely a matter of conformity would be a serious mistake. The comments that follow are based upon the pioneering work of Zeinab Radwan. Many women, her research indicated, wear the veil to conform to pressures from fathers and husbands (Radwan, 1982). In Saudi Arabia, the full veil is both a social and political requirement. The Saudi religious police do not look kindly on women who refuse to wear a full veil in public.

But social pressure, according to Radwan, was only part of the picture. Many women, according to Radwan's research, chose to wear the veil as a fulfillment of their religious obligation. As a sign of piety and virtue, the veil also improved a woman's eligibility for marriage. This was a matter of vital concern in a culture that demanded marriage and considered spinsters to be a burden.

From a more pragmatic perspective, wearing Islamic dress offers a degree of protection against predatory males. This is particularly important in Egypt and other progressive countries in which women had been integrated into the universities and workforce. Islamic dress also cuts down on clothing costs, not to mention expensive hair care. The wife of a Jordanian friend quipped that she wore the headscarf to escape the constant pressure to dress "excessively" Western at diplomatic functions.

Finally, the pressures of the era of Islamic resurgence would see the veil become a political statement. Each of the three main components of the Islamic movement had its own veiling preference. The Islamic democrats were content with a simple headscarf, while the Muslim Brotherhood found the niqab (eyes visible) preferable, and the radical extremists required the total veil, eyes and all.

The battle over the veil was vicious. Egypt launched a bitter campaign to prevent teachers, nurses, and other government employees from wearing heavy veils at work. The official explanation for the government's position was that students found it difficult to communicate with teachers whom they couldn't see. Some children claimed to be frightened of teachers dressed from head to toe in black, while others referred to their fully veiled teachers as "UFOs or extraterrestrial beings (*Egyptian Gazette*, March 21, 2009). The government also rejected full veils on the grounds that they were conveying a sexist and radical version of Islam to their pupils.

The veil wearers countered that it was their right to wear a full veil to class and were defended by woman's rights activists who argued that a woman had a right to select her clothes, regardless of faith. For them, it was a matter of personal freedom rather than religion. The veiled teachers also maintained that their dress was far less damaging to the morals of their students than that of their questionably dressed female colleagues.

The minister of health told nurses wearing the full veil to either remove the full veil or lose their jobs. In one fell swoop, 9,630 Egyptian nurses, or nearly10 percent of the country's female nurses, were faced with losing their jobs. This was an awesome figure, given the fact that Egypt faced a severe shortage of qualified nurses (Fauda, 2000).

Why all the uproar? The Egyptian government feared that the veil-wearing teachers and nurses were serving as a political symbol for the Muslim Brotherhood, Egypt's main opposition group and potential victor in anything approaching fair elections. Did the government succeed? Not really. The full veil became "all the rage" (*Egyptian Gazette*, March 21, 2009).

The situation was a little trickier for men, who began wearing beards in ever-larger numbers. More than a symbol of piety and masculinity, beards also conveyed support for fundamentalist groups. Anwar Sadat, then president of Egypt, went so far as to outlaw the wearing of beards in the weeks before his 1980 assassination. No one listened, but his frantic order was a clear indication of the power of dress as a political symbol.

The situation in Saudi Arabia and other conservative states was quite the opposite. Men got along by wearing beards, and women were forced to wear the severest form of veil in public. Religious police harassed those who violated the norm. This is not to suggest that many Saudi women didn't accept the veil as a religious obligation, but merely to note that the pressures to conform were overwhelming.

THE ARAB PSYCHE AND AMERICAN FRUSTRATIONS

Social Deviance: The Fox against Society

Beni Adam's struggle to get his share of the cake and a bit more during the era of Islamic resurgence remained much as it had been during the era of flawed independence. The fox ruled. It couldn't be otherwise, for the era of Islamic resurgence had added yet another layer of fear and confusion to the environment inherited from its predecessor.

All of the Arab psyche's time-tested strategies for outfoxing the government remained in force during the era of Islamic resurgence. They also sapped the energy of both the jihadists and more moderate organizations such as the Muslim Brotherhood and Hizbullah. The fox was all about "me" and not about faith. The players may have changed, but the game was the same.

Appearances became more important than ever during the era of Islamic resurgence, as people attempted to strike an acceptable balance between appearing religious but not too religious. Mosques were overflowing as never before, but what did that mean? The outpouring of prayer at government-approved mosques was a profound sign of the power of the Islamic movement in the progressive states, but it meant little in Saudi Arabia where the security forces closed markets during the five designated times for prayer. Religious police were even more obtrusive and kept track of the laggards. Did this mean that mosque attendance anywhere was a good indicator of religiosity? Perhaps, but it was also an indicator of the fox's innate ability to play it safe.

As always, the fox hovered near the centers of power during the era of Islamic resurgence. He didn't have much choice in the matter, because that was where the best pickings were to be found. The Islamic resurgence, however, had dramatically increased the risks of being associated with corrupt and oppressive regimes that might collapse before the Islamic onslaught. The trick was to be close, but not too close.

Just to add an element of complexity to the picture, the Muslim Brotherhood and more extreme religious groups often urged their supporters to appear moderate in their religious views as a means of placing them in the political hierarchy and the security forces. When the time was ripe, they would act.

This offered clever foxes the opportunity to have the best of both worlds. They could milk the government for money and influence while surreptitiously forming a fifth column for the Islamists. If the government fell, they were on the winning side and had nothing to fear from the victors. If the Islamists lost, business simply continued as usual.

Alas, the security services were aware of the game and trusted nobody. Even the slightest doubt could lead to prison, death, and the collective punishment of the families involved. Far scarier were the rumors spread by colleagues desperate to get a step on their peers or, for that matter, other moles attempting to curry favor with a superior. The more the Islamist tide surged, the more governments arrested anyone and everyone suspected of treason. What choice did they have? Survival of the regime and its minions was all that stood between them and a most ghastly revenge at the hands of the Islamists. No wonder the fox, that cleverest of animals, was also the most skittish.

Venality continued to be the norm during the era of Islamic resurgence. Stealing from the government and evading its laws remained a badge of honor rather than a matter of immorality. To the contrary, the Islamists viewed any act that weakened an immoral government to be moral, especially if they shared in the proceeds. The varieties of venality were covered in the previous chapter, and nothing changed.

Time and Space and the Islamic Movement

Time was critical, as the tyrants attempted to crush the Islamists before the wave of Islamic emotion overran the government. The struggle was brutal and laced with violence on all sides. By the 1990s, the outcome remained very much in question.

The Islamic movement, itself, was divided by issues of time. The Muslim Brotherhood and Hizbullah were willing to go slow while they consolidated their position and weakened the tyrants from within. Not so the jihadists, who lived for the moment in hopes of an eternity in paradise. As for the Sufi, their concern with time focused on achieving unity with God and, perhaps, the end of time. The establishment ulema urged patience with the tyrants until God was ready to judge them.

The diverse elements of the Islamic movement also struggled for the control of space. The Muslim Brotherhood and the establishment clergy competed for control of space in mosques and religious schools. It was there that they would win converts and indoctrinate the faithful. The jihadists did the same, but they were even more concerned with establishing mini-caliphates in remote isolated areas that would serve as base camps for the training and servicing of jihadist militias. Their success in Iraq, Algeria, and Afghanistan requires little elaboration.

All struggled for control of the street and the university campuses, the usual winner being the Muslim Brotherhood and Hizbullah in their respective areas. Governments could win fraudulent elections by embarrassing margins, but it was the moderation, organizational sophistication, and welfare services of the Muslim Brotherhood and Hizbullah that were in tune with the needs of the Arab psyche. It was they, accordingly, who controlled the Arab street.

For all of the conflicts, there was one element of space on which all members of the Islamic movement could agree. This was the need to liberate Palestine and Jerusalem from Israeli control. Israel, in the Muslim view, remained the last major piece of occupied space in the Muslim world. Whoever could achieve that goal would send a message of God's grace as powerful as the Ayatollah Khomeini's seizure of Iran.

Economic Behavior

The influence of the Islamic resurgence on economic behavior took a variety of forms. Islamic banking soared. Not only did it conform to Islamic law, but financial returns were often better than those paid by traditional banks and investment schemes. Interest wasn't allowed by Islamic law, but profit sharing was. The rich played the field, putting some of their money in Islamic banks and investing the rest in Western securities. Investment in long-range projects in the Arab world declined during the era. It was too risky.

For the rest, people played the fox in a desperate effort to get along. The poor, in particular, turned to the welfare services of the Muslim Brotherhood and Hizbullah in their respective areas.

RED-FLAG ISSUES: EXTREMISM AND VIOLENCE

The surge of religious emotions during the era of Islamic resurgence had a profound impact on all of the red-flag issues traced throughout the course of this book. That impact has been generally negative and has set the stage for a dramatic increase in U.S. frustrations in dealing with the Arab world and its environs.

Extremism Versus Moderation

The expansion of Islamic extremism in its various forms has been discussed at length throughout this chapter. It continues unabated today. Why did religious extremism soar during the era of Islamic resurgence? The answer is simple. It soared because all of the known causes of religious extremism also soared. These included fear, frustration, despair, hopelessness, helplessness, alienation, oppression, deprivation, humiliation, betrayal, and anger. For an increasingly frantic Arab psyche, God had become the solution, the only solution. Everything else had been tried and failed. Everything else, that is, with the exception of democracy.

Violence Versus Reconciliation

The era of Islamic resurgence (1979–2001) was arguably the most violent era of Arab and Middle Eastern history up to this point. There were foreign wars such as U.S. attacks on Iraq and Libya, Arab-Israeli wars such as the Israeli occupation of Beirut and the bombing of an Iraqi nuclear reactor, regional wars pitting Iraq against Iran and Kuwait, proxy wars between Algeria and Morocco, internal civil wars in Lebanon, Sudan, and Algeria, Islamic revolutions in Iran and Afghanistan, and wars of national liberation that pitted the Palestinians against the Israelis and the Kurds against the Turks and Iraqis.

More striking than the quantity of violence during the era of Islamic resurgence was the intensity and variety of violence that characterized the era. Suicide bombers, collective punishment of civilian populations, aerial bombings, gassing of minorities, ethnic cleansing, and bombs detonated by remote control all surged to the fore.

All indicated a marked change from earlier conflicts in which civilian populations were spared and military casualties were reduced by posturing. In the past, battle lines were drawn, but most people had time to flee or surrender (Grossman, 2009). No longer. The object of violence was to terrify people into submission by killing as many individuals as possible, whatever their station in life. Battle lines were fluid, unpredictable, and unavoidable. Political torture, killings, feuds, and other forms of violence long associated with the Arab world kept pace, buoyed by the wave of violence that had settled on the region.

The question is, how much of this violence do we want to attribute to religious extremism and how much is better attributed to occupation, foreign meddling in Arab affairs, megalomaniacs such as Saddam Hussein and Qadaffi, and repressive governments that fostered fear, frustration, hopelessness, helplessness, alienation, betrayal, and anger? So many causes of violence have been identified over the years that it would take volumes just to describe them all. Suffice it to say that all were present in spades during the era of Islamic resurgence.

Frankly speaking, it is probably impossible to sort the whole thing out. Everything was connected to everything. For many jihadist groups, by their own admission, killing and violence had become an end in itself. Political violence followed suit, as tyrants used jihadist attacks as a justification for crushing all forms of political opposition in the name of fighting terror. Saddam Hussein attacked Iran out of fear of the ayatollah's Islamic revolution, and he attacked Kuwait out of greed and megalomania. Saudi Arabia was next on his agenda.

So why did the Saudis and Kuwaitis fund Saddam Hussein's war against Iran when the writing was on the wall? The answer is fear. The Saudis and Kuwaitis feared the Ayatollah Khomeini and his Islamic revolution more than they feared Saddam Hussein. Saddam Hussein could be bought, but the Ayatollah Khomeini was a saint who had proclaimed the Saudi king a kafir (infidel) and called for his overthrow by violent means. The Saudis were also confident that the U.S. would protect them from Saddam Hussein, but they also knew that nothing could protect them from an internal rebellion sparked by Iran and its radical Arab allies.

Israel was shaken by an intifada (ground shaking) in the occupied territories, as Palestinian youth fought Israeli forces with stones and Molotov cocktails. The intifada spawned religious organizations such as Hamas, but the intifada was not initiated by religious groups. Up to this point, it was largely secular Palestinians who had led the struggle against the Israeli occupation. No longer. Israel now found itself engaged in a war of religions, the outcome of which was iffy. The Arab psyche had changed, but American and Israeli assessments of the Arab psyche had not.

Nor was fundamentalism limited to Islamic fundamentalisms. Jewish fundamentalism pushed for the incorporation of the Occupied Territories into Israel on religious grounds. Were they not the ancient Jewish kingdoms of Judea and Samaria? Christian fundamentalists in

America, some sixty million strong by Israeli count, vowed to stand by Israel and support its claim to the Occupied Territories and the lands beyond. Believe me. Sixty million Americans who can agree on anything do have a profound impact on American policy in the Middle East.

Fragmentation Versus Cooperation

Dreams of Arab unity fueled during the Nasser era had given way to dreams of Islamic unity. They, too, proved elusive as Muslim hopes of rebuilding the Muslim nation, or Umma, floundered on the issues of sectarianism, ethnicity, the nature of an Islamic state, power struggles among religious luminaries, and the bitter theological debate over the best way to serve God. The fear and distrust so deeply embedded in the Arab psyche allowed temporary alliances, but little more.

It was the same within countries, as tyrannical leaders ruled by force and the fragmentation of society. None were legitimate, so fear and distrust were the only assets at their disposal. They certainly couldn't allow the freedoms of speech and assembly.

What most Muslims could agree on was the principle that the Muslim world should be free of foreign influence. As a result, an endless series of Muslim unity conferences could agree on liberating Palestine from Israeli occupation, but they could not find a way to focus their awesome human and material resources on achieving this and related goals. Even criticism of the U.S. was muted, for many of the attendees were in America's pocket. All they could do was talk. Only the jihadists were willing to take action.

Tyranny Versus Democracy and Inequality Versus Equity

Pretenses of democracy became more of a farce during the era of Islamic revival, and human rights faded from the agenda. Anyone suspected of being an Islamist in the more secular Arab countries was tried in closed military courts rather than civilian courts open to the press. The fate of the convicted was a security secret and seldom revealed. Woman's rights had made significant progress under the modernizers, but now retreated under the pressure of Islamists. Religious freedom declined, as the tyrants dictated "acceptable" sermons to the clergy and growing legions of religious police prowled.

The tribal kingdoms had never acknowledged the legitimacy of either democracy or human rights. Democracy, the Saudi king candidly stated, was not part of Saudi culture. It was the same in the area of human rights. In line with their tribal background, rights were collective rather than individual. The good of the state had to come before the rights of the individual, and it would be the king who decided what was good for the state.

What this meant, in effect, was that the Arabs lacked a peaceful means of resolving their conflicts, and could choose extremism, violence, or withdrawing into the ethereal world of the Sufi.

Ironically, the one spark of democracy in the Muslim Middle East was the Islamic Republic of Iran, an Islamic state. Iran didn't conform to the Western concept of democracy, but authority was divided between a supreme guide, elected by Iran's religious elite, and a parliament and president elected by popular vote from among religiously qualified candidates. It wasn't much, but it was a start and served as a model of what might be if the Islamists seized power in the Arab world.

Turkey had also experimented with rule by a moderate Islamic party, but the military nullified these efforts. The only Arab country to approach democracy during the era was Lebanon. Tragically, sectarian and clan tensions could not be overcome, and this beautiful country dissolved into a fifteen-year civil war that dragged on until 1990.

Stagnation Versus Growth

Growing extremism and violence paralyzed effective governance in the Arab world as tyrants, shaking on their thrones, suppressed every hint of opposition, especially that of a religious hue. Bureaucrats and other government employees, including the military, played the fox while they either chose sides or bided their time, waiting for the dust to settle. As a result, few governments in the region were able to meet the social and material needs of the population. Stagnation followed, as did oppression, fraud, nepotism, and corruption.

It was the same in the private sector, as uncertainty dulled investment and violence scared away tourists from this historic region. Billions of dollars also fled the region to safe financial havens in Europe and North America. The oil kingdoms continued to consume without producing. Even the factories that appeared here and there were turn-key operations that foreigners built and operated. Something had to shake the Arab world from its political and economic stagnation, but what?

CHAPTER 7

TERROR, REPRISALS, AND THE ARAB PSYCHE

Welcome to the era of terror and reprisals. You know it well. It began with the September 11, 2001 terrorist attacks on the U.S. and dragged through bloody U.S. occupations in Iraq and Afghanistan, and just about everywhere else America ventured in the Middle East.

The major protagonists during the era of terror and reprisals were the United States and the Arab psyche. I mention the U.S. along with the Arab psyche because it took two to tango. And what a strange dance it was, with the most powerful nation that the world had ever known on one side, and the most battered and confused of Arab psyches on the other.

Why, then, was the United States going from defeat to defeat in a losing struggle to crush terror, curb Islamic extremism, provide a steady flow of oil to the world economy, and assure the survival of Israel? These, at least, were the stated goals of the White House as it announced its war on terror.

This topic will be debated for decades. The task of this chapter is simply to illustrate how the Arab and neighboring Muslim psyches frustrated American policy at virtually every turn. Perhaps the misunderstandings of the past can be avoided in the future.

The chapter begins by tracing the environment of the era, and then looks at how the Arab psyche attempted to deal with its violent and chaotic environment. It was this lethal blend of environment and psyche that were the core of U.S. frustrations in the Middle East in the short decade between the terrorists' attacks of 2001 and the popular uprisings of 2011.

THE ENVIRONMENT OF TERROR AND REPRISALS

The environment of terror and reprisals can only be described as horrendous. Arabs couldn't escape from jihadist terror, nor could they escape from American reprisals. Both combined to create a domestic environment of doom and despair.

The International Environment
The international environment during the era of terror and reprisals began with grisly pictures of the World Trade Towers and the Pentagon erupting in flames. Jihadist terror that had reigned in the Middle East for decades had finally struck at the heart of the United States. Reprisals would follow, but what kind of reprisals?

A recently elected George W. Bush, a man with little experience in foreign affairs, was faced with a war unlike any America had ever known. There were no massed armies to bomb or front lines to fortify, only shadows that dissolved into the throngs of the innocent. The enemy wore no uniforms except, perhaps, the ubiquitous beard. Even that could be abandoned for religious purposes. They were motivated by visions of a paradise in heaven, and they courted death. Wealth and other earthly concerns were irrelevant.

Two facts, however, were clear. First, America was at war with Islamic jihadists, a minute if virulent strain of a broader Islamic movement that was sweeping the Islamic world. Second, the center of jihadist fanaticism was the Arab world and its Muslim environs.

Crushing Terror: The Great Debate
The question was how to go about defeating the jihadist fanatics who had now attacked the United States. There were two basic views on

the topic. The Europeans favored a surgical strategy that focused on al-Qaeda and other jihadist fanatics. Their bases would be attacked, and all efforts would be made to prevent jihadist venom from infecting the vast majority of Muslims who wanted nothing more than to get on with their lives as best they could.

Little was to be gained, the Europeans argued, by inflaming the emotions of the world's 1.5 billion Muslims. A narrow group of jihadists could be destroyed if they were isolated from the mainstream of the Muslim community, but not if they became its hero.

George W. Bush's advisors, headed by Vice President Cheney and a group of conservative strategists referred to as "neo-cons," argued that the security of the United States and Israel demanded no less than the use of America's awesome military and economic power to create a new Middle East free of Islamic extremism in all of its manifestations, jihadist and otherwise(Frum and Perle, 2003).

In their view, the jihadist fanatics were merely a symptom of a deeper fanaticism that had griped the Islamic world. Attacking the jihadists, in their view, might bring temporary relief, but would not cure the disease of Muslim radicalism. If extremism existed, in the neo-con view, terror would follow. The jihadist could not function, their argument continued, without a broad base of support. Destroy the base, and you destroy the jihadists and all other threats to American and Israeli interests. Ironically, the name al-Qaeda means "base" in Arabic.

The first step in the Bush plan was attacking the Afghan bases of al-Qaeda. This was followed by a full-scale attack on Islamic schools, charities, and financial institutions even remotely linked to extremist activities. An awesome list of potential terrorist organizations was also targeted for destruction, few of which posed any direct threat to the U.S. Such, President Bush proclaimed, would be the core of America's crusade against terror. Crusade was an unfortunate choice of words, and the U.S. State Department was quick to clarify that the U.S. had not declared war on Islam. Muslims, however, were not convinced.

These measures were but the initial steps in the neo-con plan for creating a new Middle East. A second stage was launched in 2003 with the invasion of Iraq, accompanied by a pledge to eliminate all state sponsors of terror in the region, not the least of which were Iran, Syria, and the Hizbullah enclaves in Lebanon. Rather than bastions of terror, all would be transformed into the bastions of democracy so essential for providing a popular foundation of America's new Middle East.

Iraq, already under America's thumb, would come first and serve as a staging ground for the invasion of neighboring Iran, a much tougher nut to crack. With Iraq and Iran out of the way, it would be a simple matter to topple an unpopular regime in Syria, the remaining vestige of anti-Americanism in the Arab world. Hizbullah, holed up in Lebanon, would wither without support from Iran and Syria. If worse came to worse, the Israelis would take it out. The same applied to Hamas, the Muslim Brotherhood, and any other group brash enough to challenge American supremacy in the region.

The British and Australians had their doubts, but tagged along to preserve their special relationship with the U.S. Other major powers, including the EU, Japan, Russia, and China dragged their feet. Most Muslim leaders warned against attacking Islam, but they took American anti-terrorist funds and used them to crush domestic opponents. They also sabotaged America's war on terror from within when it suited their purposes. Very foxy.

In the meantime, the U.S. struggled to keep the lid on the Arab world by propping up its favored tyrants, all of whom ruled by terror.

In retrospect, the neo-con plan was flawed, and its authors have embarked upon a sickening pageant of blame and counterblame. Senator, and later presidential candidate, John McCain claims that he told Secretary of Defense Donald Rumsfield that his plan to invade Iraq was dead before it started, while Rumsfield said the plan was sound and blamed its failure on those charged with executing it (*The Guardian*, February 3, 2011). Those responsible for carrying out the neo-con plan countered by blaming their failures on a plan that was little more than a wish list. They also complained of a lack of adequate support from Washington. Everyone blamed the intelligence community for flawed information. The recriminations are still pouring out and paint a picture of American leadership that was more confused than the Arab psyche. Whatever the case, the buck didn't stop anywhere.

The International Islamic Movement

American efforts to forge a new Middle East were only part of the Arab psyche's international environment. The Islamic movement, in all of its variations, had also gone global. The Muslim Brotherhood was linked to several Islamic social and financial networks in Europe, as was Saudi Arabia, supporters of a brand of Islam far more repressive than that of the Muslim Brotherhood (Nada, 2002). Jihadist networks, for their part, had become increasingly centralized under the leadership of bin-Laden and his al-Qaeda organization. Al-Qaeda had branches in some sixty countries, supported by innumerable sleeper cells waiting to come to life with a wave of the hand. It also possessed a financial network that Western security agencies found difficult to penetrate.

Neither the Muslim Brotherhood nor the jihadists intended to be passive bystanders while the United States dismantled an Islamic faith of which they were the vanguard. If American pressures got too hot in one country, they merely shifted resources to another. The jihadists, as the Europeans had warned, seemed intent on provoking blatant American attacks on Islam as a means of igniting a war of religions in which there was no room for moderation. Sooner or later, according to their strategists, Muslims would be forced to topple their tyrants and drive the U.S. from Arab and Islamic lands. The bloodier the revolution, the better.

Much like America's effort to make a new Middle East, the global face of Islam was also evolving and adapting, but none more so than the jihadists. When the core of al-Qaeda was put to flight, it merely splintered into thousands of homegrown cells, many of which blossomed in Iraq, Yemen, and other countries in which there had been little if any al-Qaeda presence prior to the war on terror. Indeed, it was al-Qaeda victories in Iraq that kept its image alive in the Muslim press. It didn't matter where you killed Americans, just so you killed them.

The Muslim Brotherhood, by contrast, was playing the waiting game as the U.S. and the jihadists struggled to destroy each other.

Pity the poor Arab psyche caught in the international crossfire between the American efforts to forge a new Middle East, the seductive slogans of the Muslim Brotherhood, and the violence of the jihadists. Sooner or later, the Arab psyche would have to place its bets.

The Domestic Environment and the Seeds of Terror

The domestic environment in the Arab world during the era of terror and reprisals remained as dismal as described in earlier chapters, with few signs of improvement. If *The Arab Human Development Report,* a United Nations publication, is any guide, things were going from bad to worse:

> *Gripped by dread of actual or potential harm from fellow Arabs and foreign powers alike, torn by conflicts and hobbled by unjust laws, too many Arabs live out an existential nightmare of insecurity that numbs hope, shrivels initiative and drains the public sphere of the motivation for cooperative and peaceful change* (United Nations, 2009, 18).

Other pressing woes stressed by *The Arab Human Development Report* were pollution, water shortages, deterioration of agricultural land, foreign meddling, governmental inability to protect is citizens, poor health services, massive corruption, slow legal systems that ignored human rights, religious extremism, disintegration of the family, epidemics, unemployment, poverty, hunger, criminal assaults on persons and private property, and deepening tensions between religious sects, ethnic groups, and social classes (United Nations, 2009, 26). A country-by-country analysis can be found of pages 262–263 of the report.

The material quality of life varied from country to country, but the constant was an ever-deepening sense of fear and insecurity. Those under occupation suffered the most, as did the refugees attempting to escape the horrors of war. This said, the majority of the Arabs suffered from most of the afflictions listed above most of the time. As *The Arab Human Development Report* notes,

> *Such fears also permeate more fortunate Arab societies which, although free from armed conflicts or occupying forces, suffer under the dead hand of authoritarian power. In many Arab countries, the ordinary person enters a police station at his or her peril, knowing that he or she is liable to be hauled away on the merest suspicion of crime or public agitation* (United Nations, 2009, 18).

The leaders of the Arab world, for all of their pomp and circumstance, were no more secure than the subjects they ruled. I was going to refer to "citizens," but an Arab friend corrected me, saying, "There are no citizens in the Arab world, merely subjects." Whatever the word used, no one doubted that there was a tragic disconnect between the rulers and the ruled in the Arab world.

Underpinning many of the region's economic and social woes was the acceleration of the global push for privatization driven by the major industrial powers. Efficiency and exports increased, but so did unemployment and the ever-widening gap between rich and poor. New wealth was created, but it went to a capitalist class that was closely linked by marriage and bribes to the ruling class. In the process, the poor, and that was most people, became ever more dependent upon Islamic welfare agencies, including those of Hizbullah and the Muslim Brotherhood.

Accompanying the global economic revolution was an equally profound revolution in communications technology. This revolution, more than any other, terrified the tyrants of the region as they saw their control of information wither away. The information revolution clearly increased the power of the Islamic movement.

Now, add a demographic time bomb to the equation, as populations exploded and swarms of Arabs were forced to live in the swelling slums of the region's major cities, often without basic water and sanitation services. A majority of the Arabs, moreover, were below the age of twenty-five, perhaps younger. They knew little of the past, but they were acutely aware of their personal trauma.

In many ways, the international and domestic environments during the era of terror and reprisals were like two sides of a vise with an ever more frantic Arab psyche caught in the middle. It was impossible for Arabs to improve their domestic environment without international pressure, and international pressure was not forthcoming because of American fears that democracy and human rights would unleash new waves extremism and terror. Catch 22, anyone?

THE ARAB PSYCHE FACES THE ERA OF TERROR AND REPRISALS

The components of the Arab psyche didn't change during the era of terror and frustration. The pressures that the Arab psyche had to deal with, by contrast, became more complex and lethal than at any prior time in the history of the Arab people.

The Battered and Confused Muslim Identity

Early psychology books talked about the "looking-glass self." You were what you saw reflected in the mirror of those around you. That was your identity. You were what other people said you were. If the Arab's and Muslim's view of themselves is what is reflected in the mirror of the West, God help us all.

The trouble is, it's not much better when the Arabs look at themselves. What do they see? They see exactly what the *Arab Human Development Report* described in our discussion of the prevailing Arab environment.

Arabs remain intensely proud of their Arabic heritage and their role as the core of Islam, but according to Hisham Sharabi, a leading Arab social scientist, they have yet to forge a clear image of who they are or how they fit into the world around them (Sharabi, 1988, 23).

The crux of the problem, according to Sharabi, is that the Arabo-Islamic psyche is stuck somewhere between the past and the present. The ways of tradition have been eroded, while the ways of the West remain a veneer that lacks substance. Tribal and religious identities remain intense, but nationalism, whether Arab or local, remains ephemeral. Some people appear traditional, while others appear modern. In reality, Sharabi warns, such differences are not as sharp as they appear. Differences between tradition and modernity in the Arab world are not black and white, but merely different shades of gray.

Motivations during the Era of Terror and Reprisals

The search for security and stability became all-consuming passions for most Arabs during the era of terror and reprisals (Meguid, 2006). How could it otherwise when a majority of people in the Arab world lived under the constant threat of violence, be it U.S. bombing, police brutality, sectarian and ethnic strife, wanton jihadist terror, crime, drug wars, domestic feuds, and honor killings?

Almost anything was better than what they had.

The urgency of other needs and wants increased apace. This was inevitable, for food, shelter, jobs, and just about every other need associated with a sustainable quality of life required some degree of security and stability. The fox did his best to fend for himself, but that only made things worse for society as a whole.

Arabs and most Muslims also felt a deep humiliation at the Western practice of stereotyping them as flawed human beings because of the heinous crimes of a few jihadists. The situation was even worse in Europe, where Muslims were blamed for everything from unemployment to drug crimes.

Western officials argued that stereotyping was justified on security grounds and that Arabs and Muslims were playing the victim and overlooking their own role in the problems of the world. Our purpose is not to argue the point, but merely to point out that these sensitivities are likely to shape Arab behavior for years to come.

Adding to the fray was an intense Muslim desire for the West to respect the rights of Muslims living in their midst and to stop desecrating the Prophet Mohammed in cartoons and political rhetoric. They demanded multiculturalism while their hosts demanded assimilation.

Democracy and human rights moved up the list of Arab wants, but were largely limited to intellectuals. For the average person, democracy remained a remote concept with little hope of achievement. Far more real were promises of salvation through Islam.

Conscience and Morality during the Era of Terror and Reprisals

What role do the motives of guilt and conscience play in an environment of violence, oppression, corruption, political decay, and collapsing social institutions? The answer, provided by Hisham Sharabi, is painfully simple: "In one's *actual* practice, one conducts oneself *morally* only within the primary structures (family, clan, sect); for the most part, one lives amorally in the jungle, in the society at large (Sharabi, 1988, 35).

The Koran urged obedience, decreeing that God would deal harshly with unjust tyrants. Judgment was His right, and not theirs. Morality demanded compliance.

While commands for obedience had long been cited as a cause of Arab passivity, the era of Islamic resurgence had witnessed a clear shift among Arabs and most Muslims toward radical interpretations of Islamic scriptures that equated morality of conscience with establishing morality on earth. If that meant resisting immoral leaders, so be it.

If anything, Western attacks on Islam had intensified the moral need for Muslims to support their faith. This didn't mean jihadist violence, but it did mean a heightened sensitivity to Western affronts to Islam and the Christian and Jewish occupation of Islamic lands.

The Emotions of Terror and Reprisal

Arab concerns with survival and stability lead naturally to a discussion of the dominant emotions of the era of terror and reprisals. All, in addition to being powerful motivators in their own right, triggered a variety of Arab responses to their wretched environment. Emotions didn't always explode in predictable ways, but the very existence of soaring emotions should have provided a most frustrated U.S. government with signs of things to come.

Fear

The most powerful of these emotions during the era of terror and reprisals was unquestionably fear. If I were to make a composite of the fears of Arab friends from a variety of countries, it would sound something like this:

> What do I fear? Everything. I fear American and Israeli bombs. I fear that the Americans will keep us in a state of perpetual chaos in order to steal our oil and protect Israel. I fear that the Americans are attempting to destroy Islam. I fear that the bickering and venality of religious leaders will deprive us of the coherent Islamic leadership that we so desperately need. I fear our leaders and the police. I fear extremist violence. I fear political instability. I fear my neighbors and their peering eyes, not to mention fears that my telephone calls and computers are being monitored. I fear my boss and my colleagues. I fear that my daughter will commit some stupidity like putting her picture on Facebook. I fear my wife, who demands more than I can provide. She also watches too many movies and has begun to resist our customs. I fear that my children won't score high enough on the universal secondary school exams to be admitted to a university. I fear for my sons, who can't get married for lack of a dowry or apartment. I fear for my daughters who may be doomed to spinsterhood. I fear pressure for globalization because I will probably lose my job and my dignity. Perhaps I fear that my children won't be able to care for me when I grow old. Want some more? Buildings are falling down, trains are crashing, roads have become a death trap, and the level of air

pollution is up to four packs of cigarettes a day. To sum it up, I fear the future of the Arab world in which some 60 percent of the population are youth without hope.

Building upon the pervasiveness of fear in the Arab psyche, a political psychologist, Michel Nehme, writes that

It is true that fear is in the mind, but a good part of its origin is in external factors and circumstances that are truly threatening. What are the foundations of fear in the Arab world? They are the manifestations of the forces for chaos, natural and human.... In a sense, every Arab construction, whether mental and material, is a component stemming from the spring of fear developed to contain chaos. Thus cosmological myths, philosophical ideologies, and political systems are shelters built by the mind within which Arab societies can rest, at least temporarily, from the siege of chaotic experience and doubt (Nehme, 2003, 21).

Hopelessness, Helplessness, Self-doubt, and Alienation

The future of most Arabs during the era of terror and reprisals seemed hopeless, and they felt helpless to do anything about it. Elections were a sham, and if they voted for the Muslim Brotherhood, they were beaten with clubs or thrown in jail as provocateurs. Even discussing politics in public was dangerous.

Most of the Arabs with whom I have worked felt alienated from the political system, but they didn't try to change it because the chances of success were minimal and the risks were terrifying. They also doubted themselves. How can we change it, they asked, when our political leaders are kept in power by the United States? No wonder some 86 percent of the Arabs surveyed toward the end of the era had an unfavorable view of the U.S. (Telhami, 2008). It's a vicious circle. Helplessness and self-doubt bred hopelessness and alienation, and hopelessness and alienation bred helplessness and self doubt (Nehme, 2003; United Nations, 2004).

Humiliation, Despair, Frustration, and Anger

I discuss feelings of humiliation, despair, frustration, and anger in the same section because they create of chain of sorts. Humiliation and

THE ARAB PSYCHE AND AMERICAN FRUSTRATIONS

despair lead to frustration because Arabs feel helpless to change things. Frustration, in turn, often turns to anger. They are angry at American policy, angry at their leaders, and angry at themselves. In the words of a modern poet, "I don't blame the tyrants, my people, I blame you" (Al-Khatib, 2010, 1).

Distortions in the Reasoning Process

The thinking-cognition process during the era of American frustrations was the same as it always had been. People tried to keep track of the things going on around them, gave their perceptions a quick evaluation, and then sorted the relevant information into manageable categories that would enable them to chart a reasonable course for maximizing pleasure and minimizing pain under the most trying of circumstances.

I keep the image of an ego alive to enable you to place yourself at the control panel of the Arab psyche during this critical era that resembled *Alice in Wonderland* more than any prior era in the evolution of the Arab psyche. Everything looked familiar, but nothing was what it seemed.

You might also want to put yourself at the control panel of the psyche of people responsible for making and implementing American policy in the Arab world and its Muslim environs. Is it possible that American policymakers were so blinded by visions of forging a new Middle East that they bit off more than they could chew?

Now add the faith-versus-science debate to the reasoning process. The surge of religious emotions during the era of American frustrations requires little elaboration. The more Muslims turned to God as the solution for their existential nightmare, the more faith was likely to shape what they saw. Faith also shaped how they evaluated and categorized what they saw, and how they used their reason to chart a precarious path between pain and pleasure in an ever-changing world. If Islamic logic had surged to the fore during the era of Islamic resurgence, it consolidated its dominance during the era of terror and reprisals.

Defense Mechanisms

The above discussion assumes that Arabs were attempting to come to grips with the reality of their existential nightmare in a logical and reasoned way. Nightmares are painful business, and the ego did its best to defend itself against them.

Which defense mechanisms were active during the era of terror and reprisals? Most of them, but probably the most prominent was projection. Americans blamed the Arabs for their frustrations, and Arabs blamed America for their misery. It worked out well for both sides, as neither had to address its own failures.

Blaming others led to the conspiracy theories which had become an art form during the era. The one I liked best was the theory that the U.S. had encouraged the September 11 terrorist attacks as a pretext for invading Iraq and other Arab countries. This theory was particularly interesting because it reflected traces of a still-active kawaga complex in the Arab psyche. Only an all-powerful kawaga could devise a plan so cruel and cunning. What hope did the Arabs have against such a foe?

The kawaga conspiracies, in turn, became an excuse for passivity. It wasn't a matter of cowardliness, but common sense. Why get slaughtered when resistance was hopeless? Why didn't the Saudis use the oil weapon to force a Palestinian state? How could they? The U.S. would destroy them. For those who wanted to believe that the Saudis weren't in league with the Americans and Israelis, there was the excuse.

In the process, the Mahdi complex also soared. Only a hero of bin-Laden's stature could counter the cunning of the kawaga. But why was bin-Laden a hero when, according to the prevailing conspiracy theories, the U.S. had put him up to the September 11 attacks? Don't look for logic in defense mechanisms. Why would the ego dwell on contradictions that undermined its whole argument? It would be too painful. Besides, American defeats in Iraq and Afghanistan suddenly made everyone realize that bin-Laden was smarter than the Americans. The Arab psyche could have it both ways: conspiracies and the God-sent arrival of a new superhero. No wonder the Americans were frustrated.

I could provide a few thousand more conspiracy theories, but they would add little. When people need a reason to do something, be it action or inaction, a conspiracy will pave the way for them. You can't understand the Arab world without understanding conspiracy theories. Nor, for that matter, can you understand American ventures into Iraq or elsewhere in the region without them. Just read the multitude of books by the American decision makers who plotted the creation of a new

Middle East. If you are still not convinced, add the wave of Islamophobia sweeping the U.S. and Europe.

Was fantasizing also in play? Absolutely. Why focus on the nightmare of the present when dreams of paradise and a return to the idealized days of the Prophet Mohammed were so much more pleasant? Were American policymakers also inclined to fantasize? What would you call their visions of building a new Middle East?

Is the Arabic Language Still Part of the Arab Psyche?

The Arabic language remained a critical part of the Arab psyche during the era of terror and reprisals. Then, as now, it was the Arab language that made Arabs truly Arab. Language was pride and ethnic consciousness, and it provided ties to the glories of the past, including the Islamic faith.

If the psycholinguists are correct, the Arabic language did more than distinguish Arabs from their neighbors. It also gave them a different cognitive framework than their neighbors. We have covered this ground earlier, but it should be noted that Persian, Turkish, and Kurdish belong to totally different language classifications than Arabic. Ironically, the only language close to Arabic is Hebrew. Arabic and Hebrew are both Semitic languages. Does that mean that Arabs and Hebrews think alike? Interesting thought, but keep in mind that the psycholinguistic branch of psychology is more speculative than empirical.

Perhaps the Arabic language was more than a link to the past. In some ways it was also a chain to the past, a chain that pulled the Arabs backward rather than forward. People who argue this point stress that formal Arabic is the language of God and cannot be altered. Prayer remains in classical Arabic, while efforts to deal with modernity rely on borrowed words or awkward perversions of classical words, both of which vary markedly from county to country.

What this meant in the context of the era of terror and reprisals was that the content and emotionalism of the Arabic language was more conducive to fostering Islamic extremism than it was in forging a secular response to American incursion in the region. Keep this point in mind as the Middle East moves toward a war of religions. The Israelis had little trouble defeating secular Arab armies, but they have yet to conquer the Islamists. Neither has the U.S.

Roadmaps and Poker

The world that the Arab psyche saw as it attempted to cope with the era of terror and reprisal was starkly different than the world that Americans saw. It was the Arab psyche's vision of the world that determined how Arabs placed their bets in dealing with a reality that was manifestly intolerable.

Perhaps America's vision of the Arab reality was equally flawed. What else would explain U.S. frustrations in Iraq, Afghanistan, and just about everywhere else in the Middle East? Psyche poker anyone?

ARAB BEHAVIOR AND U.S. FRUSTRATIONS DURING THE ERA OF TERROR AND REPRISALS

Arab behavior in the decade between the terrorist attacks on the U.S. in 2001 and the eruption of popular revolutions in 2011 was overwhelmingly shaped by the need to survive the twin scourges of terror and reprisal.

The discussion of Arab behavior during the era follows the pattern of earlier chapters, albeit with a special focus on how the Arab preoccupation with survival frustrated U.S. efforts to stamp out extremism and terror. The Arab psyche didn't plan or coordinate its efforts to stymie the U.S. during the era. It just came naturally.

Political Behavior

The trauma of terror and reprisals further blurred the vague lines separating political, social, and economic behavior in the Arab world. It couldn't be otherwise when the dominant themes of the era were attack and survival. The three categories are retained as areas of emphasis.

Expressing Identity: Nationalism, Tribalism, and Religiosity

Identity patterns during the era of terror and reprisals were more complex than at any previous time in Arab history (Khashan, 2000). The same observation was made in earlier chapters, and with good cause. In each case, the Arab psyche became more complex in order to keep pace with an ever more complex environment. Identity patterns followed suit.

Islamic emotions continued to sweep the region during the era of terror and reprisal, but bitter sectarian conflicts fragmented them. Debates over how best to serve God were equally divisive. Establishment Islam, having been corrupted by its submission to tyrants and tribal kings, found its hold over the masses eroded by the lure of the Muslim Brotherhood and an endless array of populist preachers.

Take, for example, Amr Khaled, the phenomenally popular Egyptian tele-preacher, whom the Western press tabbed the Islamic Billy Graham. A former member of the Muslim Brotherhood, he was expelled from Egypt in 2001 for discussing issues on his satellite programs that Arab governments found to be excessively sensitive. Among others, these included poverty, corruption, and immorality. His telecasts continued from London, as did his spectacular popularity in the Arab world. So great was his popularity, it was rumored that he was to be a candidate for the Egyptian presidency.

So bitter was the fragmentation of Islamic identities that hopes of Islamic unity all but disappeared. The only things that Arab Muslims were able to agree on were the dangers posed to Islam by America's war on terror and the need to end Israeli occupation of Muslim land.

Arab nationalism was alive, but not well. Feelings of Arab ethnicity were deeply embedded in the Arab psyche and manifested themselves in hostility toward the U.S. invasion of Iraq and the Israeli humiliation of Palestinian Arabs. They also played themselves out in Iraq, as Arab Shia increasingly resented the dominance of Iranian ayatollahs. As always, Arabs found it easier to blame their woes on external forces than to sacrifice for the good of the Arab nations. The fragmentation of Muslim identities reviewed above didn't help matters. Many Arab Muslims simply found it difficult to disentangle their Islamic and Arab identities. Hopes of Arab unity, while a hot topic among intellectuals, continued to fade.

Now add family and clan identities to the mix. By and large, they dominated Arab calculations of pain and pleasure as they struggled to survive in the "jungle" on a daily basis. While Arab intellectuals may have differed on issues of Islam and Arabism, they were unanimous on the central role of kinship ties in Arab life. Some praised it and some condemned it, but all agreed that family-clan-tribal considerations influenced all dimensions of Arab life.

As Tariq Habib, an expert on psychological illness, explained on the Al Arabiya program *Enlightenment* that religious Saudis put their loyalty to the Islamic Umma before their loyalty to the Saudi state, while the less-religious Saudis put their tribe or their village/town first. He found this to be disturbing, given the fact that the Saudi nation provides more welfare for its citizens than any other country. He blames this negative situation on an education curriculum that stresses religion and culture while placing minimum emphasis on nationalism. He goes on to criticize the lack of skilled teachers and the poor teaching of nonreligious subjects in Saudi schools (Habib, 2009).

Not to be outdone, the moderator of the Al Jazeera program *In Depth* introduced the topic of national identity in the Gulf with the comment, "The question of identity in the Arab Gulf region has become the most pressing, complicated, and painful of questions." Guests on the program considered language, Islam, and "roots" to be the core of the Gulf identity, along with the warning that "nationalism had yet to become more than government slogans" (Al-Zafiri, 2010).

This didn't mean that local identities were without significance. Despite all of Iraq's internal turmoil, victories of the Iraqi soccer team unleashed a rare moment of national rejoicing. Sadly, it also brought charges that selection of the team's governing body was selected on sectarian grounds. Bloody conflict over an Egyptian-Algerian soccer game almost resulted in a rupture of diplomatic relations between the two countries. In both cases, the intensity of mass emotions spoke of more than sports. They were also a warning of pent-up emotions waiting to be unleashed against their ruling tyrants.

The Arab Identity and American Frustrations

The identity patterns traced above suggest that virtually every dimension of the Arab identity can trigger an outpouring of emotions against outsiders. They also suggest that no dimension of the Arab identity is strong enough to galvanize the Arabs into a unified force capable of resisting the West or solving their own internal problems.

The U.S. has found each of these features of the Arab identity to be profoundly frustrating to its efforts to create a new Middle East or, for that matter, to deal with the old Middle East. The ease with which affronts to the multiple Arab identities can ignite emotions against outsiders has played a major role in fueling anti-Americanism in the Arab world. Simultaneously, the Arab inability to work together deludes the United States into thinking it can control the Arab world with a simple show of force. The same Arab inability to work together has frustrated the U.S. war on terror by creating weak states in which violence and extremism flourishes.

Just how much latent hostility the U.S. would face in its efforts to create a new Middle East became apparent from Muslim reactions to the September 11 attacks on New York and Washington. A *Times of London* poll conducted shortly after the September 11 attacks found that approximately 11 percent of Britain's two million Muslims believed that there was some justification for the attacks. An additional 40 percent condemned the attacks but believed that bin-Laden's war against the U.S. was justified (*Sunday Times*, November 4, 2001). During the same period, the *Arabic News* disclosed a secret Saudi intelligence survey that revealed that 95 percent of educated Saudis supported bin-Laden's cause (*Arabic News*, January 29, 2002). Reports of a supporting nature were provided by related polls, most of which displayed admiration for American democracy but harshly condemned its role in the Middle East (Palmer and Palmer, 2008).

The polls, in turn, were paralleled by a marked increase in Islamic dress and Islamic separatism in Europe, as well as increasing tensions between Christian and Muslim communities in the Middle East.

Also alarming was the sharp increase in Muslim hostility toward the U.S. that accompanied American attacks on Islamic educational institutions, Islamic charities, and Islamic financial institutions. As a congressional investigation acknowledged in 2003, "The bottom has fallen out of [Muslim] support for the United States (*New York Times*, February 5, 2004).

The freefall of Arab and Muslim support for the U.S. continued with the American occupation of Iraq which mass protesters and Islamic clerics of all stripes bitterly condemned. What choice did the tyrants have but to go along? The deep penetration of American forces into Pakistan and Yemen, and the threatened destruction of Iran, also inflamed Islamic emotions. Arabs didn't like Iranians, but this was an Islamic issue that signaled an intensification of America's war on Islam.

Arab hostility, it is important to note, did not translate into hostility toward individual Americans working in the region, but frustration with U.S. policy was clearly building.

The Obama administration made a concerted effort to ease Arab and Muslim sensitivities by putting on a smiling face, but American policy changed little. The withdrawal of all but fifty thousand U.S. troops from Iraq in 2010 was heralded as a new beginning in Arab-American relations. What it really heralded was a U.S. acknowledgment that its Iraqi venture was a dismal failure. The Arab psyche took heart.

It is not just Washington and Tel Aviv that had a talent for triggering the sensitivities of the Arab psyche. Given the complexity of Arab identity patterns, anyone and anything was capable of triggering a wave of anti-Western emotions in the Arab and Muslim worlds.

Take, for example, the crisis that erupted in 2006 when a Dutch newspaper published derogatory cartoons of the Prophet Mohammed. Massive anti-Dutch protests were unleashed throughout the Arab world, and diplomatic relations with Holland were strained to the breaking point. Everyone jumped on the bandwagon, including the dictators for life and the tribal kings. Again, they had no choice. They couldn't risk appearing anti-Islamic. Were the protesters careening through Cairo and other major cities solely concerned with affronts to their religion? No. The cartoons were used as a pretext for demonstrating against their leaders. Who knew when a protest would catch fire and a pro-American regime would be no more?

A repeat performance occurred in 2010 when the preacher of a small church in Gainesville, Florida, threatened to burn the Koran on September 11 in commemoration of the Muslim attacks on the U.S.

It made the local papers one day and was headline news on the Middle Eastern and European satellite channels the next. The issue was only defused when America's lead general in Afghanistan warned that the Koran burning could cost American lives. President Barack Obama and Secretary of State Hillary Clinton also asked this unknown preacher not to burn the Koran. He is no longer unknown, and at last report he was speaking to right-wing groups in Europe.

The plight of the Palestinians became even more sensitive because, in addition to being an affront to Islam and Arab nationalism, Israeli occupation of Palestinian territories stands as a blatant reminder of

Arab impotence. The Arab press was almost masochistic in its bloody portrayals of the Israeli slaughter of Palestinian civilians during the era, perhaps hoping to shock the Arab and Muslim worlds into action.

Imagine, then, the stir created in the Arab and Islamic worlds when Israel's former chief rabbi, and the spiritual leader of Israeli's leading religious party, called for a "Palestinian genocide," to cite the headline in the *Jerusalem Post*. Actually, he said, "God should strike them with a plague" (*Haaratz*, August 30, 2010). More headline news on Arab and Muslim satellite channels. More wounded pride. More shouting and cursing. More anti-Americanism. More hand wringing by the leaders of the Arab world, and more sympathy for the Islamists.

Why should unfortunate comments by an Israeli rabbi trigger anti-American emotions? Because large numbers of Arabs and Muslims viewed American and Israeli policy as being one and the same. All very frustrating.

This didn't mean than anyone upset with American policy was a terrorist. Almost all Arabs were upset with American policy, but only a minuscule fringe of Arabs and Muslims were terrorists or actively supported terror. Don't forget, the victims of terror were overwhelmingly Arab and Muslim.

As past kawagas have learned to their dismay, it is difficult to rule the Middle East by force alone. Force is part of the equation, but it didn't achieve American goals in either Iraq or Afghanistan. Nor, for that matter, have the Israelis had much success in quelling Palestinian emotions. Like it or not, American efforts to achieve its goals in the Middle East may have more to do with making friends and influencing people than they do with holding a gun at their heads. People march when the gun is present, and turn against their oppressors when it is not.

Even more frustrating for the U.S. and Israel was the realization that the region was seething with militias that, in addition to being heavily armed with rockets and other powerful weapons, had mastered the art of mining highways and detonating remote-control devices targeting Western troops. Kawagas have always been reluctant to take casualties, and the Israelis more so. On several occasions, they have willingly traded hundreds of Arab prisoners for one abducted soldier.

This, then, brings us to the cruelest of all frustrations confronting the U.S. in the Middle East during the era of terror and reprisals. The

U.S. could bomb the world out of existence, but occupation and lesser displays of force were proving ineffective.

Perhaps the best solution to America's frustrations was to abandon occupation while working to transform the countries of the Arab world into viable entities that were able to reduce extremism and violence by meeting the needs of their people.

This thought has been the focus of development scholars since the end of WWII, but it remains largely a dream. The crux of the problem is that the Arab states aren't really nations in the Western sense of the word. Most are collections of competing clans, sects, and ethnic groups held together by dictators via a blend of force and corruption.

The result of the Arab identification and loyalty patterns traced above was that the U.S. was dealing with Arab political leaders totally lacking in legitimacy who ruled by force and corruption. If the force waned, the system dissolved into a battle of tribes and sects.

Internal chaos was only part of America's frustrations with Arab identity patterns during the era of terror and reprisals. Sects and tribes did not recognize national borders, and conflicts in one country spilled over into neighboring countries like a contagious disease. Take, for example, the case of Iraq. Jihadist (al-Qaeda) groups did not have a presence worth mentioning in Iraq prior to the U.S. invasion, but they exploited the chaos of the U.S. occupation to become major actors in Iraqi politics. From there, their venom spread to Saudi Arabia and Yemen. The Kurds, for their part, used massive U.S. assistance to establish a virtual state within a state in northern Iraq. Assistance to enduring Kurdish revolts in Turkey, Iran, and Syria followed. Hizbullah, in turn, used its dominant position in Lebanon to strengthen Shia militias in Iraq.

Searching for Strong Bases of Group Support and Expressions of Loyalty

The ever-deepening chaos that gripped the Arab world with the advent of the era of terror and reprisals forced people to cling to their clans and other core groups with a renewed sense of urgency. To whom else could they turn? Governments were as ineffective as they were rapacious, and warring sects and occupation authorities were destroying everything in sight.

If traditional core groups couldn't provide security or other needs, people looked to charismatic religious groups or powerful warlords, both of whom boasted their own militias, secret or otherwise. Such tendencies were particularly strong among youth, migrants to the region's bursting slums, and residents of areas thrown into chaos by civil strife and American invasions.

It was all very predictable and remains so today. How else could people protect themselves and their families when every country in the region was either under the boot of tyrants, coping with occupation, wracked by civil war, riddled by sectarian conflict, suffering sustained terrorist atrocities, or threatened by external attack?

Tribes, once declining in influence, became major actors (warlords) in Iraq, Afghanistan, and most of the oil kingdoms. Charismatic sectarian groups, such as the Sadarists in Iraq and Hizbullah in Lebanon, became kingmakers in their respective countries. While unable to rule by themselves, they had enough power to assure that no one else could rule effectively either. Added to the fray were gangs of thugs, many masquerading as jihadist groups, who existed only to rob, ransom, and extort money from the rich. One had to get along.

In the process, individuals found themselves under even greater pressure to conform to the norms of their groups, all of whom were authoritarian and controlling. People had no choice, given the prevailing atmosphere of group conflict based on fear, distrust, hostility, and vengeance. After all, life had been reduced to a simple zero-sum game. It was them or us.

In some cases, tribal and sectarian loyalties overlapped, while in others sectarian militias fought tribal militias for control of territory and resources. Such conflicts were frequent, as alliances made to fight a common enemy dissolved into conflicts over political control. Alliances with terrorist groups such al-Qaeda became part of the game and followed the same on-again-off-again pattern.

American Frustrations Resulting from Support and Loyalty Patterns

Having sunk ever deeper into the morass of the Arab world, the U.S. lurched from strategy to strategy in its effort to create a new Middle East in an environment of ever-deepening group conflict that threatened the transformation of the entire region into a swamp that bred extremism, violence, and anti-Americanism. I use the word "lurch," because the U.S. pursued so many conflicting policies at the same time that it was hard for the Arab psyche to keep score. The American public didn't try. It was too painful.

This phase of American frustrations concentrates on three U.S. efforts to manage the group conflict that fueled terror and undermined stability in the region: elections, divide and conquer, and strengthening the security forces of regimes that supported the United States. The discussion focuses on Iraq because that was the major battleground between the U.S. and the Arab psyche during the era. The same pattern was being adopted in Afghanistan and other emerging swamps in the region.

Faced with the reality that its occupation of Iraq had turned into a nightmare, the U.S. gave up its initial policy of imposing a puppet regime on the Iraqis. Instead, the U.S. decided to allow the Iraqis to elect a leader whom, they hoped, would cooperate with the occupation authorities in bringing peace and development to a country in a virtual state of civil war.

The logic was compelling. People would be provided with the opportunity to express their views free of the influence of their core tribal and religious groups. A method would also be provided for resolving conflicts by peaceful means. In the process, America would emerge as the champion of democracy. Rather than being an occupying power, the U.S. would be the supporting partner of a democratically elected Iraqi government.

People in Iraq, to America's frustrations, did vote their interest. They voted for their core tribal and sectarian groups. Where else did they have to turn? Certainly not to a provisional government hastily cobbled together by the occupying power. Besides, few people believed that the elections had been free and fair, which of course they weren't. How could they be when they were conducted in the middle of a civil war in which large sections of the country were beyond the control of the United States or its provisional government?

A series of Iraqi elections served only to put an unstable, pro-Iranian regime in office. It also unleashed an interminable power struggle that immobilized the government and deepened sectarian, ethnic, and tribal conflicts. The Kurds took their share of the cake and ran, while the only thing the Shia could agree on was inflicting revenge on the Sunni while they fought among themselves. The Sunni, the big losers in the elections, hunkered down in their core groups, and jihadist terrorism flourished. The U.S., it seems, hadn't bothered to study the Arab psyche.

Parallel elections in Afghanistan followed the same script, but the farcical elections in Egypt, Jordan, and other countries allied with the U.S. were different. As long as the tyrants could keep the lid on group conflict, the U.S. had little interest in fair elections. The U.S. may have talked democracy, but leaked U.S. diplomatic documents tell a much different story.

This divergence in U.S. policies raised questions about why the U.S. was only interested in free and fair elections when it was bogged down in the middle of civil wars while turning a blind eye to blatantly fraudulent elections in Egypt and elsewhere.

Whatever the case, America was blamed for suppressing democracy in countries where it might have had a chance of taking root and was criticized for imposing elections in countries where the forces of terror and extremism were in the best position to win. Very frustrating.

Perhaps holding elections in countries locked in civil wars might have provided the U.S. with an avenue for reconciling group conflicts, if Washington hadn't pursued a simultaneous policy of playing one group off against the other, a ploy employed by the kawaga throughout history and perfected by the British. Let the Arabs fight it out while the kawaga kibitzes. In the case of Iraq and Afghanistan, this meant arming tribal militias to fight al-Qaeda and its allies, who had been encroaching on tribal territories.

This led to some much heralded tactical victories, but their luster faded as the newly empowered tribal militias fought to secure their own territories against all comers, including the U.S. Much like religious sects, the tribal militias were more interested in expanding their own control rather than building a nation or helping the Americans. If one tribal leader became too powerful, the others became jealous and turned on him. Remember, tribes are nations, and all they were doing was attempting to keep a balance of power among themselves while repelling the Americans and al-Qaeda, neither of whom were in Iraq prior to the invasion. When American and tribal interests clashed, the tribal militias were armed and ready. Some even made alliances with al-Qaeda.

Al-Qaeda, for its part, temporarily shifted its activities from the tribal areas and began blowing up Shia sections of Baghdad and Shia holy cities such as Najaf. As al-Qaeda predicted, their attacks precipitated Shia retaliation against all Sunni, many of whom were already hostile to the U.S. What better formula for turning Iraq into a swamp where al-Qaeda could breed? Leaders were killed, but they were soon replaced by local leaders with tenuous ties to bin-Laden and the al-Qaeda leadership. That wasn't of great concern to al-Qaeda, as long as chaos was brewing and the deadly jihadist organization could claim yet more victories against the Americans.

The process was repeating itself in Afghanistan, Pakistan, and just about every other swamp in the region. Getting caught in the middle of civil wars, declared or not, was an open invitation to frustration. It had to be. Things were just too complex for the kawaga to keep track of. Besides, al-Qaeda and other anti-American groups understood the psyche of the region. The Americans didn't.

Having been frustrated by its hastily contrived elections and the confusion caused by its divide-and-rule tactics, the U.S. adopted a strategy in both Iraq and Afghanistan that focused on building a dedicated, native security force that could control the country until democracy took hold and blatant corruption was reduced to manageable proportions. The U.S. had kept friendly regimes in power for decades by "advising" their security services. They knew the drill, or so it seemed.

U.S. confidence, however, was misplaced. As noted above, the U.S. was not dealing with random individuals in Iraq, but with members of groups whose interests were often adverse to those of the U.S. The military was not blind to this practice in Iraq, and it frankly admitted that it had failed to produce an effective government fighting force in either Iraq or Afghanistan. The trainees much appreciated the arms, training, and money, but much of it was simply diverted to destroying the American-imposed regime rather than supporting it.

The tensions produced by the era of terror and reprisals also began to undermine the loyalty of "friendly" governments and the effectiveness of "friendly" security services, such as those in Egypt and Saudi Arabia. The U.S. had counted on friendly Arab countries to stand by

America in its war on terror. None did so. Their leaders feared that the issue was so sensitive that their security services might rebel rather than fight. Arabs didn't like to kill other Arabs and Muslims simply to please the kawaga. It was part of their psyche.

If America's tribal kings and puppet dictators had confidence in their security services, why did they allow the anti-American demonstrations to go on for so long? That was the crux of the issue. The primary role of Arab militaries was to keep the regime in power. Fighting foreign enemies was secondary. Far worse, military establishments and secret services had become a law unto themselves. Oppression and mass fear increased apace, as did mass hostility toward their rulers. When workers at an Egyptian military factory demanded better safety measures following deaths caused by an exploding boiler, for example, they were jailed for obstructing national security. It was the same everywhere. No one cared as long as the security services kept the regime in power. But the pot was boiling.

The Arab security forces, themselves, had become wracked by the climate of fear permeating the region, not to mention sectarian conflicts, penetration by the Islamists, the micromanagement of superiors, and the watchful eye of the secret police. Not only were senior commanders nervous about their subordinates, but all of the reigning tyrants had their special royal or presidential guards designed to keep them in power if the security forces should rebel.

The Saudis attempted to solve the problem by having two armies, a regular army and a national guard, each designed to counter the other in the case of an attempted coup. The national guard was based heavily on troops from loyal tribes, and it was under the direct command of one of the senior Saudi princes. The regular army was under the command of a rival prince from a different mother. Were the Saudis nervous? You'd better believe it.

The U.S. also began to doubt the effectiveness of Arab militaries, a case in point being Wikileak's exposure of American embassy cables noting the decline of the Egyptian military, but taking solace in its continued ability to keep the Mubarak regime in power. They were soon proven to be wrong again.

On the brighter side, the Saudis spent their billions on American military equipment. The Americans weren't sure that the Saudi military would be allowed to use their fancy equipment for fear of rebellion, but it gave the Saudi royal family the image of power, boosted the American economy, and made Saudi Arabia's tribal kings even more dependent on the U.S. Who else could advise them on all that fancy American technology?

With all of these advantages, who cared if the Saudi Army couldn't fight? The Israelis cared. Not about the inability of the Saudis to fight, but about billions of dollars in sophisticated equipment that would fall into the hands of the Islamists should the regime fall. Who knew, for that matter, how much Saudi equipment was finding its way into the hands of resistance groups hostile to Israel? The U.S. did sell the Saudis $60 billion of arms from 2010 to 2011, and that was over Israeli objections. Even then, the quality of the equipment was downgraded to ease Israeli fears. The U.S. equipment was sophisticated enough to fight Arabs and Iranians, but not to fight the Israelis. The Israelis weren't convinced, and Saudi Arabia, a key American ally, was humiliated, again. It was almost enough to make a conspiracy-prone Arab psyche believe that the Saudis, U.S, and Israel were in cahoots.

Social Behavior

Conformity and an Obsession for Control: The Sexual Powder Keg

As in the past, most Arabs continued to conform to the political and social pressures of the day, whether they supported them or not. It was dangerous not to. If the police and the religious fanatics weren't lurking, family and neighbors were.

The era of terror and reprisals made the need for control and conformity even more urgent. The problem began with the conflicting identity and loyalty patterns discussed above and was accentuated by America's war on terror. Take, for example, the Muslim obligation of giving to the poor. Was donating money to an Islamic charity, a traditional act of piety and conformity, now an act of terror? One never knew. American authorities even accused the Saudi royal family of funding terrorist charities, and much to their humiliation, they were forced to repent in public. Were the Saudis really trying to control donations to suspect charities, or was their act of contrition merely a hollow gesture of forced conformity imposed by the U.S. imposed? In many cases, contributions were simply diverted to clean charities that subcontracted with less-clean charities, and they to far less-clean charities until the money trail was lost altogether (Palmer and Palmer, 2008). Saudi hands were clean, and the U.S. was frustrated.

For women, the decision to veil or not to veil became ever more politicized during the era of terror and reprisals. Far more significant in the long run was the emergence of gender relations as the prime source of social and political change in the Arab world. The veil was the symbolic battleground between traditional patterns of control and conformity on one hand, and social change on the other.

I don't know if the U.S. understood the potency of gender relations as a catalyst for modernity, but the jihadists surely did. Tradition was based on female subservience, and there was no greater threat to the jihadist vision of Islamic purity than the liberation of females from the total physical, social, and psychological domination of males (Altorki, 1986). Indeed, the first measures the Taliban introduced upon seizing power in Afghanistan were the total veiling of women and the closing of girls' schools. The Saudis maintained veiling but promoted female education on the condition that there was no mingling of the sexes.

The Muslim Brotherhood and Hizbullah, by contrast, faced the dilemma of finding a compromise that would allow women to play a more active role in society while still serving as the bastion of morality and family values. They knew that they couldn't return women to a time warp of seventh-century Arabia, but neither were they willing to see the sexual revolution go forward.

The stress of changing gender relations was also painful for men during the era, as they found it difficult to keep pace with changes in women's attitudes that were far outpacing their own (Baydoun, 2007). Education and docility seldom mix, and Saudi Arabia, that bastion of social and religious conservatism, suddenly found itself with more female than male students in its universities. It is true that there was no mingling of the sexes, and female unemployment was rampant, but the world of Saudi females was clearly changing more rapidly than that of Saudi males. Female students were not even on the same planet with the religious police, who equated the exposure of a naked eye with seduction and sin. Bahrain, far more liberal than Saudi Arabia, opened its first sex shop in 2010. According to *Spiegle Online*, it was doing a booming business to both males and females (October 2, 2010).

The best illustration of the tension between traditional and modern feminine roles that I have encountered was in an elementary Arabic language textbook designed largely for Lebanese Christians. The wife, a gorgeous creature dressed in stunning Paris fashions and spiked heels, cautions her children, immaculately dressed and sparkling clean, not to disturb their father as he returns exhausted from a hard day at the office. She rushes to greet him as he sinks into a comfortable chair, and she prepares a sumptuous dinner while the kids play quietly. In the next picture, the same woman, spiked heels and all, is teaching school. Presumably, she also has a job.

I have met a large number of wives in diverse Arab countries and, without exception, found them to be a far cry from the docile stereotype so common in the Western media. All were educated and had liberal husbands which makes them an exceptional group. Nevertheless, they represent the upper end of an accelerating cycle of change (Altorki, 1986). All were accepting of male dominance, but not without dignity and a clear sense of their own rights.

Arab women, in general, are now increasingly educated and, in sharp contrast to earlier eras, find education and the prospect of a good income to be an advantage in making a good marriage. They are also becoming increasingly selective about who and when they marry, the timing and number of children they want, and just how subservient they intend to be to their mothers-in-law.

For all of its changes, Arab society continues to demand marriage and children. Few fears among women are greater than that of spinster-hood. It is not that they can't face life without a man, merely that they can't face society without marriage. As the Egyptian press described the situation toward the end of the era of terror and reprisals,

> Because of the pressure on the girl, she often finds herself forced to get married as early as possible. She no longer enjoys her right to choose her partner. She chooses from the best from a bad bunch of offers in order to escape from the specter of spinsterhood, say specialists (*Egyptian Gazette*, March 16, 2010).

Speaking on the Al Arabiya TV program *Enlightenment*, the prominent Saudi writer, poet, and columnist, Abdullah bin Bakhait, cited a recent study issued by the Saudi religious police, the Committee for the Promotion of Virtue and the Prevention of Vice that justified the need for polygamy by warning that 1.5 million unmarried Saudi females currently faced spinsterhood. The standard of spinsterhood was any maiden who was not married in her nineteenth year.

An interesting aspect of the discussion was bin Bakhait's view that polygamy was unnatural and, although technically allowed in Islam, had aggravated a crisis of spinsterhood by allowing wealthy men to marry four wives, while the average youth couldn't afford to marry one. Bakhait understood the need to curb flirting in malls, but he took sharp offense at the religious police harassing a couple sitting in a restaurant before first ascertaining whether the woman in question was the wife, sister, or daughter of her companion. Sitting in a restaurant with a suitable male relative is not a sin in Saudi Arabia (Bakhait, 2008).

How was a woman to marry and avoid the scourge of spinsterhood when dowry and housing costs have become prohibitive? Necessity is the mother of invention, and large group marriages of one hundred couples or more are now taking place throughout the Arab world, many sponsored by religious authorities in order to prevent a further decay of Islamic morals. In Gaza, group weddings are being used to provide husbands for wives widowed by Israeli attacks. Many of the new husbands are drawn from within the kinship network of the bride (*Al Arabiya*, July 19, 2009). Even Saudi Arabia, that most conservative of countries, held its first group marriage in 2009. Common-law marriages are also increasing in the more progressive Arab states.

Added to the fray is the struggle of young females to conform to traditional demands for purity while peer pressures demand the relaxed sexual norms of satellite TV. The internet and Facebook are now evading even the restrictive laws of Saudi Arabia as couples, unable to meet in public, exchange pictures and coded messages. Alas, this often results in abuses, as immature or predatory males share the pictures, usually no more than a partially veiled face, with their friends. And predatory males there must be, for the Saudi religious police recently announced the stunning discovery that some ninety thousand Saudi license plates contained sexual references.

The Saudi religious police struggled to stay on top of things during the era of terror and reprisals by imposing severe penalties on even the most minor of moral infractions. When a female graduate student consulted too ardently with her major professor by telephone, both were whipped. In a notorious case of gang rape, the Saudi court was decisive in its verdict. The girl was at fault for being provocative. At the very least, the situation would never have occurred if she had conformed to the customs of Saudi society (Ismael, 2007).

The above stories, reported by the Saudi press and relayed by Arab satellite networks, have led to growing complaints against the Saudi religious police. In some case, irate Saudis have even attacked members of the religious police. It wouldn't have happened in an earlier era, but it is happening now. Even stranger is the fact that these events are being talked about in the Saudi press. Clearly, gender relationships were a potent force for change.

For women who give in to the temptations of love, Chinese fake-virginity kits are available for a few dollars. Egyptian authorities outlawed them under pressure from religious leaders, but that just increased their cost (*New York Times*, October 6, 2009). Virginity can also be restored for about three thousand dollars at a Paris clinic (BBC, April 24, 2010).

Conformity and American Frustrations

For all of the changes occurring in the Arab world during the era of terror and reprisals, the desire for continuity and belonging assured that conformity would remain a key element of Arab behavior. Behavior patterns change, but like the culture on which they are based, they changed slowly. Youth struggled to conform to the more traditional values of their parents and grandparents while pursuing a modern lifestyle among their peers (Melikian, 1981).

What this meant in terms of U.S. frustrations in dealing with the Arab world during the era of terror and reprisals was that Arab attitudes and behavior were changing too quickly for the comfort of America's pet tyrants and too slowly for the Arab world to embrace the modern values of the West. It also meant that the region was becoming polarized between people seeking an Islamic solution to their woes and those preferring a secular path. This conflict was so deep that no Arab country could escape it.

It would also be a mistake to ignore gender tensions as a source of America's frustrations during the era. One doesn't have to be a Freudian to understand that the harsh restrictions on sexual activity, including late marriage, were an underlying source of frustration in Arab society. Of themselves, they were unlikely to lead to revolt, but frustrations do play a role in fueling anger, extremism, and violence. The fit isn't perfect, but when you add sexual frustrations to oppression, unemployment, humiliation, and the rest, America had a real mess on its hands.

Social Deviance: The Fox against Society

American efforts to create a new Middle East provided the fox with unparalleled opportunities to ply skills honed by the eras of independence and resurgent Islam. The only change was the target, and what a wonderful target the Americans were. They were rich, generous, arrogant, careless, confused, desperate for love, gullible, and impatient. You name it, the Americans had it. The only trouble was that they were trigger happy.

Positioning: Capturing the Kawaga

The key to playing the fox with the U.S. was positioning, to be close but not too close. How else could the fox play with fire without getting burned? The truly clever fox gained the permission of his group to associate with the U.S. The group acquired arms, money, influence, and information. The fox used the same arms, money, influence, and information to bribe superiors, peddle influence, evade the rules, shake down innocents, force sexual favors, trade wasta, put relatives in key positions, inflict vengeance on enemies, and perpetrate all of the other species of venality discussed throughout earlier chapters. It was a win-win situation. The fox was helping the group by doing well for himself. In the process, his status within the group increased, often to the point of establishing his own subgroup of supplicants.

Some foxes offered the U.S. advice. Others worked in U.S. embassies and military establishments. Many informed Arabs made a cottage industry of selling insights and analysis to the Americans. The information they didn't have, they simply made up. Either way, most had their own axe to grind. Some dribbled the information out in small doses just to whet the appetite of American diplomats and intelligence agents. The more intriguing the stories, the better. I'm not sure whether the Americans were being duped, or it was simply a game they played to fulfill their official duties. Diplomats and intelligence agents had to talk to somebody, and informed Arabs were knowledgeable and spoke English. This was important, for a recent government report indicated that only 5 percent of the CIA agents during the era spoke a foreign language. Some diplomats even talked to me, but it wasn't the same. No mystique. On second thought, maybe selling curious information to the Americans was bigger than a cottage industry. It paid much better than their academic positions and was a sure path to research grants and visas.

Perhaps the greatest fox of all was Ahmed Chalabi, who positioned himself to take over Iraq well before the U.S. invasion had begun. Clever fox that he was, Chalabi beguiled the U.S. administration into believing that he could deliver the Shia community to the Americans if he were made the leader of a liberated Iraq. He knew that he couldn't achieve power on his own merits, so he convinced the Americans to do the trick for him.

That was just the beginning. Once in power, he would use the American support to destroy his Shia rivals at the same time that he used American fear of the Shia and Iran to make the U.S. ever more dependant upon him. The game was a simple as it was brilliant. Play the Shia against the Americans, and the Americans against the Shia. It almost worked, but not quite, so Chalabi offered the same deal to the Iranians while paving the way for a comeback with the Americans.

Not far behind Chalabi was an Iraqi defector codenamed "Curveball" who, determined to overthrow Saddam Hussein's regime, convinced German intelligence that Saddam Hussein had a secret biological weapons program. The Germans passed the information to the Americans with warnings to the CIA that it wasn't "watertight," but it was this information that the U.S. and its allies used to justify their attack on Iraq (*Guardian*, February 17, 2011). The then-director of the CIA disavowed any knowledge of German doubts until two years after the war had started.

The process of capturing the kawaga repeated itself up and down the line, as competing individuals and groups sought to strengthen their positions by cooperating with the U.S. to gain money and arms, both of which could be used against the U.S. when need be. In the meantime, the fox relied on the U.S. for protection. The process was the same in Afghanistan, Pakistan, and all of the other swamps in the making.

For those who couldn't work for the American government directly, there were ample opportunities to link up with a USAID contractor or to affiliate with one of the thousands of nongovernmental organizations (NGOs) descending on the region to help Arabs in need. Their organizations skimmed off most of the money that well-meaning people and gullible governments donated. Some NGOs did a great job, but they were in the minority.

There was lots of money available, and the kawaga also used the NGOs to appear concerned for human rights and to put pressure on its puppet dictators should they disobey. It could be a coincidence, but every time an Arab dictator stood up to the United States, he was faced with a wave of protests demanding greater democracy and human rights. The dictator backed down, and the protests disappeared. Think I am being cynical? Check the record yourself.

Even better than the run-of-the mill contractors and NGOs were the private security firms that provided mercenaries to the U.S. government and its allies in Iraq, Afghanistan, and God knows where else. While the typical contractors and NGOs did well financially by promising to do good for humanity, the mercenaries, the Big Boys, did unconscionably well by carrying out covert operations discouraged by military rules of conduct. Rough estimates placed the number of Big Boys in Iraq in the range of thirty thousand to fifty thousand (Fainaru, 2008).

The U.S., like most kawagas before it, began its Middle Eastern ventures confident of its ability to control both its informants and its contractors. The more the U.S. realized that it was being duped by informants and contractors alike, the more frustrated it became. Not only was the information provided by reliable sources unreliable, but the blatant graft of U.S. contractors became a national scandal. The Big Boys, for their part, killed and maimed with such abandon that their actions inflamed local populations already seething with hostility at the U.S. invasion. Why weren't they reined in? Simple. No one seemed to be in charge of the mercenaries. Not the American government, not the U.S. occupation authorities, and not a fragmented Iraqi government preoccupied with lining its pockets, shipping arms to its pet militias, and seeking revenge against Iraqi Sunni.

Religious NGOs, while sincere, inflamed Muslim emotions by attempting to convert Muslims to Christianity. Religious hostilities soared and, in some cases, resulted in the murder of the missionaries. This provoked a domestic crisis in the U.S. and forced overextended

U.S. troops to provide protection for the missionaries. If it wasn't one thing, it was another, and things kept getting worse.

Next on the list of America's frustrations was its realization that deals made with individuals and groups were temporary alliances that shifted with every change in the fortunes of war. The fox was only concerned with his own interests and didn't give two damns about the interests of his country or the U.S. Today's ally was tomorrow's adversary. Such was life in the land of the fox.

Appearances, Dissimulation, and American Frustrations

Appearances and dissimulation during the era of terror and reprisals continued to be two sides of the same coin. Appearances gave the impression that things existed when they didn't, while dissimulation gave the impression that things didn't exist when they did. To quote an Israeli journalist whose name escapes me, "We all lie. It's part of our psyche."

The importance of appearances soared to new heights in Iraq and Afghanistan, as the fox schemed to convince the kawaga that he was loyal, effective, and trustworthy. More than ever before, the fox had become a master of disguises, pretending to support the Americans while simultaneously filtering money and arms to his group or militia in order to gain its approval. Along the way, he filled his pockets, helped his family, and traded wasta to get from others what he couldn't take directly. Don't forget, *The Arabian Nights* took place in Baghdad.

As always, appearances focused on displays of wealth and influence. Both were vital in giving the impression of power, the key element in the Arab psyche's calculus of whom to support and whom to betray. Caution was also vital. Appearances of too much power made superiors nervous, while excessive displays of wealth brought hoards of relatives and invited kidnappings by the rapacious gangs that roamed freely in Iraq, Afghanistan, Algeria, and other swamps of the region. Bankers and politicians lived a very precarious existence in these countries, as did known supporters of the U.S. and Israel.

The capacity to kill has always been an element in the facade of those who would aspire for power, be they a political leader, general, or jihadist emir. More than ever, this was the case during the era of terror and reprisals. All conflicts, large and small, were transformed into a deadly game of chicken played with rockets, F-16s, collective punishment of civilians, and suicide bombers. Israelis spoke openly of their "crazy strategy" to justify the carnage of their devastating Cast Lead attack on the Gaza Strip in 2008 (BBC, March 13, 2009). The world condemned the attacks, but the Israelis had made a statement: "We are crazy enough to risk all if our security is threatened." Iran is now playing the same game with great effect. Does that mean there may soon be nuclear war in the region? I hope not, but the war cries of the tribal era have clearly given way to the rattling of nuclear sabers.

This situation was not only frustrating to the United States, it was also very dangerous. The escalation of conflict had become so brutal and so pervasive that it was beyond the control of the United States or any alliance of major powers to control. The looming U.S. defeat in Iraq and Afghanistan sure didn't help things. The Arab psyche sensed weakness, and its fear of the U.S. and American puppets was collapsing.

Adding to America's frustrations was the pervasive role of appearances and dissimulation in the region during the era of terror and reprisals. Both made it virtually impossible for the U.S. or anyone else to gather accurate information about the realities that the U.S. had to deal with in pursuing its interests in the region, Afghanistan and Iraq being cases in point. A bad show all around.

Offense as the Best Defense and American Frustrations

As the importance of appearances intensified during the era of terror and reprisals, so too did the need to save face. No one could afford to let down his guard, even for a moment. It was too risky. As always, offense became the best defense. Errors were denied and accusers vilified. No accusation could be left unchallenged, lest silence be interpreted as an admission of guilt and embolden others to pursue their attack. If denial failed, subordinates were forced to take the blame.

If sins were too visible to be swept under the table, they were blamed on outside forces. The U.S. or Israel were the obvious targets, but a competing sect, clan, country, or terrorist organization would do.

Paranoia? Not necessarily. Israeli spy networks permeated the region, and "dirty tricks" were part and parcel of Israeli defense strategy. The CIA had perfected dirty tricks during the Cold War and now applied them from covert bases in Iraq, Afghanistan, Pakistan, Yemen, and wherever the opportunity presented itself (*Washington Post*, September 23, 2010). Arabs and neighboring Muslim countries played the same game. It was all part of doing business in the Middle East, but that didn't make it easier for the people who lived there.

Paranoia or not, the pervasive game of blame and counterblame kept tensions in the region at a feverous peak. No one knew whom to believe or who their leaders would lash out at in a frantic effort to divert attention from their own miscalculations. Remember, the Arab psyche doesn't allow its leaders to be wrong.

Take, for example, the assertion of Mahmoud Ahmadinijad, Iran's president, that the Holocaust was an American plot to justify the settlement of Jews in Palestine. Perhaps the man is demented, but more likely, it was a defensive ploy to divert mass attention from his own domestic failures and to rile Muslims against American sanctions on Iran's nuclear program.

The ability of the U.S. to achieve its core interests in the region required an atmosphere of stability and compromise. This could not be accomplished in the prevailing atmosphere of blame and counterblame that fueled the conspiracy theories rampant in the region. All major players, be they countries, groups, or individuals, lived in constant fear of attack. Counterattacks were the Arab psyche's option of choice, so the cycle of attack and counterattack became self-perpetuating. The jihadists benefited from the violence and were able to gain footholds in the Arab world where none had existed before.

Adding to the confusion was the reality that not all of the conspiracy theories overwhelming the Arab psyche during the era of terror and reprisals were without foundation. Western books such as *Spies and Lies* were translated into Arabic and widely reviewed by Al Jazeera and other Arabic satellite channels (Al Jazeera, September 25, 2010). Wikileaks joined in by providing the Arabs with a daily soap opera of American and Israeli conspiracies.

These and similar revelations came as little surprise to anyone familiar with the region. The danger of Wikileaks exposing U.S. diplomatic cables to the public was that they gave credibility to all of the Arab conspiracy theories, real and imagined. They also made it very difficult for the U.S. and its puppets to pretend that they were sincerely interested in promoting democracy in the region or seeking an equitable peace between the Israelis and the Palestinians. How, for example, was the leader of the Palestinian Authority to gain support among the Palestinians when the cables revealed that he was cooperating with Israel to crush the Hamas movement that controlled the Gaza Strip? Survival was the PA's main concern, not Palestine.

In the meantime, the conspiracy mill had shifted into high gear, and the Arab penchant for exaggeration and embellishment was having a field day. After all, if all of the conspiracies revealed by Wikileaks were true, could others be far behind?

Whenever America thought that it had things calmed, a new crisis would emerge to keep the pot boiling. Take, for example, the case of the Coptic (Christian) bishop in Egypt who sent Egypt's sectarian tensions soaring by proclaiming that verses of the Holy Koran hostile to Christianity had been added during the reign of the Prophet's successors? In Muslim eyes, this assertion undermined the cardinal belief that every word of the Koran was revealed to the Prophet Mohammed verbatim by the Archangel Gabriel over a period of some twenty-three years (*Egyptian Gazette*, September 25, 2010). To put things in context, this is like saying that the Torah was not revealed to Moses.

Venality and American Frustrations

Venality in the Arab world is best defined as "beating the system" and includes everything from evading traffic laws to grand theft. And why not? Tyrants and occupiers were illegitimate and brutally oppressive. Morality wasn't an issue. To the contrary, ripping off the system continued to be a badge of honor and, more often or not, a prerequisite for survival. Even when people wanted to play by the rules, what good did it do them when no one else did? It didn't make sense to the Arab psyche, and the do-gooders were viewed as either fools or exceptionally clever foxes.

The political systems of the region were built on venality, nepotism, favoritism, corruption, and connections. They would collapse without them. What this meant for the U.S. during the era of terror and reprisals was that it could only keep puppet regimes in power by promoting oppression, corruption, nepotism, favoritism, and connections. The system was elaborated upon in Chapter 5. It had rotted even further under the pressures of the era of terror and reprisals.

This situation left the U.S. with a difficult choice. Should the U.S. act morally in dealing with the political systems of the region, or should it be practical and pragmatic? The choices were too daunting for the U.S. to deal with, so each branch of the American government pursued its own course as it saw fit.

Take, for example, the curious scenes in Iraq and Afghanistan, as some branches of the U.S. government were putting intense pressure on corrupt puppet regimes to clean up corruption, while the CIA was playing the Middle Eastern game by providing the same leaders with money for bribes and kickbacks.

The same conflicts were occurring in Egypt and Syria, as the U.S. State Department was putting pressure on puppet governments to be more humane at the same time that the darker forces in the U.S. government were sending terror suspects to the very same countries for torture. Rendition, they called it.

If this were not frustrating enough, the United States forced Hamid Karzai, its arranged dictator in Afghanistan, to apologize in public for being corrupt at the same time that the CIA was keeping him in power by funding his corrupt regime.

The Taliban and others could only interpret America's public humiliation of their puppet prince as a sign that they were about to dump him. Coincidently, it was shortly after their public humiliation of Karzai that the U.S. opened indirect negotiations with the Taliban, its main target in a failed nine-year effort to pacify Afghanistan. Oh, did I mention that Karzai was also taking money from the Iranians and that the Afghan minister of the interior was a warlord with his own army? (*Washington Post*, September 27, 2010).

America's inability to resolve its morality-pragmatic dilemma resulted in its ending up with the worst of all possible worlds. Corruption and oppression continue unabated, while puppet leaders were weakened and the religious extremists emboldened.

Capping U.S. frustrations was its growing realization that it was never going to end extremism and violence in the Middle East by perpetuating corrupt and oppressive leaders who were even more venal than their subjects. Take, for example, a Saudi monarchy that blamed girls for crimes of rape at the same time that the young princes were enjoying sex and drug parties carefully avoided by the religious police. It is the same everywhere. Wikileaks just happened to catch the Saudis.

Distrust, Suspicion, and American Frustrations

Ironically, the more successful the fox became in beguiling the kawaga and plying his trade for personal gain, the more he courted suspicion within his core group. Treason and double agents were everywhere in the Arab world, and while people admired the fox, they didn't trust him. Superiors feared that a successful fox would use his newfound influence, however much it helped the group, to replace them. I use the word "fear" rather than "suspicion" because few people in the Arab world had any doubt about the matter. Don't forget, they were also foxes.

Peers, for their part, feared the growing influence of their colleagues, but weren't sure what to do about it. They knew the drill, for it was the same as theirs. Family and very close friends would come first, and then the circle would expand to lower levels of trust. Those left out of the circle were doomed to ignominy. And thus the cruel question. Should they curry the favor of the more clever foxes or destroy them? Perhaps they could do both.

The United States, like the British kawaga before it, didn't want to rule the Arab world directly during the era of terror and reprisals. Rather, it wanted to establish moderate regimes compatible with American interests, including the maintenance of anti-terror bases on their territory. If Iraq and Afghanistan were any indicators, the U.S. couldn't rule a Middle Eastern country directly even if it wanted to.

No factors frustrated America's idealistic dream of a new Middle East more than the pervasive fear and distrust that permeated the Arab and Islamic worlds. It was fear and the accompanying distrust that bred the extremism and violence engulfing the region, much as it was fear and distrust that prevented the Arabs and most of their Muslim neighbors from building effective nations with flourishing economies.

Economic Behavior

Terror and reprisals dampened legitimate economic behavior. Innovation, always a weak point in the Arab psyche, declined, as did investment. It was too risky. Individual productivity also declined, as unemployment soared and fear sapped the energies of government workers. This led to a scarcity of goods and a booming black market in just about everything.

The energies of the fox, by contrast, shifted to smuggling and extortion. This was certainly the case in Iraq and Afghanistan. It was also the case in Egypt, as the Israeli-American blockade of the Hamas-controlled Gaza led to the construction of a vast network of underground tunnels between Egypt's Sinai Peninsula and Gaza. Arms, food, and medical supplies were the main items smuggled into Gaza, but some tunnels were so vast that they even accommodated cars. It was the same in Iran, as items prohibited by the U.S. poured across Iran's porous border with Iraq. Some had even been stolen from the U.S. supply depots. The U.S. blockade of Syria was largely symbolic, but was easily circumvented by Lebanese smugglers.

Where to start? How about by acknowledging that blockades don't work? The Israeli-American blockade of Gaza could cause a humanitarian crisis among poor Palestinians, but it didn't clip the wings of Hamas. The most lasting effect of the blockade, now lifted, was irreparable damage to Israel's reputation as a humane and peace-loving country. Don't be shocked. The matter is widely discussed in the Israeli press. The Israelis discuss such issues freely. So do the Europeans.

The U.S. blockade of Iran was an inconvenience, but it didn't stop the Islamic republic from building nuclear facilities capable of manufacturing weapons of mass destruction. Nor, for that matter, did the U.S. sanctions prevent Iran from developing rockets capable of delivering those weapons, perhaps as far as Israel. America's coveted oil fields in Iraq, Saudi Arabia, and the Gulf sheikhdoms were clearly placed at risk.

While legitimate economic activity suffered, it was the gangs of smugglers, many linked to zaims, tribes, terrorists, and extremist groups, that prospered. As a result, the U.S. had to pump ever-larger sums into Iraq and other friendly countries just to keep their economies afloat. In the meantime, the price of oil soared, and the U.S. economy grew shaky. Perhaps the U.S. couldn't afford to create a new Middle East.

Now, add drugs to U.S. frustrations. The production of cocaine and other drugs flourished because it was exceptionally profitable and couldn't be controlled. People were going to do whatever was required to survive. That is basic psychology. They were also going to incline toward products that were safe and easy, and that produce huge profits.

That's economic theory. It also describes the ease of producing drugs in the swamps of the Middle East.

RED-FLAG ISSUES: BAD SHOW ALL AROUND

Religious extremism continued to soar during the era of terror and reprisals, and violence continued to set new records in variety and intensity. Fragmentation became the norm at both the local and regional level. Tyrants ruled by whim and continued to make a mockery of democracy. In the process, they drove the masses to ever-greater despair. There was no equality or equity, and hopes for development and a better future continued to fade.

Why didn't the whole thing explode?

CHAPTER 8

RAGE, CHAOS, AND THE ARAB PSYCHE

Why hadn't the Arab world exploded in anger given the decades of despair and humiliation described in the preceding chapter? Or as the moderator of the Al Jazeera program *Opposing Views* posed the question, "Why are Arabs more tolerant of tyrants than any other people on the face of the earth?" (Qassem, 2010). This wasn't his view alone, for the question had earlier been posed to the program's viewers, 75.3 percent of whom agreed with the proposition that the Arabs were indeed, the most docile people on earth.

THE ARAB WORLD EXPLODES

No sooner had Al Jazeera program aired than the Arab world erupted in rage, as Arab youth poured into the public squares of Tunis and Cairo screaming for jobs, dignity, and justice. What a marvelous sight it was, with banners, chants, and inciters hoisted on the shoulders of their colleagues like the poets of old.

The explosion began in Tunis on December 17, 2010, when a young fruit peddler was stopped by a female inspector as he hawked his apples. She seized his apples. He grabbed them back. She slapped him. A scuffle ensued, and he was beaten by two of her colleagues (*Washington Post,* March 26, 2011.) Other reports say the peddler was selling vegetables, but the results were the same. Angry and humiliated, the vendor demanded restitution from the local authorities who brushed him aside. His fruit gone and his honor destroyed, the vendor set himself ablaze in front of a public building. Less than a month later, mass protests had forced Tunisia's president of twenty-three years, a close ally of the United States, to flee the country.

The suicide by flames could well have been written off as insanity if the humiliation and despair of the fruit peddler had been his alone. It was not. Other protest suicides followed throughout the region despite warnings by government clerics that the Koran banned suicide (*Egyptian Gazette*, January 19, 2011). As the president of the Arab Federation of Psychiatrists noted, "Many people with no outlet for their own frustration, despair, and helplessness, understood how he must have felt and saw him as a kind of role model" (Okasha, 2011, 1).

Approximately six weeks after the Tunisian riots, it was the flames of Egypt, the mother of the Arabs, which electrified the Arab masses and sent revolution and violence spiraling throughout the Arab world. The Egyptian uprising, like that sparked by the fruit vender in Tunis, came as a surprise to everyone, the U.S. included. After all, protests were nothing new in Egypt. There had always been student demonstrations in Cairo, but all had collapsed in a few days under the boot of the tyrant. As a protest organizer in Egypt later confessed, "We went out to protest that day and expected to be arrested in the first ten minutes, just like usual" (El-Ghobashy, 2011). The riot police also assumed that the January 25 protests would unfold according to script, with an operations colonel noting that, "Our preparations for January 25 were as per-usual, and the instructions were not to molest demonstrators" (El-Ghobashy, 2011).

What was new in the Tunisian and Egyptian explosions was the steadfastness of Arab youth in the face of armed security forces firing live bullets, clubbing the demonstrators from horseback and camelback, and dragging female protesters away for virginity checks (*Al-Masry Al-Youm*, April 31, 2011). Iraqi youth had braved American forces, and Palestinian youth had defied Israeli tanks, but never had there been a sustained popular revolt against tyrants who ruled the Arab world. Military and religious coups, yes, but not the displays of mass resistance that confronted the tyrants in the spring of 2011.

The era of rage and chaos had begun. I term the latest era of Arab history the era of rage and chaos because explosions of rage shattered the past with little regard for the future. A new order will evolve, but it will take time, lots of time. There will be lots of false starts as the tyrants cling desperately to power while the protesters struggle to forge a new political system that will give voice to their dream.

With this thought in mind, the final chapter will examine why the Arab world exploded in rage after decades of servility. It will also trace the stages that the Arab revolution is likely to pass through in its enduring search for stability, food, freedom, justice, jobs, and dignity. Finally, the chapter speculates on what comes next, based upon the study of the Arab psyche and Arab behavior that have been traced over the course of Arab history. Along the way, it addresses America's likely frustrations as it attempts to cope with a new Middle East far different from the new Middle East that it had once hoped to build.

There is no guarantee that the trends of the past will continue into the future because of the possibility of new and cataclysmic changes in the Arab environment, such as a nuclear war between Israel and Iran, American reprisals for a new and devastating jihadist attack on the United States, or the appearance of a new hero reminiscent of Nasser or the Ayatollah Khomeini. The possibilities are endless. Until that time, think of this stage of the discussion as a checklist to help you keep score as the era of rage and chaos evolves over the coming years.

WHY THE ARAB WORLD EXPLODED: THE ENVIRONMENT OF RAGE

Why, then, did the Arab world explode in rage after decades of servility? The answer to this question will be debated for decades, but the key elements in the explosion are not hard to identify.

The despair of the Arab masses had transformed the Arab world into a vast tinderbox waiting to explode. All that was required was a spark. How else can one explain how the self-immolation of a fruit peddler could topple a Tunisian tyrant who had ruled uncontested for twenty-three years, and unleash a chain of uprisings that would stretch the length and breadth of the Arab world? There was no conspiracy or planned uprising, merely one blaze triggering another. The Tunisian spark landed first in Egypt, where it prompted a Facebook call for demonstrations in sympathy with the Tunisians. The author of the Facebook revolution admitted, with some embarrassment, that he had no idea that he would precipitate a revolution (El-Ghobashy, 2011).

The explosion, however, was more than a matter of grinding poverty and a dismal future without jobs or any hope of a better life. It was also a matter of profound indifference on the part of the tyrants. Tribal kings and presidents, alike, believed that their security services and American power could keep them in power forever. As a result, they became impervious to the public mood while implementing American demands for economic globalization and cooperation with Israel. The former deepened economic hardships while the latter assaulted Arab pride, but none more so than Egypt's cooperation with U.S. and Israeli efforts to starve the Hamas government in the Gaza Strip out of existence.

The Saudis had similarly been damaged by their cooperation with Israeli and U.S. efforts to crush Hizbullah. Israeli forces struck Hizbullah strongholds in Lebanon, including Beirut, while the U.S. and Saudi Arabia publicly blamed Hizbullah for the carnage. The Israeli attacks turned out to be a disaster for Israel. Their forces retreated, and Hizbullah grew stronger. The Saudi monarchy, the protector of Islam, was left holding the bag and openly complained that the Americans hadn't kept their part of the deal (Obaid, 2006).

Why, many Arabs wondered, had their leaders helped Israel kill Arabs and Muslims? What kind of Arabs and Muslims were they? The answer was simple. The tribal kings and presidents for life had joined the U.S. and Israel in a silent agreement to stamp out all forms of Islamic extremism that threatened the existing order. The Arab masses were not part of the deal.

The uglier the public mood became, the more the tyrants retreated to their palaces while the security forces ran the country, a situation graphically described by Mona El-Ghobashy:

Mubarak's [Egypt] was not a police state because the coercive apparatus routinely beat and detained people. It was a police state because the coercive apparatus had become the chief administrative arm of the state.... Officers are free to work out their own methods of revenue extraction, sometimes organizing the urban drug trade. Patrolmen routinely collect tribute from taxi and microbus drivers and *shopkeepers, while high-ranking officers partner with landowners or crony businessmen* (El-Ghobashy, 2011, 2).

Ghazi Al-Taube, a leading Al Jazeera commentator, concurred, but noted that this was nothing new (Al-Taube, 2011). Arab leaders, in his view, had always been isolated from the masses. Some may have been more enlightened than others, but with the exception of the early days of Islam, there had always been a disconnect between the rulers and the ruled. Force and tyranny were the norm and not the exception. As a result, there simply were no mechanisms available for the masses to express their grievances other than protests and violence. The tighter the lid was sealed, the more mass hostilities festered, until they exploded in violence. This was the case for the rage of 2011, much as it had been the case in the violent explosions that accompanied the era of Islamic resurgence. The contexts were different, but the root causes were the same (Palmer and Palmer, 2008).

The explosion of 2011 should not have been cause for undue surprise. Protests had become increasingly frequent in the preceding years, most organized by students. It was they, desperate, idealistic, and intensely sensitive to the humiliations of Arabism and Islam, who were the vanguard of protest in the Arab world. They were also well educated, articulate, computer savvy, and yet to be cowed by the threat of arrest.

Students were the most vocal of the diverse centers of rage in Arab society, the nature of which varied from country to country. In Egypt, other key centers of rage included neighborhoods inflamed by police brutality, labor strikes ignited by low wages and grinding hours, farmers forced from the land by real estate developers, and professional associations chaffing under regime control. Foremost among the latter were the lawyer, teacher, medical, engineering, and press syndicates, many of which had fallen under the influence of the Muslim Brotherhood (El-Ghobashy 2011).

Adding to the "desertion" of the professional syndicates was a general disaffection among a small, if vibrant, middle class that was finding itself so squeezed financially that it could no longer maintain the lifestyle to which it had been accustomed. As a leading member of Egypt's ruling party later acknowledged, "I didn't expect the middle-class people to come together that way and be that effective" (Badrawi, 2011).

A graphic illustration of the link between political and economic discontent is found in survey data provided by Gallup/Dhabi that indicated that 91 percent of the Egyptians viewed themselves as either "struggling" (60 percent) or "suffering" (31 percent) (Gallup, Inc., 2011). These figures were parallel to those in Tunisia, Yemen, the Palestinian Territories, Libya, Jordan, and Morocco. Not only was the quality of life in these countries miserable, but it was also declining, a classic formula for revolution.

Now, add "waithood," to the despair and frustration of young Arabs. "Waithood" is a term reflecting the length of time required to gain financial security adequate for marriage. Arab society demands marriage, and yet among Egyptians "aged 15 to 22, 39% are working, but only 5% are married. Low percentages of marriage among men persist through the 23 to 29 age bracket.... Fewer than half (41%) are married" (Younis, 2010).

The centers of rage in countries such as Yemen, while headed by the students, centered on tribal and sectarian conflicts, either of which could flare up at a moment's notice. In Bahrain and Iraq, sectarian differences also came into play.

In years past, protests from the diverse centers of rage, while increasing, were sporadic and uncoordinated. This allowed the security forces ample time and resources to cope with the crises on an individual basis. Enough force was used to convince the masses that rebellion was futile, while stopping short of gratuitous violence that might trigger larger protests.

This formula broke down during the era of rage, as Facebook and other avenues of social networking tilted the advantage in favor of the protesters. Facebook and its cohorts shaped the revolution in at least three ways. Perhaps the most powerful message of Facebook revolution was simply, "You are not alone." As protests proliferated, the message became, "We number in the millions." Then came the message, "We can win."

Beyond this, social networking enabled all of the diverse centers of rage within a country to coordinate their activities and face the security forces with overwhelming numbers that were beyond their capacity to control. As a senior police official in Egypt would later concede, the protesters "outnumbered the security forces by a million or more [and led to] confrontations with angry people and indescribable hatred to the government" (Al-Shurouq, March 23, 2011).

The explosion, however, was more than the coordination of centers of rage known to the security forces. Facebook and other avenues of social networking had given birth to a new and powerful group that was beyond the control of the security forces. For lack of a better term, I refer to it as the Movement of the Dispossessed, a term borrowed from earlier Shia uprisings in Lebanon (Norton, 1997, 47).

The group had no identity, no organizational structure, and no ideology other than desperation and hopelessness. Nor, for that matter, did it possess a national identity or a religion. Wretchedness in the Arab world was pervasive and played no favorites. It was this wretchedness that provided a critical mass of people willing to stand firm against the tyrants. It had become their only hope. The dispossessed were nothing new in the Arab world, but now they had found a way to share the intensity of their agony and humiliation.

Undoubtedly, the global satellite networks played their role in preparing the ground for the uprisings. Al Jazeera led the way, with exposés of everything from corruption in the Arab world to American efforts to crush Arab resistance movements. The program on corruption in the Arab world concluded that Arabs spent about one-third of their income on bribes (Al Jazeera, July 7, 2010). This formula meant that the rich got most of what they wanted, while the dispossessed got nothing. Far worse, the ability of the rich to buy government officials meant that they were free to exploit the dispossessed at will. Were the dispossessed angry? Count on it.

Viewers watching the program on American efforts to crush Arab resistance movements, in turn, were invited to vote on the question, "Do you support Arab, Israeli, and American efforts to prevent weapons going to Arab resistance movements?" The result: 93.2 percent of the voters favored arming Arab resistance movements (Al Jazeera, May 13, 2010). Call-in surveys aren't reliable in scientific terms, but these results sure were inflammatory in a region primed for revolution.

Other tantalizing programs covered secret prisons in the Arab world, not to mention relentless portrayals of the U.S. as a wounded power locked in a vortex of defeats from which it could not escape. The message was clear. The kawaga's days are numbered, and he will desert his Arab tyrants much as he deserted the Shah of Iran.

Add to this the soaring popularity of the Muslim tele-preachers. Even tame tele-preachers such as Amr Khaled, the Arab Billy Graham, preached a message compatible with the views of the Muslim Brotherhood. His speeches had been softened to mollify the state censors who praised his moderation, but left ample room for reading between the lines (Khaled, 2011). Remember, Arabs had made an art form of reading between the lines, especially when the key content was in the sound and rhyme rather than the words. Talk shows had been allowed as a means of enabling people to let off steam. In retrospect, this was a failed strategy that merely informed the masses of how discontent their fellow citizens really were.

One way or another, the pressures leading up to the era of rage tapped the full range of emotions discussed earlier, including despair, humiliation, anger, revenge, Arabism, and religious zeal. Combined with the explosion of information and misinformation, there was so much adverse information pelting the Arab psyche that it couldn't dodge its misery even if it tried.

An Egyptian commentator summed the recipe for the explosion: "Ingredients: A corrupt ruler, a bunch of corrupt communities and 80 million ounces of naive Egyptian society. Preparation: Preheat oven to inferno level. Mix all the ingredients to a smooth consistency, then pour the mixture into a large pan. Bake for 30 years and bon appetite!" (Salama, 2011).

All of the stimuli that led to the Arab explosion of 2011 will come into play in this discussion that speculates on what comes next as the Arab world struggles to create a new political order that is both stable and capable of meeting the aspirations of its citizens.

STAGES IN THE ERA OF RAGE AND CHAOS

While the era of rage left no country of the Arab world untouched, the revolution of rage has progressed much faster in some countries than others. And a revolution it is, for neither the Arab world nor the Arab psyche will ever be quite the same again. Coups come and go, but not revolutions.

Egypt and Tunisia are in the forefront of the revolution of rage, while Saudi Arabia lags behind. This said, the revolution of rage is passing through several stages that even the most firmly entrenched tyrants in the Arab world will find difficult to avoid. The lines between the stages outlined below are often blurred, for revolution is a fluid process that ebbs and flows with the tide of events. The intensity of deeply entrenched conflicts may dull glimmers of democracy, and one tyrant may fall only to be replaced by another. In the meantime, the Arabs will struggle to create a new political order that is both stable and capable of meeting the aspirations of its citizens. When this goal is achieved, the era of rage and chaos will have come to an end.

Stage One—Pre-Revolution: The Game of Protests and Measured Repression

Protests had increased steadily throughout the Arab world in the decade preceding the Arab explosion. None had seriously challenged the authority of the regime, and all had been dispersed by the security forces within a few days. It was a game of sorts, as the dispossessed let off steam while the tyrants demonstrated the invincibility of their security forces. People could protest against the Americans and the Israelis and even economic shortages, but under no circumstances were they allowed to protest against the tyrant. They remained inviolable.

Intellectuals and the leaders of docile opposition parties mumbled inanities about the need for greater democracy at the same time that their hands were in the till. Rather than deserting the tyrants, Arab intellectuals provided them with the illusion of legitimacy (Bidwan, 2011). The few who stood their ground were arrested but seldom maimed for life. That, too, was a game of sorts, as they became heroes.

Egypt had led the way in this process, with almost a decade of student demonstrations protesting the war in Iraq and a seemingly endless array of minor labor disputes. The Saudis, by contrast, had suffered through a spate of respectful petitions begging a beneficent king for greater representation and increased rights for women.

The protests had little impact on policy as the tyrants, confident of their authority, continued to cooperate with U.S. and Israeli efforts to crush radical Islamic currents that threatened to destabilize the region. Some even raised food prices, a sure guarantee of public protest.

The game, while largely an illusion, set the stage for the Arab revolution in several critical ways. In part, the early protests were a training ground, as the protesters found their voice and pushed the limits of regime tolerance. The Egyptians and the Tunisians were far better trained in the game of protest than the Saudis who, by and large, refused to play the game.

The game, illusion or not, lulled the tyrants and the United States into a false sense of security. The game seemed to work so well that both seemed to believe that it could go on forever.

While the security forces plundered and intellectuals were bought off, the pain of the masses grew unbearable. They cried in silence, but no one was listening because all of the avenues for expressing their grief, including the press and the intellectuals, had been bought off by the government. The Muslim Brotherhood did well in the faux elections, but never ran enough candidates to challenge the government. They too, were doing well by playing the game. It was part of their strategy.

Stage Two—The Game Changes: Challenges and Incitement
The game changed when the protesters violated the rules by attacking the regime and refusing to disperse in the face of standard security measures. To the contrary, most called for "days of rage" that would pit the tyrants against the dispossessed.

The tyrants countered with a combination of brutal force and vague promises of jobs, but the protesters stood their ground. This forced a confrontation with the regime that it couldn't sidestep. Most blamed the protests on "outside influences," and called out their pet intellectuals, sports heroes, movie stars, and clergy to sing the praises of the regime. Saudi Arabia was short on movie stars, but had lots of clergy. A promised day of rage was countered by official religious decrees declaring all sit-ins and protests to be a violation of Islamic law (Al Arabiya.net, March 5, 2011). Least there be any doubt on the matter, the Saudis printed 1.5 million copies of a religious decree issued by senior Saudi clerics denouncing any form of protest and calling on the Saudi population to "stand united behind its wise and legitimate leadership" (*Guardian*, March 29, 2011). The monarchy vowed to uphold Islamic law by crushing all disturbances challenging its authority. The Saudi foreign minister also vowed to "cut off any finger raised against it," a threat presumably aimed at Iran (*As-Shark Al-Awsat*, March 10, 2011).

The initial day of rage failed to explode in Saudi Arabia, but in a prime example of Arab doublespeak, a commentator on the Saudi-owned *As-Shark Al-Awsat* chortled, "Everyone was surprised when this day of rage turned into a silent Bayaa (pledge of allegiance) which saw the Saudi public wordlessly express their support of their leadership" (Alhomayed, 2011). That is how Saudis express their opinions. Wordlessly.

The international and regional media also entered the fray at this stage, vilifying Arab tyrants for slaughtering unarmed civilians who demanded nothing more than food, dignity, and a breath of freedom. The protesters, now cast in the role of heroes and martyrs before a global audience, held their ground.

This was all very frustrating for the U.S., the global champion of democracy and human rights which stood by its tyrants while pleading for moderation.

Stage Three—Populist Protests Become a Revolution

The more the protesters held their ground, the more formal organizations such as the Muslim Brotherhood, labor unions, professional associations, token opposition parties, and tribes were forced to enter the fray. It was risky, but they had little choice in the matter. The window of opportunity had opened, but who knew for how long? All had been tainted by their cooperation with the tyrants. It was now their turn to stand up and be counted. They could either side with the people and claim leading positions in the coming regime, or to use the Egyptian phrase, they could suffer the curse of the pharaoh.

The Muslim Brotherhood was particularly important, for it had historically provided the most vocal opposition to the tyrants, spoke with the authority of Islam, and could draw upon an organizational network that spanned the globe.

This said, the choice had not been easy for the Muslim Brotherhood, a conservative organization guided by very old men wary of plunging into uncharted territory. They knew the game and were willing to bide their time while the outrages of the tyrants paved the way to power. A populist revolution with strong secularist leanings was not part of the Muslim Brotherhood's game plan. While the elders preached moderation, it was the younger members of the Muslim Brotherhood who seized the moment and supported the revolution.

It was the participation of the better-organized groups in society that tipped the scale in favor of the protesters. Indeed, one of the key reasons that the days of rage had difficulty taking off in Saudi Arabia was the lack of a civil society. There were no independent groups in Saudi Arabia that were not under the control of the royal family. The tribes, the foundation of Saudi society, were bought off, as was virtually everyone else in the kingdom. The main exception to this rule was the Shia who predominated in the oil-rich Eastern Province. They did protest, and paid the price of brutal oppression.

The expansion of the protests into a full-scale revolution sewed doubt in the minds of security units and ordinary police. Some, sensing the power of the revolution, stopped firing on the protesters. In a few cases, units in the military and security police defected to the side of the revolutionaries, but it was far from altruism. In the case of Yemen, the defecting commander was a half-brother of the tyrant who had been pushed aside by the tyrant's son and his three nephews. In the process, new "family" military units were created to serve as a counterweight to the regular security services. The alienated half-brother of the president didn't defect to the protesters, but to Yemen's most powerful tribal leader and the second most powerful man in the country. Why had this powerful tribal leader turned on a regime that he had once supported? He had no choice. His power, too, had also been eroded by the tyrant's family (Hermann, 2011).

Palace coup or not, everyone pretended that it was a populist uprising against a despicable tyrant. The leader of the rebellious tribe, for example, assured the media that, "It is in fact a popular youth's movement and a divine will.... The tribes left their weapons in the houses and went to the squares seeking freedom and change." Curiously, this statement was issued after the rebellious sheikh's presumed shelling of the presidential palace. I say presumed shelling, because the palace could have been shelled by the president's brother or even religious groups in the north.

When the Al-Shark al-Awsat interviewer asked the rebellious sheikh if his brother had been attempting to overthrow the regime by financing the protests, the sheikh responded, "My brother, Hamid, has been one of the youths of the peaceful opposition very early on and he warned of a popular protest if the regime continued with its arrogance and intransigence"(*Al-Ahmar*, June 19, 2011).

As a general principle, the entrance of better-organized groups into the revolution threatened to rob it of its spontaneous and populist nature. Emotionalism gave way to fragmentation as key political, religious, social, and economic groups jockeyed for control of the uprising. In Egypt and Tunisia, the major divide was between the Islamists and the secularists. In Bahrain, the revolution was transformed into a sectarian conflict. In Libya, it was a tribal conflict. In Yemen, it smacked of both tribalism and sectarianism.

American policy made tepid moves to support the democratic revolutionaries, but even they were opposed by both Saudi Arabia and Israel. Israel feared that the revolutions would incite the Palestinians, scuttle its secret deals with the tyrants, and lead to a surge in anti-Israeli emotions as Islamic fundamentalists rose to power. The Saudis controlled the region by funding the tyrants and well understood that the Arab revolution would eventually reach their doorstep.

Stage Four: The Final Battle

Threatened with a total loss of control, the tyrants faced a critical choice. They could either flee, or they could rally their troops and fight to the death. This period was relatively brief in Tunisia and Egypt. The fall of the Egyptian pharaoh, as Egyptians referred to Mubarak, alarmed other tyrants, and they began to watch the protests with greater care. For many, it was too late. Yemen, Libya, and Syria were turned into bloodbaths as tyrants vowed to die on their thrones. Security forces unleashed tanks and aircraft on civilian populations, slaughtered those who attempted to flee, and raped the young women who had been left behind. The Saudis invaded Bahrain to salvage the throne of a Sunni king, who had lost control of what had become a Shia uprising supported by Iran. Gentle it wasn't, as medical personnel in Bahrain were arrested to prevent testimonies about the brutality of Saudi troops (*Guardian*, April 23, 2011).

The choice to fight to the end wasn't always the tyrant's decision alone. They couldn't have survived for decades without a vast network of military, economic, and bureaucratic support. The military often had the final choice on the matter. Their heads, too, were on the block, and in some cases, the security elite sacrificed the ruling tyrants in the hopes of salvaging their own authority. This was clearly the case in Tunisia and Egypt.

This was not an easy choice in Yemen, Libya, Syria, or other countries in which the entire security apparatus was under the control of a single clan, or at best, a narrow segment of the population. In the case of Yemen, all of the key military leaders were close relatives of the tyrant, and all of the elite units had been selected with an overwhelming concern for loyalty. Revenge being what it is in the Arab psyche, few believed that the revolutionaries would show mercy on their former jailers and hangmen. This narrowed the choice to fight or flight. The situation was even tighter in Syria, where the vast security apparatus described earlier was under the control of the minority Alawi sect, the survival of which remained questionable if the regime fell. It was much the same in Libya, where the military was under the control of the tyrant's family, clan, and supportive tribes.

More than ever, a frustrated American government "winged it" by supporting some tyrants, imposing meaningless sanctions on others, and in extreme cases, openly bombing the headquarters of their former allies. Such radical steps came only after the tyrant's fate was sealed and the U.S. was scrambling to save what it could of its humanitarian reputation.

Stage Five: Freedom Rings
The passing of a tyrant unleashed an explosion of freedom unlike the Arab world had ever seen. The press, now free, ran nonstop exposés of the corruption and oppression of the fallen regimes, not to mention their secret deals with Israel and the U.S. Exiled opposition leaders of all stripes returned to their home countries and riled the masses. They were joined by political prisoners who had been released from jail when the protesters sacked the headquarters of security agencies. Incriminating records of police brutality were also seized and made public. The tyrants and their henchmen were jailed and their assets frozen. The official parties of the tyrants were disbanded and replaced by an explosion of political parties reflecting every conceivable political

view, including those sponsored by the Muslim Brotherhood, the Salafis, and the Sufi. New parties even emerged to represent the remnants of the old regime. At one point, the Tunisians had 110 new political parties. Unity there wasn't.

Stage Six: Chaos Reigns

Temporary governments were hastily cobbled together following the fall of a tyrant, but they were invariably weak and indecisive. Tunisia managed to have three prime ministers in twenty-four hours. Most temporary regimes were remnants of the old regime, with a strong representation of the security forces who, despite their past record, promised elections and a smooth transition to democracy. National committees consisting of the protesters and other major groups were formed to guide the process. Bickering became the norm, and competing transition committees often vied for authority. What one agreed to, the other rejected.

While the generals attempted to guide things from on high, the local police went on strike to demand higher wages or simply stayed home to avoid mass retribution for sins of the past. In some cases, the police stayed away because of revenge. If the revolutionaries wanted freedom, let them have it. Either way, crime became rampant as thugs and criminal gangs roamed at will. Some were joined by hardened criminals who had been released from prison by the tyrants in a frantic effort to sew confusion among the protesters. Bureaucracies, for their part, became immobilized, and the economies careened toward collapse.

Not only did chaos grip the liberated countries, but the Movement of the Dispossessed began to unravel as the diverse centers of rage turned against each other in anticipation of the coming battle to form a new political system. The lines between the Islamists and the secularists were particularly sharp, but so were differences between business and labor groups, each demanding a new system to its liking.

The security forces seized upon the chaos to reestablish their authority. Complaints of police brutality and corruption increased apace. Mobs protested the abuses of the security force, but that had become the only thing that they could agree upon. The prevailing joke in Egypt began with a question, "Where are we protesting today?" Answer: revolutionaries in Tahrir Square, pro-Mubarak demonstrators outside

Mustafa Mahmoud, the Muslim Brotherhood in front of parliament, thugs outside police stations, the Salafis outside churches, Christian Copts in front of the Television Building, and the country's silent majority at home on the internet (Wahish, 2011).

Stage Seven: Positioning for the Future

As exhilarating as unrestrained freedom may have been, the chaos that accompanied the collapse of authority proved to be as threatening to the Arab psyche as the rule of the tyrant. The advent of elections, however ill defined, forced the diverse groups to ease their conflicts and form alliances that would give them at least a share of power in the new era. The pattern of alliances varied from country to country, but most centered on three key issues: Islam versus secularism, order versus freedom, and capitalism versus social welfare, including guaranteed jobs and subsidized everything. The Muslim Brotherhood, security forces, and the business community began to coalesce into one camp, while the unions, homeless, jobless, leftist intellectuals, and destitute inclined toward the other. The former had money, power, and organization. The latter relied on numbers, emotion, social networks, and what remained of the Movement of the Dispossessed.

Nothing, however, was as neat as it seemed. The urban poor inclined toward the Muslim Brotherhood, while tribal and sectarian loyalties often trumped other considerations in the rural areas. The Muslim Brotherhood, for its part, vehemently denied alliances with the hated security forces and disavowed any desire to assume power. The secularists weren't convinced, as story after story warned of an Islamic state supported by the security services and pandering to the rich.

In a curious irony, the protesters who had demanded immediate elections now protested to delay them because they feared a victory by their better-organized opponents. The Muslim Brotherhood and the business community, by contrast, sensed victory and demanded immediate elections. Democracy, they declared, must have its due.

To their dismay, the security forces refused to play along. The longer they could delay, the greater the likelihood became that it would be they, the remnants of the tyrant's palace guards, who ruled the country. Elections would be held, but not to worry. The security forces had a great deal of experience in conducting rigged elections. They had done it for decades.

Stage Eight: Creating a New Political Order

Elections offered the path to a new political order, but the results were often inconclusive and divisive, as protests and rumors of coups proliferated. The clearest result was the success of Islamic groups, such as the Muslim Brotherhood, in securing a dominant plurality of votes. They vowed moderation in a moral framework, and they were careful not to provoke a coup or sew fear among very nervous American leadership. Israeli grew more nervous by the day.

What Comes Next?

Speculation is risky business. It is best, accordingly, to base speculations about the Arab future on firm anchors that have stood the test of time. Of these, four come readily to mind. First, the events described in this chapter have altered the course of Arab history. Much like the French and Russian Revolutions, the ancient regimes of the Arab world were shaken to the core. Some have perished. Others are clinging to an uncertain future. Whatever the case, the Arab world can never be the same as it was in the decades before the popular revolutions of 2011.

Second, the new Middle East that emerges from the Arab Spring of rage will continue to be shaped by eras past. Much as the Prophet Mohammed was forced to adjust to the tribal reality that prevailed in seventh-century Arabia, so the era of rage will have to deal with the reality of the Arab psyche and Arab behavior described in the preceding chapters. The new, as in the past, will continue to be grafted on the old. Things will evolve, but they will evolve slowly and in fits and starts.

Third, the direction that the new Arab world takes will have much to do with its ability to solve the riddles of extremism, violence, fragmentation, tyranny, inequality, and economic stagnation that have haunted it through the ages. If the Arab world can do so, its future looks bright. If it fails to do so, an extended period of rage and rebellion awaits.

Finally, the ability of the Arab world to forge a world of religious moderation, nonviolence, unity, democracy, equity, and economic growth will be shaped by the melding of environment and psyche that have guided the discussion throughout this book. Both remain vital to shaping Arab behavior, and you can't have one without the other.

The remainder of this chapter outlines the major trends in the evolving Arab environment and the ways in which the Arab psyche is attempting to cope with its ever-changing environment. Both will have much to say about the key red-flag issues outlined above. There are no guarantees, but the discussion suggests ample cause for both optimism and pessimism. At the very least, a guide will be provided for charting the Arab future as it transverses the stages outlined in the preceding section.

THE EVOLVING ARAB ENVIRONMENT

The evolving Arab environment includes dramatic areas of change as well as the relentless lure of the past. The dead hand of the past, to borrow a phrase from the various *Arab Human Development Reports*, is very much a part of the Arab present. More than ever, the evolving Arab environment is also being shaped by regional and international forces beyond Arab control.

Areas of Dramatic Environmental Change
The most dramatic change in the evolving Arab environment is the transformation of the powerful and confident tyrannies into weak and uncertain governments subject to collapse at any moment. For those who prefer social science jargon, strong states are giving way to weak states.

Conversely, weak and docile populations are giving way to empowered populations confident of their ability to overthrow tyrannical leaders. It is now the masses that are on the offensive and the tyrannical elites that are on the defensive.

This is a transitional process in which the political institutions forged by the tyrants are crumbling, but have yet to be replaced by new political institutions with a broad base of mass support.

Social taboos are also crumbling, but none more so than the liberation of women. This, too, is a transitional process with a long way to go, but imagine, if you will, the stir caused by showing the film *Our National Hymen* in Tunisia and Egypt (Awadalla, 2011). The Saudis are even debating allowing women to drive and have promised them the right to vote in local elections a few years hence.

The growing sophistication of social networking and the explosion of a global satellite media will continue to spur dramatic change. The media exposure will fuel protests, while social networking will make them virtually unstoppable without violent repression. Over four million Egyptians accessed Facebook during January 2011, the first month of the revolution. This figure had jumped to over five million a month later.

Satellite coverage of events in the Arab world is keeping pace. As a result, violent repression may decline in utility as the world cringes at yet more grisly pictures of tyrants slaughtering and raping innocent civilians.

The shifting balance between the tyrants and the masses is also being tipped by the proliferation of independent political parties, professional associations, labor and student unions, and feminist groups, to mention but a few. Egypt alone has witnessed an explosion of thirty thousand nongovernmental organizations, dedicated to everything from promoting healthcare and eradicating illiteracy to creating jobs and promoting democracy. The tyrants viewed most NGOs as a subversive foreign presence, but the organizations are now playing a critical role in forming a civil society in the Arab world. The process remains weak, but it is growing. Even Saudi Arabia has established a human rights organization. Powerful it is not, but it is clearly a sign of changing times. A variety of diverse Islamic groups are also becoming a vibrant part of the political landscape, and could well emerge as the dominant part of that landscape.

While many of the forces of change outlined above are of a positive nature, this is hardly the case in the economic sphere. The economies of the liberated countries have been devastated by the chaos accompanying the Arab revolution and will take a long time to ease. The economic situation in Saudi Arabia is much better, but unemployment, a key indicator of political unrest, hovers around the 10 percent mark. Oil revenues abound, but to what avail? Much of the kingdom's oil wealth is absorbed by blatant corruption, the need to prop up fellow tyrants, undermining democracy in the liberated countries, paying their own citizens not to work, hiring foreign mercenaries, and buying billions of dollars of sophisticated American weapons downgraded to prevent their use against Israel. That probably means that they will also be ineffective against Iran, America's main foe in the region. The Saudi defense budget in 2010 was $43 billion and growing, not bad for a country that is so worried about its own forces that it relies heavily on Pakistani mercenaries to protect the regime (Downing, 2011).

The Dead Hand of the Past

While the balance between the tyrants and the masses has shifted in favor of the latter, it would be naive to believe that the security forces, clans, sects, and economic interests that prospered under the rule of the tyrants will simply fade away. Even when heads roll, the core of the old regime will remain. They can't be fully dislodged, because their removal would result in total chaos. After all, they are the only ones who know how to run things.

Nowhere is the dead hand of the past deader than in the massive bureaucratic systems of the Arab world. Immobilized by an uncertain future, government officials are becoming more lethargic, corrupt, and unresponsive than ever. Their numbers are also expanding, as weak leaders struggle to build popular support by dumping legions of unemployed youth in government organizations with little regard for skills, bureaucratic needs, or talents. The Saudis announced that they were creating sixty thousand new positions in the security forces. If people loved their king as much as American pundits say they do, why do they need sixty thousand more people in their security services? Why not dump them in an already moribund bureaucracy as the Saudis have done for years?

The tyrants cling to power by promising reforms while slaughtering all who dare to stand in their way. Unable to stand on their own, they have formed a league of tyrants, as monarchies as distant as Jordan and Morocco have joined the Gulf Cooperation Council, a mutual-defense organization that will enable monarchs in any sector of the Arab world to come to the aid of their endangered colleagues. Just to be on the safe side, many of the monarchies have employed Western security firms to import mercenaries with operatives from countries as distant as Columbia (New York Times, April 16, 2011). It's the Middle Ages all over again, as beleaguered sultans turn to foreign mercenaries to protect their thrones. But who will watch the mercenaries? Recall that it was the mercenaries who deposed the sultans of yore.

One way or another, coups and revolutions remain a constant threat in both the liberated and tyrannical countries. The liberated countries fear that the military or the Islamists will use the prevailing chaos as a pretext for seizing power, while the monarchies simply don't trust their own security services. Why else would they rely on foreign mercenaries to keep themselves in power?

Forces beyond Arab Control

The regional environment will also do its part to shape the Arab world, as Israel struggles to retain control of the occupied Palestinian territories and Iran extends its position as the dominant power in the oil-rich Gulf. The probability of conflict between Israel and Iran remains strong, as does continued Iranian support for Hizbullah and other Shia political organizations in Lebanon, Iraq, Yemen, and the Gulf states, including Saudi Arabia.

Turkey, for its part, will continue to serve as a beacon for moderate Islamic rule and urge the Arabs to institute moderate Islamic democracies as the safest path to stability and progress. This makes both Israel and the U.S. very nervous, and also poses a threat to the Saudis, who are opposed to democracy in any form, Islamic or otherwise. One fair election and the monarchy could well be gone.

Finally, we come to al-Qaeda and its clones that remain active throughout the Arab world and have benefited from the chaos that has accompanied the Arab revolution. Al-Qaeda also shares a common religious philosophy with Salafi groups that are now being accepted as legitimate political movements in the rush to freedom and democracy. The Salafis promise moderation, but remain intent on transforming the Arab world into a time warp of seventh-century Islam.

The international environment also threatens confusion, as the U.S. remains torn between its goals of fighting terror, preserving Saudi oil, and supporting Israel. This was tricky in the past and will probably become impossible in the future. Defeats in Iraq and Afghanistan have weakened the U.S., and it has become wary of future ventures in the Middle East. The more the U.S. supports Saudi Arabia and Israel, the more it loses the Arab psyche.

The U.S. rejoiced at the assassination of bin-Laden in 2011. The Arabs and their Muslim neighbors wonder why it took the greatest power on earth ten years and an estimated $3 trillion to kill one man, who now serves as a saintly source of emulation for Islamic fanatics throughout the world. They also wonder why the U.S. is negotiating with the Taliban and the Muslim Brotherhood. Could it be that the U.S. is willing to accept reasonably moderate Islamic governments in the Arab world and its environs? No wonder the Israelis and Saudis are worried.

The U.S. also finds itself at odds with a growing array of global powers that reject American leadership in the region. The EU is intent on stabilizing the region at all costs, including a forced peace between Israel and the Palestinians. Russia, China, and Japan muddy the Arab waters to serve their own interests, most of which involve oil and few of which involve Israel.

As a result, a frustrated U.S. will probably keep jumping from crisis to crisis while it simultaneously preaches democracy, supports tyrannical kings in the Gulf, urges liberated countries to drop their hostility toward Israel, vetoes a Palestinian state, drops drones on suspected terrorists, keeps a foot in Iraq, and mends its fences with former foes such as the Taliban and the Muslim Brotherhood. Sooner or later, it may have to make peace with Iran. Each new change in American leadership will also reshuffle the deck. That, too, is part of the Arabs' looming environment.

THE EVOLVING ARAB PSYCHE

How, then, is the Arab psyche attempting to cope with the dramatic events surveyed above? The discussion that follows approaches this question by examining the diverse components of the Arab psyche and their likely impact on Arab behavior in the years to come. Before embarking on this venture, four empirically grounded observations about the psyche—all psyches—are in order.

First, as discussed throughout the book, the Arab psyche, like all psyches, will attempt to maximize pleasure while minimizing pain. The era of rage has presented the Arab psyche with unknown opportunities for change and dramatic improvements in its quality of life. Unfortunately, the unparalleled opportunities for change have come with unparalleled dangers. It will take the Arab psyche time to find an acceptable balance between pain and pleasure. As there are so many Arab psyches, this process may vary dramatically from group to group. Rural peasants, for example, are unlikely to find the same balance as urban students. This being the case, broad generalizations can be dangerous.

Second, psyches tend to be "sticky." They gradually adapt to a changing environment rather than rushing to keep pace with it. Barring intense motivations for change, the Arab psyche has historically preferred the known to the unknown. This tendency was a key factor in explaining Arab docility in the face of brutal tyranny. Indeed, it was only when life had become intolerable that Arabs braved death to challenge their tyrants.

Third, contagion is a two-way street. The revolutions in Tunisia and Egypt helped to trigger revolutions in the broader Arab world. The brutal violence that accompanied the revolutions in Libya, Yemen, and Syria, by contrast, injected an element of caution and apprehension into the revolutionary process.

Finally, collapsing social and political institutions often lead the psyche to search security and stability by following a strong leader. This has consistently been the case for the Arab psyche in the past, and it could well be the case in the future. If so, tyranny will continue to be the norm.

While the above observations offer insights into the way the Arab psyche will cope with the future, much will also depend on the way the era of rage and chaos influences Arab identities, motivations, and the Arab psyche's ability to comprehend the world of change swirling around it. All of the observations discussed are very much in evidence, but remain speculative because they lack a firm empirical base.

Arab Identities in the Era of Rage

Judging from the rhetoric that has accompanied the era of rage, most Arabs have retained their core identities of family, faith, and Arabism. Local nationalism, class awareness, and images of tradition and modernity are gaining ground. Added to the fray are new identities of "revolutionary" or "reactionary" that cross the lines of faith, family, class, and links to tradition. The revolutionaries, while weighted in favor of the youth, are not of one stamp and share no common ideology. This fragmentation, of itself, will assure that the path of revolution will remain stormy and uncertain.

The strength of the Arab identity is evidenced by the ease with which the Arab explosion spread from one country to another. It is this shared sense of empathy or mutual understanding that makes events in one part of the Arab world of vital interest to all Arabs.

This said, prevailing expressions of Arabism remain vague and focus more on addressing Israeli humiliations of Arab pride than on reviving dreams of an Arab state (*Al-Masry Al-Youm,* April 13, 2011).

As Saad Ibrahim, a noted Arab sociologist, also notes, feelings of Arabism, while pervasive, break down when local issues are involved:

> There will always be two dimensions. The first one is the pan-Arab dimension: every Arab person from Iraq to Morocco feels that they have something in common: they all watch Al Jazeera, listen to Egyptian and Lebanese songs, watch Egyptian movies. If an Arab country is playing a match against a non-Arab country, everyone will cheer for the Arab team. But if it is Algeria and Morocco playing soccer, then you can see how strong country loyalty is. It is just as strong as pan-Arab feeling (Ibrahim, 2011).

Arabs do scream for the home team at soccer matches. No doubt about it. Does that mean that either Arab identities or local identities can transcend the emotional level and motivate Arabs to work together for their common good? Arab psychologists are apprehensive. One Egyptian psychologist warned that "it would take years and a lot of work to turn the newfound positivity and national pride among Egyptians from a temporary high into a sustainable change…in order to dispel the negatives that decades of oppression have instilled into the Egyptian character" (Afify, 2011).

Islamic identities, by contrast, have been sharpened and polarized during the era of rage by the explosion of Islamic satellite channels and Islamic political parties, and by the return of exiled religious leaders. People are also increasingly aware that they may soon have to choose what role they want Islam to play in their lives.

The strengthening of Islamic identities, in turn, has sharpened both secular identities and minority identities. The Arab media throughout the region has increasingly focused on the growing divide between Islamists and secularists. They also warn of growing intolerance between Christians and Muslims and deepening tensions between Sunni and Shia. Non-Arab groups have similarly seized upon the chaos to press for their own independent countries, the Kurds and Berbers being a case in point.

Class identities, while never particularly strong in the Arab world, are also becoming sharper as the struggle to create a new economic order continues. The growing influence of labor unions reflects this trend. A shared sense of class victimization fueled the Movement of the Dispossessed. Indeed, it is that shared sense of economic victimization that is one of the movement's main sources of cohesion.

Elections, too, are sharpening and polarizing Arab identities. Pity the poor Arab psyche forced to choose between candidates ranging from communists to jihadists and all stages in between. Not only is the range of choices bewildering, but it also could be dangerous. Who knows if the elections will be fair or if the winning candidates will graciously step down if they lose future elections? For that matter, who knows if there will be future elections? The Arab psyche has a long memory.

Despite the sharpening and polarization of Arab identities, most Arabs continue to want some of this and some of that. Most will be reluctant to make a firm commitment to the future until the dust of the era of rage has settled. As such, they are likely to avoid choices that may prove dangerous with each new turn of fate. This will certainly be the case for the bystanders and sleepers who continue to constitute a large percentage of the Arab population.

Arab Motivations in the Era of Rage and Chaos

Basic visceral needs for security, stability, food, shelter, jobs, and the rest are the same as they have always been and will not change. It was the inability of the tyrants to meet these needs that fueled the Arab explosion. It is the continued inability of the Arab countries to meet these basic needs that will fuel the explosions of the future. The chances are that they will also fuel violence and extremism.

This is all the more the case, because the protesters who ignited the Arab revolution assumed that the fall of the tyrants would fulfill their acquired wants as well as their basic needs. They would have it all: power, plenty, and security in an atmosphere of dignity, equality, equity, freedom, and democracy. Lest one underestimate the potency of learned needs, don't forget that it was the humiliation of a Tunisian fruit peddler that triggered the Arab explosion. Most Arab reviews of the revolution also place pride and dignity on par with material needs.

Emotional Triggers in the Era of Rage

The emotions of despair, frustration, anger, hopelessness, humiliation, and disgust fueled the Arab explosion. The Arab explosion wasn't caused by fear, but by the stronger emotion of total despair. It was despair and humiliation that trumped the fear that had kept the tyrants in power. At least in the view of some Arab commentators, the protesters had nothing left to lose, not even their pride (*Opposite Opinions*, Al Jazeera, January 16, 2011. In Arabic).

In the liberated countries, the Arab explosion gave way to the emotions of victory, joy, hope, power, pride, efficacy, and revenge, all of which have become frayed in the frantic task of transforming dreams into reality in the difficult environment described above. Frustrations are soaring, and fears of a stolen revolution are pervasive. The longer it takes for the revolution to rekindle the emotions of hope and confidence in political authorities, the more the negative emotions of fear, anger, frustration, and revenge will reign.

It is now the tribal kings and princes who must deal with the emotions of despair, frustration, anger, hopelessness, humiliation, and self-disgust. The fear of the masses pales in comparison to the fear of their leaders, who cling in desperation to their thrones.

Things, however, aren't quite as simple as they seem. The masses in Saudi Arabia and the other well-heeled monarchies fear the chaos and the unknown as much as they fear the oppression of their leaders. Even greater is the fear of a final battle that would leave thousands dead and maimed. Few may be willing to risk a reasonable quality of material life for the wanton slaughter that accompanied the revolutions in Libya, Yemen, Syria, and elsewhere. As noted earlier, contagion is a two-way street, and the experience of revolutionaries in Syria, Libya, and Yemen has clearly raised the barrier of fear in the oil monarchies.

This doesn't mean that the revolution won't come to Saudi Arabia, the bastion of tribal monarchy in the Arab world, but it probably means that it will be a slow process. The centers of rage in Saudi Arabia are growing and include a much abused Shia minority, oppressed women, a Western-educated middle class that craves a breath of fresh air, jealous tribes, and a religious elite fearful of fresh air.

Al-Qaeda and other jihadist groups also lurk, Saudi denials notwithstanding. In their view, the Saudi monarchy is the last bastion of American influence in the region. Just think what the jihadists could do with all of the Saudi oil wealth, not to mention the massive store of weapons that the monarchy has purchased from the U.S. The oil weapon could cause global economic chaos while funding untold terrorist attacks on America and its allies.

Many American commentators equate Saudi submissiveness with love of the king, but that sure isn't my impression. Rather than love of a tribal king, the thought that haunts many Saudis is, "Just think of how much more we could have if we ruled the country rather than our medieval kings. Wealth, power, dignity, and intellectual freedom await." It just takes courage. Alas, the fear factor is strong in Saudi Arabia, and perhaps the Saudis aren't desperate enough for courage.

Can the Psyche of Rage be Rational?

One way or the other, the reasoning process during the era of rage and chaos is being stretched to the breaking point, as people struggle to sort out the momentous events swirling around them in a manner calculated to maximize pleasure and minimize pain.

The problem begins with the intense media coverage of the constantly changing events in the region. There is simultaneously too much information to keep track of, and too little information about what is really happening. Most media coverage is biased, and speculation is rife with little basis in fact. Now bring rumors and conspiracy theories into play. Nothing in this *Alice in Wonderland* world is what it seems, so who is one to believe?

The more savvy Arabs try to keep track of what the U.S. and other major powers are saying, but to what avail? The major international actors are chasing after events with no clear idea of how to change them. The Arabs may think that the U.S. knows what it is doing in the Middle East, but I'm not sure that many Americans do.

Don't forget the influence of the faith-versus-science debate on the reasoning process. Which basis of reasoning is likely to be most effective in helping people deal with the tumultuous events unfolding around them, the model of Western science or the model of Islamic science? The answer to this question depends upon whether individuals believe in their own ability to shape things or are more inclined to rely on God.

However the Arabs attempt to answer this question, their decisions are likely to reflect enduring personality traits that change far slower than the mercurial and fleeting emotions triggered by the era of rage and chaos. This being the case, the personality traits likely to dominate the Arab future are authoritarianism, collectiveness, an overriding concern for stability, and the search for a savior, religious or otherwise.

The above discussion assumes that Arabs are attempting to come to grips with the reality of their chaotic environment in a logical and reasoned way. This is probably a flawed assumption. Emotions are the driving force in the era, and while potent motivators, emotions are seldom rational. Joy, anger, and the rest lead to instant and dramatic actions, many of which serve only to perpetuate chaos and unleash a rash of contrary and contradictory emotions.

How long, for example, can the thrill of victory last before it triggers cries for revenge? For that matter, how long can the thrill of victory last before it gives way to the agony of defeat? Cries of revenge set in almost immediately after the successful Arab revolutions. They were soon followed by desperate cries to "save the revolution," as security forces reasserted their power and threatened to steal victory from the hands of the revolutionaries.

Fear is probably the most rational of human emotions because it is directly linked to human survival (Hawkins, 2002). This doesn't mean that fear is a positive force for change and development. To the contrary, fear in the Arab world has led to submission, distrust, and inaction, three of the greatest foes of a true Arab revival. Perhaps courage and despair are more rational than fear. It was they that overcame the barrier of fear in the Arab world and led to popular demands for a bet-ter way of life.

Defense Mechanisms

Least rational of all are the psyche's defense mechanisms. The whole purpose of defense mechanisms is to make irrational behavior seem rational, be it violence or passivity. Of these, the defense mechanisms that are likely to have the greatest influence on the era of rage and chaos are projection, rationalization, and displacement.

Projection is simply the fine art of blaming others for personal fail-ures. As in the past, projection has come to the fore during the era of rage, as the revolutionaries blame each other for their squabbling and inability to forge a coherent path for the future. The tyrants aren't far behind, as they blame their atrocities on overzealous and poorly trained security forces. Both the revolutionaries and the tyrants are increas-ingly weaving their projections into conspiracy theories. The tyrants accuse the revolutionaries of being agents of Israel and the U.S., while the revolutionaries blame the Saudis for financing counterrevolutionary groups and Islamic extremists hostile to secular democracy (Al-Masry Al-Youm, May 8, 2011).

The greater danger is not the content of conspiracy theories that people tend to discount, but growing signs that the Arabs are dodging responsibility for their own failings by blaming others rather than put-ting their own house in order. "When will the Arabs abandon this con-spiracy complex and stop denying mistakes and searching for a scape-goat?" asks Dr. Aaidh Al-Qarni, a Saudi-born cleric whose book, Don't Feel Sad, has sold millions (Al-Qarni, 2011). The question is rhetorical, and no answer is provided. Perhaps there is none.

Rationalization merely furthers the process by allowing both the revolutionaries and the tyrants to convince themselves that their actions, however illogical, are necessary and morally justified. More than an excuse for avoiding responsibility, rationalization becomes an excuse for violence. Far worse, it becomes a call for violence. Sin must be eradicated, and enemies must be destroyed.

Just to make the circle complete, add selective perception (cogni-tive dissonance) to the list. People tend to see things that make them look good while avoiding information that suggests that their actions have been flawed. They certainly don't want to accept shame or guilt. It is too painful.

But it is worse than that. The interminable negotiations between the Arabs and Israelis, and the Arabs and the United States, are intentionally vague to allow each party to see what they want to see. There is no meeting of the minds, but agreements are reached, however futile they may be. The same is true of negotiations between the U.S. and Israel and among the Arabs themselves. This certainly is not a good omen for the rapid transition of the era of rage and chaos into an era of development, stability, and democracy.

Language

More than ever, the soaring emotions of the era of rage will find reflection in the strong inclination of the Arabic language toward exaggeration and embellishment. One sees this reflected in the political and religious rhetoric of the era. The line between the two is often vague.

Yet the language of the Arab revolution, for all of its embellishments, is also becoming the language of the internet and Facebook. It is the language of anonymity devoid of identity or the peering eyes of neighbors.

Roadmap and Future Poker

What makes the era of rage and chaos so dangerous to the Arabs is that neither rage nor chaos are conducive to charting a clear path to the achievement of their diverse wants, be they innate or learned. The rage that triggered the Arab explosion is weakening the social and political institutions that guided the Arab world for decades. It may be a long time before the revolutionaries are able to replace them with viable alternatives. For the moment, at least, the Arab psyche is in limbo.

So on to the game of future poker. The poker expression that comes to mind is "betting on the come," a wonderful way of saying that you are risking all on the next card to be dealt. The protesters risked all and opened the door for a much dreamed-of Arab revival. Others will follow, and it is now the tyrants who must bet on the come. Will the U.S. step in and save their thrones, or will it turn against them? Or more likely, will the U.S. continue to vacillate as it has done in the past?

This, while probable, will assure the U.S. even greater frustration in the years to come.

Again, you may want to place yourself in the role of the Arab ego as it attempts to place its bets on the future. Maybe not. Kawagas are not Arabs, and viewing Arab options through the eyes of a kawaga could be dangerous. Very dangerous.

RED-FLAG ISSUES AND THE ARAB FUTURE

The explosion of Arab rage marked a dramatic departure from established behavior patters as the Arab masses, at long last, stood up to the tyrants. Will the Arab explosion of 2011 serve as the catalyst for an new Arab revival, or will the chaos that has marked the early years of the Arab revolution continue to torment the Arab psyche for years to come?

The answer to this question depends largely on the ability of the Arabs to put moderation above extremism, reconciliation above violence, cooperation above fragmentation, democracy above tyranny, equity above inequality, and economic development above stagnation. The environmental and psychological trends reviewed above offer ample cause for both optimism and concern.

The red-flag issues are treated collectively because all are mutually dependent. Development, democracy, national unity, equity, and the ability of governments to meet the needs of their people all depend upon the existence of a reasonably stable environment that promotes law and order without stifling creativity and the free flow of ideas and political views. Conversely, it is difficult to have any of the above if the price of law and order is the brutal oppression of the past that choked the creativity and locked the Arab in an existentialist nightmare. You can also put democracy first if you like, but it all comes out the same. It is hard to solve one of the red-flag issues without addressing them all.

Optimism

Optimism comes with the Arab explosion of 2011 that broke the yoke of tyranny and laid the foundation for the revival that Arab philosophers have dreamed of since the collapse of the era of enlightenment a

303

thousand years ago. Sheikh Jamal Qutb, a leading religious scholar at the venerable Al-Azhar University, summed up the impact of the revolution by saying, "Egypt recovered from its psychological illnesses after the eruption of the 25 January revolution.... The complexes that filled the souls with bitterness were resolved...after the end of the period during which...poverty, and backwardness reached a level man would not impose on animals" (Qutb, 2011). Unlike Qutb, the senior leaders of Al-Azhar did not support the revolution. How could they? They were part of the ruling elite.

The Arab genius for creativity, while dormant, has not been totally crushed. Arab scientists serve the West, where they prosper in an environment of enlightenment that had been denied them in their own countries. Perhaps the new environment created by the Arab explosion will again see Arab genius serve the cause of an Arab revival.

Optimism is also to be found in an increasingly educated Arab youth who are less tied to the past than their elders. Arab youth, at least 60 percent of the population and growing, have tasted freedom and long to escape the crippling political and social pressures that have denied them a viable future. This is certainly the case for Arab women, who are leading their own social revolution.

More than just having tasted freedom, Arab youth now know that popular uprisings can dislodge their tyrants, however formidable their security forces. They also know that they have a critical mass sufficient to defy the tyrants. In the process, docility and passivity are giving way to a sense of hope, efficacy, and self-confidence, all of which were missing in the past. The challenge will be holding on long enough until the tyrants fold or the world community comes to their aid.

Other signs of optimism abound. The global environment offers a free flow of information and personal communications unheard of in decades past. Arab youth understand networking better than the tyrants and keep inventing ingenious techniques for exploiting networking skills that will keep them ahead of the tyrants. The tyrants are struggling to keep pace, but they lack the mental agility of their adversaries.

Beyond being networked by the computer cloud, Arabs are increasingly being networked by a civil society consisting of multiple political parties, professional associations, labor and student unions, feminist groups, and neighborhood alliances. The process is just beginning, but is growing rapidly and being aided by foreign labor, business, feminist, and welfare organizations.

What this means, is that the future of the Arab revolution is not just about individuals. It is about organized groups that have a far greater capacity to make their voices heard than individuals. They also have a far greater staying power than lone individuals, who are vulnerable to the boot of the tyrant. Adding to the importance of the voluntary associations is their ability to bring together individuals from diverse kinship and religious backgrounds, a major weakness of Arab society in the past.

Arabs also sense that America's efforts to impose its will upon the region have failed, and that the world order established in the wake of the September 11, 2001 attacks on the United States is crumbling. Perhaps the Arabs are less awed by the kawaga than they once were, although that remains to be seen.

Whether or not this is the case, the U.S. is putting pressure on its tyrants to appear more humane and more sensitive to the issues of democracy and feminist equality. Within six months of the fall of the Egyptian tyrant, the Saudis announced that women would be allowed to vote in local elections, scheduled for three years down the road. The last round of local elections was cancelled, but even the acknowledgment of the women's right to vote was a cataclysmic change in Saudi political, social, and religious policy. The Saudis hastened to clarify that this decision was the gift of an enlightened and compassionate king and had nothing to do with American pressure. I doubt it, but such a dramatic change in Saudi policy indicates that the monarchy is running scared.

Finally, I believe that it is safe to assume that the vast majority of Arabs do not want to live under tyranny, be it the tyranny of tribal kings or the tyranny of Islamic extremists intent on returning the Arab world to a time warp of seventh-century Arabia. This is not an attack on Islam, for the Arab enlightenment flourished in an environment of moderate Islam. It could do so again if enlightened Islamic rule produced stability and national cohesion, met the needs of the people, stimulated development, and provided the Arabs with the ability to reconcile their conflicts in a nonviolent manner. Moderate Islamic rule has been profoundly successful in Turkey. Does this mean than it can work in the Arab world? This is a hot topic of debate throughout the Middle East and will be discussed shortly.

Pessimism

Unfortunately, the pessimistic side of the ledger is equally persuasive. Collapsing political systems have to be rebuilt from scratch, a difficult task for countries coping with chaos or facing the prospect of civil war. Until rebuilt governments can prove their effectiveness, the need for survival will leave Arabs with little option but to cling to their core groups and play the fox. Recall Neguib Mahfouze's warning that "revolutions are made by dreamers, carried out by brave people, and seized by the opportunists."

Rebuilding new and effective political systems requires firm and decisive leadership, neither of which are the hallmarks of weak governments, democratic or otherwise. The temptation to rely on a new tyrant will be strong.

Effective governance capable of meeting the needs of the people also requires a strong economic base. Aside from oil and tourism, Arabs produce little. Oil wealth is squandered, and post-revolutionary violence has crippled tourism. It will take a long time to get the Arab economies to reach the point at which they can meet the escalating demands of their populations. Foreign loans and grants can help, but only if they are going to effective governments that can use them to the best advantage. Unfortunately, the temptations of corruption loom large, as weak leaders and their sycophants make hay while the sun shines.

To make matters worse, counterrevolutionaries, whether domestic or regional, have a vested interest in perpetuating chaos. The supporters of the old regime, including senior military officers, will use the chaos as an excuse for a return to autocratic rule. If this occurs, more bloody showdowns between the military and the protesters are probable, if not inevitable.

The centers of power in the liberated countries, moreover, have vastly different visions of what their new political system should look like, the major divide being between the Islamists and the secularists. This is a divide that will be difficult to bridge without conflict.

Turning to practical matters, Arab bureaucrats will presumably play a key role in implementing the new political system, a scary thought seeing that the Arab bureaucrats survived their entire lives on corruption, subservience, and the avoidance of responsibility. This is a poor formula for creating a political system capable of building legitimacy and social cohesion by meeting the needs of its population. Keep in mind that it is the bureaucrats and the opportunists who will manage the billions of dollars in aid pouring into the liberated countries.

The picture for democracy is also bleak as the Arabs, while allowed to vote in fraudulent elections for meaningless legislatures, possess little experience in democracy. The Egyptians have had more experience with faux democracy than most. Yet, Mohammed El Baradi, former head of the UN Atomic Energy Commission and once the leading candidate in Egypt's first presidential election of the liberated era, candidly stated that eighty percent "of the Egyptian population were not prepared for democracy" (El Baradi, 2011). Civil society may be emerging, but as El Baradi notes, it still has a long way to go. For the moment, the most powerful groups throughout the Arab world are the Muslim Brotherhood, the military, and core tribal, sectarian, and ethnic groups, many of which have their own militias.

A majority of the Arab masses, at least in the short run, are likely to remain sleepers and bystanders while the situation sorts itself out. It is hard to have a functional democracy without commitment. It its even harder to have a functioning democracy when the predominate emotions and traits are collectivism, fear, authoritarianism, hero worship, distrust, vengeance, appearances, revenge, face-saving, blaming others, intolerance, and a zero-sum approach to conflict.

Undermining all of the red-flag issues is the prevailing violence that is reaching record proportions as tyrants slaughter at will, and country after country approaches civil war or faces occupation by regional or foreign powers. Extremism follows in the wake of violence, or perhaps it is the other way around. Whatever the case, both violence and extremism will explode unless the riddle of the red-flag issues can be solved.

CHOICES BEFORE THE ARAB PSYCHE

At least seven choices face the Arab psyche as it looks to the future. All are possible, given the circumstances in the diverse Arab countries.

Long Live the King

As the Arab revolt of 2011 continues on its uncertain path, it is possible that exceptionally rich oil monarchies, such as Saudi Arabia, will be able to survive the revolutionary surge with a combination of economic incentives, a further strengthening of their security forces, and a gradual easing of social restrictions. Deep reforms leading to a diminishing of the king's power are virtually impossible. The survival of an antiquated tribal monarchy would be placed in jeopardy.

Even if the Saudi monarchy can survive the internal threat, it will also have to deal with revolutions on all sides, not to mention pressure from Iran and Israel. I wonder what the U.S. would do if it had to choose between Saudi oil and Israeli security?

Perpetual Rage and Chaos

Of the remaining choices, the most probable is a perpetuation of the era of rage and chaos. Continued chaos is probable because there are so many issues to be sorted out, so few resources to go around, so much fragmentation in Arab society, so much external meddling, and so much fear and divisiveness in the Arab psyche.

With so much pain and so little pleasure during the era of chaos, the Arabs will be driven to produce a stable political order. But what kind of order will it be?

Western Liberal Democracy

The preferred choice of the protesters was a Western-style democracy that established stability, growth, a food supply, morality, and equity through the rule of law and the peaceful resolution of the bitter conflicts that have haunted the Arabs throughout the ages. As discussed earlier, the authoritarian and divisive nature of the Arab psyche will make this difficult and unlikely in the near future. This certainly has been the case with past Arab experiments with Western democracy. Lebanon claims to be a democracy, but it is really a system for dividing resources among competing sects, feudal zaims, and ethnic enclaves. The U.S.-established democracy in Iraq is a farce. The pseudo democracies of the Gulf are merely charades that allow people to vote and squabble while the royal families make all the key decisions. Optimists claim that this is a step in the right direction that will grow with time. For the moment, it is a charade for political control.

Military Rule

A probable solution for the chaos produced by the revolution of rage is a coup by the security forces. Arab militaries still possess a preponderance of coercive force and should have little difficulty seizing power. The military is also adept at exploiting the fear factor which is deeply entrenched in the Arab psyche.

Things, however, are not quite that simple. The generals have been discredited by their attachment to the tyrants. The curse of the pharaoh is not easy to shake. The slaughter of innocent protesters has also robbed the military of much of its legitimacy. The masses have tasted power, and the one issue on which the Islamists and secularists can agree is the prevention of another corrupt and oppressive military dictatorship. Revenge is also a major feature of the Arab psyche, and it is awaiting its turn to settle scores with the pharaoh's hangmen.

The looming question for many people is, can the Arab militaries provide stability? The answer is not at all clear. They couldn't save Mubarak, the pharaoh of tyrants. All in all, thoughts of a discredited military leading the path to democracy and development seem terribly naive. They didn't do it when they were in power. Why, discredited by their slaughter of innocents, should they do it now? Past behavior suggests that they will simply plunder and rape while they have the opportunity.

Islam Lite: The Turkish Model

Since assuming office in 2002, Turkey's Islamic Justice and Development Party has built Turkey into the world's seventeenth largest economy, consolidated Turkish democracy, brought Turkey to the doorstep of membership in the European Union, made Turkey a key player on the international stage, and established Turkey as a dominant power in the Middle East. The sick man of Europe has awakened.

This success was achieved by a program that blended Islamic morality, economic liberalism, and secular democracy. Added to the mixture was Tayyip Erdogan, a leader whose charisma rivaled that of Nasser. His followers call him "Papa," and he swept to victory after victory by playing the victim against Turkey's legacy of military oppression. He also played the Islamic card by defending the right of Muslims to wear Islamic dress, and he played the nationalism card by taking a hard line against

Kurdish separatists. He has also played upon Turkish pride by opposing Israeli-American efforts to crush the Hamas government in the Gaza Strip and by defying the U.S. blockade of Iran. He vows a willingness to cooperate with both Israel and the U.S., but only on Turkey's terms.

The success of moderate Islamic rule in Turkey has led both Arab and Western analysts to suggest that the Turkish model may be the solution to Arab woes. Turkey is selling the model, calling on Arabs to follow Turkey's path of pursuing Islamic morality within a secular political framework. Secularism promotes democracy and development, while Islam promotes morality and equity. The state is secular, but individuals are Muslims, Turkish pundits have duly labeled the Turkish model "Islam Lite" or "neo-laicism" (Hurriyat Daily News, September 15, 2011).

The Turkish model has refuted claims that Islam is incompatible with democracy, development, and the other red-flag issues discussed throughout this book.

Does this mean that Turkey can serve as a model for Arab development? Many Arabs take hope from the Turkish success. Turkish culture, they note, is very similar to Arab culture. Tribalism and Islam shaped both. While the fit isn't perfect, the Turkish experience in nation building is closer to the Arab experience than a model of development and democracy born in the British Isles. The Turkish leader also portrays the image of an Islamic leader with whom the secularists can live. Muslims can have their headscarves, and secularists can have democracy and economic growth.

Religious and cultural similarities, of themselves, do not mean that the Turkish model is transferable to the Arab world. Indeed, looking at the differences between the Turkish and Arab experience may help to illustrate the vast differences that exist between the Arabo-Islamic psyche and the broader non-Arab Islamic psyche.

The topic is complex, so the discussion is limited to a few key points. The Turkish psyche evolved in a far different historical environment than that of the Arab. They were the conquerors of much of Europe and had never suffered the humiliation of Western colonialism that the Arabs consider to be the source of their psychological woes. Turkish nationalism, by all indicators, is more intense than the vague sense of Arabism that permeates the Arab world. Perhaps this is because Turkish society has always been more cohesive than Arab society. It certainly hasn't been diluted by some twenty-four local identities or the deep and abiding schism between Shia and Sunni. While minorities abound, Turkey is more than 95 percent Muslim, the vast majority of whom are Sunni Muslims. While the Arabs struggle over religious schisms, the Turks are preoccupied with crushing Kurdish desires for an independent country. This is a nationalist issue that unites the Turks and not a religious issue that divides them.

Seeing that language has played such a prominent role in the earlier discussion, it would be remiss to ignore the fact that Turkish is a vastly different language than Arabic. It was written in the Arabic script until WWI for religious reasons, but the fit between the Arabic script and Turkish sound patterns was awkward. If the psycholinguists are correct, this would mean that Arab thought patterns are closer to those of Israelis than to those of the Turks.

Language aside, there can be little doubt that almost a century of forced modernity has left Turks far more westernized than the Arabs. The appeal of Islamic morality is strong in Turkey, but Turks, while accepting an Islamic government, are less likely than the Arabs to fall prey to a Salafi vision of retrogressive Islam. Just in case they are, the Turkish military establishment that imposed forced westernization of the Turkish public is alive, if subdued. Governments that strayed from the secular line were overthrown in the past, and the threat of a military coup, a constant topic of discussion in the Turkish press, serves as a moderating check on the zeal of Turkey's moderate Islamic leaders.

Practical problems further deflate optimism about the applicability of the Turkish model to the Arabs. As an Egyptian analyst warns, the Arab revival is not a matter of this model or that. "It has to do with hard work to create economic prosperity. It has to do with the rule of law, clean elections and working to respect human rights even when strong prejudices are in place" (El Amrani, 2011). No model will work until the Arabs get these and the other red-flag issues in place, and they have a long way to go.

Besides, where are the Arabs to find the equivalent of Turkey's Justice and Development Party? Similar parties in the Arab world remain in the embryonic stage and have yet to prove that they can accomplish anything. Unlike the Turkish Justice and Development Party which has the stage to itself, the Islamic Lite parties in the Arab world are over-shadowed by the Muslim Brotherhood and must compete in elections with a much fragmented Islamic electorate that extends from the Sufis to the jihadists.

For the moment, at least, the Islamic Lite parties in the Arab world lack a charismatic leader comparable to Turkey's Tayyip Erdogan. They, too, may need a "papa" to succeed.

Finally, there are those who worry that the Turkish model is merely a temporary stage that may eventually evolve into an Islamic state based upon Islamic law. I don't think so, but Turkish secularists remain skeptical.

Islam Center: The Muslim Brotherhood and Hizbullah

There can be little doubt that the Muslim Brotherhood, Hizbullah, and similar radical-moderates will play a dominant role in shaping the future of Arab politics in their respective areas. The current discussion focuses on the Muslim Brotherhood because it is the dominant Sunni Muslim organization in the world. This is not to diminish the importance of Hizbullah, but merely to note that Hizbullah was an Iranian creation whose role in shaping the future of Arab politics may have more to do with the fate of Iran than it does with domestic Arab politics.

There are so many reasons to expect the Muslim Brotherhood and other radical-moderates to play a dominant role in shaping the future of Arab politics that a simple list will do. Most of the points have already been elaborated in the earlier discussion.

Most importantly, the Muslim Brotherhood is a perfect fit for an Arab psyche that is predominantly conservative, intensely Muslim, and very Arab. While Arabs have a deep respect for the Turkish leader, they don't want an Iranian or a Turk to lead them.

The Muslim Brotherhood's vision of economic development blends Islamic morality with economic liberalism and resonates well with an Arab psyche that wants both. It also makes it easy for the Muslim Brotherhood to cooperate with the business community. Indeed, the Muslim Brotherhood claims to have the same program as Turkey's Justice and Development Party. This, however, is not entirely accurate. The Justice and Development Party advocates Islamic morality within a secular framework. The Muslim Brotherhood is not clear on the matter.

It advocates democracy and is willing to cooperate with secular groups to win elections, but it wants democracy to work within an Islamic framework rather than a secular framework. Islam comes first. This may also play well with a majority of the Arabs.

In addition to its seductive vision of Islamic morality blended with economic liberalism, the Muslim Brotherhood knows how to play the victimization and humiliation cards that were key to the success of the Justice and Development Party in Turkey. The Muslim Brotherhood suffered the boot of the tyrants, and it raised the banner of resistance to U.S. and Israeli domination of the region. In so doing, the Muslim Brotherhood has cast itself in the role of Arab hero and Islamic martyr, a combination that will serve it well in the future.

The Muslim Brotherhood's record of providing help and hope to the poor also plays well with the Arab masses. It has a record of effectiveness and honesty that promises effective government. It also promises stability with tinges of compassionate patriarchal rule. This is not a problem for an Arab psyche that is both patriarchal and fears chaos.

Finally, compare the organizational capacity of the Muslim Brotherhood with the disarray of competitive groups. The Muslim Brotherhood knows how to win elections and can control the street at will. There may be doubts about the future intentions of the Muslim Brotherhood, but for the moment, it has established itself as the firm middle ground between secularism and jihadism. The question is, can it bring peace, stability, freedom, and prosperity to the Arab world?

Islam Heavy

The only option left is rule by Salafis intent on a returning the Arab world to a version of Islam in the seventh century. The Salafis gained twenty-five percent of the vote in Egypt's first post-revolutionary parliamentary elections, and they may have a stronger voice in more traditional countries such as Yemen, Libya, and Saudi Arabia. The script is still being written.

Splintering

The above scenarios assume that the countries of the Arab world will remain much as they are today. This is a risky assumption, for pressures are already building to divide the Arab world into more cohesive ethnic and religious units. Each, in turn, will have to deal with the options outlined above. This process has already taken place in Sudan, and Iraq may not be far behind. I doubt if this is what the U.S. had in mind when it launched its effort to build a new Middle East, but there you have it.

Each of the main Arab futures outlined above promises to frustrate U.S. efforts to build a Middle East compatible with its goals of stemming terror and religious extremism, assuring the steady flow of oil to the world economy, protecting Israel, and maintaining America's strategic position in this vital region.

Keeping the kings in power will force the U.S. to choose between oil and Israel. It wasn't this way in the past, but the Saudis, in particular, are now playing the anti-Israeli card in a desperate effort to build domestic and regional support. They also continue to fund Salafi groups throughout the region, all of whom are violently hostile to the U.S. and Israel. Which of America's goals is dominant? Is it fighting terror, securing oil, or preserving greater Israel? It is doubtful that the U.S. can have it all. How frustrating.

Continued rage and chaos serves only to produce the instability and confusion that breeds religious extremism and terror. Instability is contagious and will certainly increase terrorist attacks on American forces and American allies in the region.

A reassertion of Arab military rule may provide the U.S. with a brief reprieve from the instability shaking the Middle East, but it will be temporary at best and increase conflict and extremism in the long run. Hopes that it will lead to democracy and moderation are beguiling and misplaced.

The institution of viable Western-type democracies in the Arab world remains a distant dream. They have little foundation in the Arab psyche and are poorly organized. As a result, weak liberal democracy will invite demagogues who thrive on anti-Americanism and revenge for Israeli humiliations.

The Turkish model, if transferable, could promote democracy, development, and stability in the Arab world. If the Turkish experience is an example, it would also lead to the isolation of Israel and stringent demands for a much reduced American presence in the region.

The dominance of the Muslim Brotherhood would be more of the same, with far less moderation. While Islam Lite accepts the practice of Islam within a secular framework, the Muslim Brotherhood and Hizbullah would not. Rather, they would accept secularism within an Islamic framework. Pressure on the American and Israeli presence in the Middle East would be far greater than under the Turkish model. As argued above, the Muslim Brotherhood and Hizbullah are well positioned to influence the Arab future in their respective areas.

American frustrations, spawned by an upsurge of Salafi and jihadist influence, require little elaboration. The U.S. can attack al-Qaeda, but the only way to stem the jihadist zeal is to meet the wants of the Arab psyche in a more moderate package. That probably means the Muslim Brotherhood. Negotiations are underway, but remain murky. The Arab psyche has taken note of America's willingness to deal with the Muslim Brotherhood, and the Muslim Brotherhood knows that it is in the driver's seat. It will deal with the U.S. but on its own terms.

If the U.S. can't find a way to meet the wants of the Arab psyche, it will lose, as past kawagas have lost. From the perspective of the Arab psyche, the U.S. is already in retreat. The American retreat began in Iraq and is being followed up in Afghanistan and Pakistan. The Arab psyche is placing its bets accordingly.

THE JOURNEY CONTINUES

Continuing updates on the evolution of the Arab psyche will be provided at www.arabpsyche.wordpress.com or contact me at arabpsyche@gmail.com.

Glossary of Arabic Terms

al-Qaeda: literally, the base; a dominant terrorist group
ayatollah: exalted Shia religious leader
bakara: gift of grace, charisma
bayaa: pledge of allegiance to an Arab leader
bedouins: nomadic Arabs
beni: son; can also be used with an era such as beni tribal or beni colonial to refer to the culture of the era.
beni Adam: the son of Adam; the Arab expression for humanity
bint: daughter or young maiden
backsheesh: small bribes
caliph: the successor to the Prophet Mohammed
Deobandi: a fundamentalist version of Islam in Pakistan
diwan: a council of advisors
emir: prince
fatwa: religious decree issued by a senior religious scholar
Hadiths: recounted sayings of the Prophet Mohammed
Hashemite: the clan of the Prophet Mohammed
inshaallah: if God wills
intifada: the earth shaking
Kuraysh: the tribe of the Prophet Mohammed
imam: prayer leader; senior religious figure
Imam (hidden): the Mahdi
jihad: internally, it is the fight against human appetites; externally, it is the fight against the enemies of Islam
jinn: spirits with supernatural powers
kawaga: influential foreign Christians
Koran: the holy book of Muslims
Mahdi: a messiah figure in Islam
madrasa: school; often attached to a mosque

mahdi complex: longing for the arrival of the Mahdi
Mamluks: slave rulers of Egypt
mufti: senior religious judge
shariah: Islamic law
sheikh: head of a tribe or Muslim religious order
Shia: the minority branch of Islam
Kaaba: the holiest shrine in Islam
shaoobi: non-Arab Muslim (derogatory slang)
Sunna: the majority branch of Islam; individual members of the sect are referred to as Sunnis
umma: the Islamic nation
wadi: an usually dry river bed
wafq: Muslim charity donations
Wahabi: a Saudi fundamentalist version of Islam
wasta: connections and influence peddling
zaim: a local power broker or warlord

Cited References

Afify, Heba. "A Peek into the Post-Revolution Psyche." *Al Masry Al Youm*, April 23, 2011.

Al Adnani, Al Katib. *Adultery and Homosexuality in the Arab History*. Beirut: Arabdiffusion, 1999. In Arabic.

Al Gosaibi, Ghazi. "Arab Poetry: A Glimpse into the Soul," http://www.jehat.com/Jehatt/en/Poets/Ghazi-al-Gosaibi.htm (accessed November 9, 2010).

Al Gosaibi, Ghazi. *My Life in Administration*. Beirut: Arab Organization for Studies and Publishing, 1998. In Arabic.

Alhomayed, Tariq. "Saudi Arabia: The Day of the Silent Bayaa." *Asharq Al-Awsat*, March 12, 2011.

Al Jazeera. "Meeting of the Arab Society for Cultural Growth Worries about the Arab Future." Al Jazeera. April 27, 2008. In Arabic.

Al-Katab, Ahmed and Mohammed Amaara. *The Sunni and the Shia Religious Unity and Political and Historical Differences*. Cairo: Maktaba In-Nafitha, 2008. In Arabic.

Al-Khalili Jim. "The 'First True Scientist.'" BBC, January 4, 2009.

Al-Khatib, Youssef. "Why Don't Arabs Revolt?" Al Jazeera. Cited in Fysal Qassem. November 25, 2010. In Arabic.

Al-Manoufi, Kamel. *The Changing Political Culture of the Egyptian Village*. Cairo al-Ahram Center for Political and Strategic Studies, 1979. In Arabic.

Al-Qarni, Aaidh. "The Arabs and the Conspiracy Complex." *Asharq Al-Awsat*, April 11, 2011.

Al Shindagah, "The Arab Psyche." Al Shindagah.com, March 1999.

Al Tabatabai, Muhammad Husayn. *Shi'a*. Qum, Iran: Ansariyan Publications, n.d.

Al-Taube, Ghazi. "Corruption in the Arab World." Al Jazeera, July 7, 2010. In Arabic.

Al-Toube, Gazi. "Why Are the Revolutions Succeeding Now?" Al Jazeera, April 21, 2011. In Arabic.

Altorki, Soraya. *Women in Saudi Arabia: Ideology and Behavior among the Elite*. New York: Columbia University Press, 1986.

Al-Zafiri, Ali. Moderator. "In Depth: The Challenges of Identity in the Gulf." Al Jazeera, April 19, 2010. In Arabic.

Al-Zaiyat, Mansour. "Sharia and Life Series: Islamic Groups and Violence." Al Jazeera. August 11, 2002. Interviewed by Mahir Abdullah. In Arabic.

Amin, Galal. *Whatever Happened to the Egyptians? Change in Egyptian Society from 1950-Present*. Cairo: The American University in Cairo Press, 2000.

Armajani, Yahya. *Middle East: Past and Present*. Englewood Cliffs, NJ: Prentice-Hall, 1970.

Awad, Hassan. "Jihad Names for Armed Groups." *Al-Wasat*, no. 622 (December 29, 2003), 10–11. In Arabic.

Awadalla, Ahmed. "National Hymen Unpacks Virginity Problems in Tunisia." *Al Masry Al Youm*, June 10, 2011.

Azm, Sadiq. *Self Criticism after the Defeat*. Beirut: Vanguard for Printing and Distribution, 1979. In Arabic.

Badrawi, Hossam. "I Didn't See It Coming." *The Cairo Review of Global Affairs*, February 21, 2011.

Badri, Malik. "The Islamization of Psychology: Its Why, Its What, and Its How and Its Who," *Islamic World*, 2010.

Badri, Malik and Uthman Uthman. "Psychological Dimensions of the Glorious Koran: Islamic Law and Life." Al Jazeera, April 4, 2010. In Arabic.

Baigent, Michael. *Racing Toward Armageddon*. New York: HarperOne, 2009.

Bakhait, Abdullah bin. "Noted Saudi Author Calls for the Abolition of the Committee for the Promotion of Virtue and the Preventions of Vice. *Al-Arabiya*, December 24, 2008. In Arabic.

Batatu, Hanna. *Syria's Peasantry, the Descendants of Its Lesser Rural Notables, and Their Politics*. Princeton, New Jersey: Princeton University Press, 1999.

Baydoun, Izza. *Masculinity and the Changing Feminine Circumstances*. Casablanca: The Center for Arab Culture, 2007.

Behrens-Abouseif, Doris. *Islamic Architecture in Cairo: An Introduction.* Cairo: The American University in Cairo Press, 1989.

Berque, Jacques. *Egypt: Imperialism and Revolution.* New York: Praeger, 1972.

Bidwan, Ali. "Parties, Elites, and Arabic Street Revolution." Al Jazeera, April 4, 2011.

Bill, James A. and John Alden Williams. *Roman Catholics and Shi'i Muslims: Prayer, Passion, and Politics.* North Carolina: University of North Carolina Press, 2002.

Bouhdiba, Abdelwahab. *Sexuality in Islam.* London: Saqi, 2004.

Boukra, Liess. *Algérie la terreur sacrée.* SA Lausanne: FAVRE, 2002. In French.

Boustani, Mahmoud. *Studies in Islamic Psychology: Vol. I and II.* Beirut: Dar al-Balagah, 2000. In Arabic.

Corrigan, John, ed. *Religion and Emotion: Approaches and Interpretations.* Oxford: Oxford University Press, 2004.

Coon, Carleton S. *Caravan: The Story of the Middle East.* New York: Holt, Rinehart and Winston, 1958.

Cox, Samuel. *Diversions of a Diplomat in Turkey.* New York: Charles L. Webster & Co., 1887.

Downing, Brian M. "Pakistan Marches to Saudi Tune." *Asia Times,* June 3, 2011.

El Amrani, Issandr. "Which Turkish Model?" *Al Masry Al Youm,* September 19, 2011.

El Baradi, Mohammed. "Stressing the Realization of All of the Demands of the Revolution in the Transitional Stage." *Al Arabiya,* April 1, 2011. In Arabic.

El-Ghobashy, Mona. "The Praxis of the Egyptian Revolution." Middle East Research and Information Project, MER258, April 6, 2011.

Elhadj, Elie. *The Islamic Shield: Arab Resistance to Democratic and Religious Reforms.* Boca Raton, FL: Brown Walker Press, 2007.

Elliot, Matthew. *Independent Iraq: The Monarchy and British Influence, 1941–58.* London: IB Tauris, 1996.

Fainaru, Steve. *Big Boy Rules: America's Mercenaries Fighting in Iraq.* Philadelphia: Da Capo Press, 2008.

Farid, Abdel Majid. *Nasser: The Final Years.* Reading, UK: Ithaca Press, 1994.

Fathaly, Omar and Monte Palmer. "Change Resistance among Rural Libyan Elites." *International Journal of Middle East Studies* (1980): 247–261.

Fauda, Emira. "10,000 Egyptian Nurses Face Being Fired Because of Wearing the Niqab." *Al Arabiya,* April 6, 2000. In Arabic.

Filiu, Jean-Pierre. *L'apocalypse dans l'islam*. Paris: Fayard, 2008. In French.

Fraser, T.G. *The Middle East 1914–1979*. London: Edward Arnold, 1980.

Freud, Sigmund. *Moses and Monotheism*. New York: Vintage Books, 1955.

Frum, David and Richard Perle. *An End to Evil: How to Win the War on Terror*. New York: Random House, 2003.

Gallup, Inc. "Egypt: The Arithmetic of Revolution: An Empirical Analysis of Social and Economic Conditions in the Months before the January 25 Uprising." Gallup, Inc. March 2011.

Gross, James, et. al. "Cognition and Emotion Lecture at the 2010 SPSP Emotion Preconference, Cognition and Emotion." Online, DOI at www.dx.doi.org/10.1080/02699931.2011.555753, 2011.

Grossman, Dave. *On Killing: The Psychological Cost of Learning to Kill in War and Society*. New York: Back Bay Books, 2009.

Gunaratna, Rohan. *Inside Al-Qaeda: Global Network of Terror*. New York: Columbia, 2002.

Habib, Rafiq. *Religious Protest and Class Conflict in Egypt*. Cairo: Sinai for Publishing, 1989. In Arabic.

Habib, Tariq. "Enlightenment: Saudi Religious Citizens Adhere to the Islamic Nation More than the Saudi Nation." Turki al-Dakhai, Moderator of the program *Enlightenment. Al Arabiya,* March 11, 2009. In Arabic.

Hamady, Sania. *Temperament and Character of the Arabs*. New York: Twayne Publishers, 1960.

Hamouda, Adel. *How the Egyptians Mock Their Leaders*. Cairo: House of Sphinx Publishers, 1990. In Arabic.

Hamzeh, Ahmad Nizar. *In the Path of Hizbulluh*. Syracuse, NY: Syracuse University Press, 2004.

Hawkins, David R. *Power vs. Force: The Hidden Determinants of Human Behavior*. Carlsbad, CA: Hay House Inc., 2002.

Heikal, Mohammed H. *What Happened in Syria*. Cairo: National Publishing House, 1962. In Arabic.

Heikal, Mohammed H. *The Road to Ramadan*. New York: Ballantine Books, 1975.

Hermann, Ranier, "A Yemeni Tribal Affair." *Qantara.de*, August 6, 2011.

Hitti, Philip K. The Arabs: A Sort History. Princeton, N.J.: Princeton University Press, 1943, 21.

Hitti, Philip K. *History of the Arabs from the Earliest Times to the Present*. 6th ed. London: Macmillan, 1956.

Hitti, Philip K. *The Near East History: A 5000 Year Story*. Princeton, NJ: D. Van Nostrand Co., Inc., 1961.

Howard, Pierce J. *The Owner's Manual for the Brain: Everyday Applications from Mind-Brain Research,* 3rd *ed.* Austin, TX: The Bard Press, 2006.

Hughes, Thomas P. Dictionary of Islam. Chicago: KAZI Pub., Inc. Reprint of the First Edition 1886.

Husaini, Ishak M. *The Moslem Brethen*. Beirut: Khayat's, 1956.

Hussain, Musharraf. *Seven Steps to Moral Intelligence: Based on Imam Ghazali's Teachings*. Leicestershire, England: 2009.

Ibrahim, Saad Eddin. "Europe Should Work for the Promotion of Democracy." *Qantara.de*, 2011.

Iraqi Ba'ath Party. *The 1968 Revolution in Iraq*. Baghdad: Arab Ba'ath Socialist Party in Iraq. January 1974.

Ismael, Faraj. "Saudi Court Orders Prison and Whipping for Girl Exposed to Seizure and Gang Rape." Al Arabiya.net, November 14, 2007.

Jabri, Mohammed. *The Composition of the Arab Psyche*. 8th ed. Beirut: Center for Arab Unity Studies, 2007. In Arabic.

Jones, William. *The Moallakat*. Poems and discussion by William Jones. Sacred Texts.com, n.d.

Keilani, Musa. *The Islamic Movement in Jordan*. Amman, Jordan: Dar Al Bashir, 1990. In Arabic.

Kerr, Malcolm. *The Arab Cold War 1958–1964: A Study of Ideology in Politics*. London: Oxford University Press, 1965.

Khaled, Amr. "Faith and Hope in Egypt." *The Cairo Review of Global Affairs*, April 19, 2011.

Khashan, Hilal. *Arabs at the Crossroads: Political Identity and Nationalism*. Gainesville, FL: University Press of Florida, 2000.

Khourshid, Farouk. *The Wondrous World of the Arab Popular Culture*. Cairo: Dar As Sharouk. 1991. In Arabic.

Lacy, Robert. *The Kingdom: Arabia and the House of Sa'ud.* New York: Harcourt, Brace and Javonovich, 1981.

Lyell, Thomas. *The Ins and Outs of Mesopotamia.* London: A.M. Philpot Ltd., 1923.

Mackey, Sandra. *The Iranians: Persia, Islam and the Soul of a Nation.* New York: Dutton, 1996.

Mahmoud, Zaki Naguib. "What's Going on in the Arab Mind?" *Al-Majella,* October 20, 1984: 32–36. In Arabic.

Meguid, Wahid Abdel. *L'attitude arabe face a la violence.* Paris: L'Harmattan, 2006. In French.

Melikian, Levon H. *Jassim: A Study in the Psychosocial Development of a Young Man in Qatar.* New York: Longman, 1981.

Mustafa, Hala. *The Political System and the Islamic Opposition in Egypt.* Cairo: Markaz Al-Mahrusa, 1995. In Arabic.

Nada, Joseph. "Interview with Joseph Nada, Commissioner of International Political Affairs for the Muslim Brotherhood." Six-part interviews by Ahmed Mansour. Al Jazeera. August 4 to October 5, 2002. In Arabic.

Naji, Abu Bakr. *The Management of Savagery: The Most Critical Stage Through the Umma Will Pass.* Cambridge, MA: John M. Olin Institute for Strategic Studies, Harvard University, 2006. Translated by William McCants.

Nash, Manning. *Primitive and Peasant Economic Systems.* San Francisco: Chandler Publishing Company, 1966.

Nasr, Sayyed Hossein. "Appendix IV" of Mohammed Al Tabatabai, *Shi'a.* Qum, Iran: Ansariyan Pub., 1971: 235–236.

Nasser, Gamal Abdul. *Speeches and Press Interviews for the Years 1954–65.* Cairo: Information Department.

Nasser, Gamal Abdul. *Egypt's Liberation: The Philosophy of the Revolution.* Washington, DC: Public Affairs Press, 1955.

Nathan, Tobie. *Psychanalyse Paienne.* Paris: Editions Odile Jacob, 1995. In French.

Nehme, Michel. *Fear and Anxiety in the Arab World.* Gainesville, FL: The University Press of Florida, 2003.

Norton, Augustus R. *Amal and the Shi'a: Struggle for the Soul of Lebanon.* Austin, TX: University of Texas Press, 1997.

Obaid, Nawaf. "Interview: Saudi-US Relations Information Service." www.saudiusrelations.org. August 22, 2006.

Ogas, Ogi and Sai Gaddam. *A Billion Wicked Thoughts: What the World's Largest Experiment Reveals About Human Desire.* New York: Dutton, 2011.

Okasha, Ahmad. "Escape from Suffering and Oppression." *Qantara.de*, February 7, 2011.

Palmer, Monte. *Politics of the Middle East.* Itasca, IL: F.E. Peacock Pub., Inc., 2002. Second Edition, Wadsworth/Thompson Learning, 2007.

Palmer, Monte, "The United Arab Republic." *Middle East Journal*, 1966.

Palmer, Monte and Princess Palmer. *Islamic Extremism: Causes, Diversity, and Challenges.* Lanham, MD: Rowman and Littlefield Pub., Inc. 2008.

Palmer, Monte, Ali Leila and El Sayed Yassin. *The Egyptian Bureaucracy.* Syracuse, New York: Syracuse University Press, 1988.

Patai, Raphael. *The Arab Mind.* New York: Hatherleigh Press, 2002.

Perthes, Volker. *The Political Economy of Syria under Asad.* London: I.B. Tauris, 1997.

Pervin, Lawrence A. *The Science of Personality*, 2nd ed. New York: Oxford University Press, 2003.

Qaradawi, Yousef. "A Conversation with Sheikh Yusuf (sic) Al-Qaradawi." *Asharq Al-Awasat*, December 27, 2010.

Qaradawi, Yousef. "Violence and the Islamic Groups, Part 1." Al Jazeera (July 7, 2001). Interviewed by Hamid Al Ansari. In Arabic.

Qaradawi, Yousef. "Violence and the Islamic Groups, Part 2." Al Jazeera (July 7, 2001). Interviewed by Hamid Al Ansari. In Arabic.

Qassem, Fysal. "Why Don't the Arabs Revolt?" Al Jazeera, November 23, 2010. In Arabic.

Qutb, Sheikh Jamal. "Asharq Al-Awsat Talks to Sheikh Jamal Qutb." *Asharq Al-Awsat*, June 1, 2011. Waleed Abdul Rahman, Moderator.

Radwan, Zeinab. *Appearance of the Hijab among University Students.* Cairo: National Center for Social and Criminal Research, 1982. In Arabic.

Rahman, Fazlur. *Islam.* Garden City, NY: Doubleday & Co., Inc., 1966.

Raouf, Wafiq. *The Vagueness of the Arab Revival.* Beirut: Center for Arab Unity Studies, 2005. In Arabic.

Romero, Anna A. and Steven M. Kemp. *Psychology Demystified.* New York: McGraw-Hill, 2007.

Said, Mohammed. *Lineage and Kinship in Arab Society before Islam*. London: House of Saqi, 2006.

Salama, Basma. "A Recipe for Corruption." *The Egyptian Gazette*, May 31, 2011.

Schneer, Jonathan. *The Balfour Declaration: The Origins of the Arab-Israeli Conflict*. New York: Random House, 2010.

Seale, Patrick. *Asad: The Struggle for the Middle East*. London: I.B. Tauris & Co. Ltd., 1988.

Sedillot, L.A. *Histoire des arabes*. Paris: N.P., 1854 in Benoist-Mechin. In French.

Shamees, A.M. *El Yemen El Hadeeth (Modern Yemen)*. Cairo: Political Books, Cairo House for Printing, 1958. In Arabic.

Shanker, Thom. "Warning Against Wars Like Iraq and Afghanistan," *The New York Times*, February 26, 2011.

Sharabi, Hisham. *Neopatriarchy: A Theory of Distorted Change in Arab Society*. New York: Oxford University Press, 1988.

Sharour, Mohammed. *State and Society*. Damascus: Al-Ahali Printers and Publishers, 1994. In Arabic.

Smith, Robertson, W. *Kinship and Marriage in Early Arabia*. Boston: Beacon Press, 1903.

Talal, Prince El Hassan Bin. "Op-Ed: The Third Arab Renaissance." *Middle East Times*, November 14, 2007.

Telhami, Shibley. *2008 Annual Arab Public Opinion Poll: Survey of the Anwar Sadat Chair for Peace and Development*. College Park: University of Maryland, 2008.

Tully, Mark and Zareer Mansani. *From Raz to Rajiv: Forty Years of Indian Independence*. London: BBC Books, 1988.

United Nations Development Program. *Arab Development Report 2009: Challenges to Human Security in the Arab Countries*. New York: United Nations Publications, 2009.

United Nations Development Program. *Arab Human Development Report 2004: Toward Freedom in the Arab World*. New York: United Nations Publications, 2004.

Warraq, Ibn. *Virgins? What Virgins? And Other Essays*. Amherst, NY: Prometheus Books, 2010.

Wahish, Niveen. "Friday's New Face." *Al Ahram Weekly*, 2–8 June 2011.

Wiet, Gaston. *Cairo: City of Art and Commerce.* Translated by Seymour Feiler. Norman, OK: University of Oklahoma Press, 1964.

Yalcin, Soner. "The Story of How Wives of Senior AKP Members Covered Up." *Turkish Daily News,* February 16, 2008.

Yassin, El Sayeed. *The Arab Personality.* 4th Ed. Cairo: Madbouli, 1993. In Arabic.

Younis, Mohamed. "Silatech Index Highlights Challenge of 'Waithood' for Young Egyptians." *The Daily News Egypt,* November 22, 2010.

Yule, Henry. trans. *The Book of Sir Marco Polo, the Venetian.* London, 1875, Vol. 1: 146–149. Cited in Philip K. Hitti's *History of the Arabs from the Earliest Times to the Present.* 6th ed. London: Macmillan, 1956, 447.

Zakriya, Fuad. *Reality and Illusion in the Modern Islamic Movement.* Cairo: Dar Quba'a, 1998. In Arabic.

CPSIA information can be obtained
at www.ICGtesting.com
Printed in the USA
BVHW041921141019
561065BV00009B/341/P